To Love and To Work

To Love and To Work
A Demonstration and Discussion
of Psychotherapy

Leonard H. Kapelovitz, M.D.

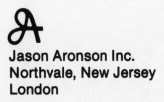

Jason Aronson Inc.
Northvale, New Jersey
London

Library of Congress Cataloging-in-Publication Data

Kapelovitz, Leonard H.
  To love and to work.

  Reprint. Originally published: New York : Grune &
Stratton, c1976.
  Includes bibliographies and index.
  1. Psychotherapy. 2. Psychotherapy—Case studies.
I. Title. [DNLM: 1. Psychotherapy. WM 420 K17t 1976a]
RC480.K28   1987   616.89'14   87-19477
ISBN 0-87668-977-2

Manufactured in the United States of America.

To Mara, Daniel, Abbey and my parents

"Freud was once asked what he thought a normal person should be able to do well. Freud is reported to have said: 'Lieben und arbeiten' (to love and to work)."

from Erik H. Erikson
Childhood and Society

Contents

Preface

To Love and To Work has been used as a textbook in numerous psychotherapy courses and also as an introduction to psychotherapy for the interested lay reader. As a textbook, *To Love and To Work* has been used most frequently in continuous case conferences because it presents an entire case, including the therapeutic action of every hour. In other courses, both clinical and theoretical, the book has been used for its essays on psychiatric diagnosis, treatment planning and technique, dream analysis, the therapeutic contract, the working alliance, transference, working through, and termination.

For the general reader who has never been in therapy, the book allows entrance into the psychiatrist's office. This has been of great value to friends and relatives of psychotherapy patients, who often feel mystified by a process in which they do not directly participate. Several readers have told me that they entered therapy themselves after reading the book because they gained an understanding of the process and saw how they would benefit from it. For those who are patients, the book provides an entree into the therapist's mind. Often patients feel that their therapists merely listen silently and passively. *To Love and To Work* describes how the therapist processes the material as it unfolds and waits until the proper moment to intervene.

To Love and To Work provides a model for intense but fairly brief psychoanalytically oriented insight psychotherapy. In an age when there is great emphasis on cost containment, it is useful to be able to apply psychoanalytic theory and understanding to therapy of short duration. In forty-four sessions, the patient followed in this book is led to examine and understand the neurotic patterns that keep him from succeeding. He not only gains insight into his own psychodynamics; he also experiences the process of psychotherapy. He identifies with the therapist's analyzing ego so that even after he has terminated therapy, he can continue the process on his own.

An author can never express appreciation to everyone who helped make the writing of a book possible. I am indebted to all my teachers, whether they were professors or patients. My wife, Abbey Poze Kapelovitz, edited this book. My colleague, Wayne London, M.D., read the manuscript and made many helpful suggestions. I am grateful to Jean Bevis, who typed the manuscript and made it possible for me to meet the publisher's deadline. Derf Vondy helped with the proofreading and provided useful suggestions and criticism. And finally, I wish to express my appreciation to "Paul Turner," who gave me permission to use the material from our work together.

Foreword

As Rene Spitz once said, both teaching and learning how to do psychoanalytically oriented psychotherapy would be substantially easier if prospective
psychotherapists could begin their learning experience by first mastering the
theory and technique of psychoanalysis. The analyst has available to him a
coherent, if incomplete, body of theoretical knowledge of intrapsychic and
adaptive functions as well as knowledge of normal and abnormal child development. He also has an extensive literature on analytic technique and theory
of technique, one basically derived from clinical psychoanalysis. The
psychoanalytic situation, with its frequency of sessions and free association,
provides the analyst with a constant check on the accuracy and timeliness of his
interventions. Psychoanalysis also facilitates the unfolding and analysis of the
transference neurosis, perhaps the best method of understanding many of the
conflictive vicissitudes of human behavior.

The vast majority of patients, however, do not need psychoanalysis,
though they may derive great benefit from psychotherapy. Psychotherapy, is in
many ways much more difficult than psychoanalysis. Psychoanalytically
oriented psychotherapy can be viewed as a kind of applied psychoanalysis; it
borrows extensively from psychoanalytic theory and only occasionally from
psychoanalytic technique. Its aim is not the analysis of the transference
neurosis, although it does deal with transferences to both the therapist and
people in the patient's life. Central conflicts and defenses may be dealt with,
but usually in well-defined areas. The frequency of interviews is less and the
duration of treatment is usually shorter. This can burden the therapist in that his
knowledge of the patient is considerably less than that of the analyst, while his
need for knowledge is as great or greater.

Dr. Kapelovitz brings to this book knowledge and experience in both
psychoanalysis and psychotherapy. The book addresses itself to insight-
directed, psychoanalytically oriented psychotherapy. It has the great virtue of
clearly presenting the entirety of a case, including the therapeutic interactions
of every hour as well as the therapist's conceptualizations about the therapeutic
process as the therapy unfolds. This book is a distinct addition to all rational
discussions of treatment, because Dr. Kapelovitz provides the reader with the

complete data base and the verbatim psychotherapeutic process, and documents his own conceptual frame of reference from both the patient and the literature. His therapeutic interventions are not the only ones which would have been helpful, and thus the case material will generally lend itself well to individual and group discussion of both the theory and technique of psychotherapy. It should prove useful to all who are involved in practicing, teaching, and learning about psychotherapy. It also presents data in a format which could serve as a research model.

In the context of psychoanalysis proper, a valid question might be raised as to why psychotherapy, not analysis, seemed the treatment of choice for this 25-year-old graduate student with problems that were clearly derivatives of an unresolved oedipal conflict. The answer lies essentially in the fact that the patient's chief developmental difficulty was his inability to quite solve the problems of the transition from adolescence to early adulthood. His conflicts were lively, as in adolescence, and successful insight and change did occur through dealing effectively with oedipal derivatives in his current life situation. This is always a difficult assessment to make early in therapy and, had the process gone less well, analysis would have been recommended. Had he again returned for treatment, analysis would have been the treatment of choice.

This is a thoughtful, candid, thought provoking book, written by a sensitive, adept psychotherapist and analyst.

Janice N. Kaufman, M.D.
Professor, Department of Psychiatry
University of Colorado Medical Center

Introduction

This book is written for the student of psychotherapy, the practicing psychotherapist, and the interested lay reader. It is based on the case history of a young man who experienced the emotional struggles of late adolescence with the help of psychotherapy. The notes that I took while treating him were later used in teaching a course in psychotherapy to third-year psychiatry residents at the University of Colorado Medical Center. This enabled the residents to study and discuss the psychotherapy of a patient from his initial telephone call to the therapist through the termination, 44 sessions later. The response of the residents who took the course and the responses of medical students, psychiatric social workers, clinical psychologists, and practicing psychiatrists who heard about the course encouraged me to use a similar format for a textbook of psychotherapy.

For didactic purposes this book is divided into three parts, corresponding to the three phases of psychotherapy. This is slightly artificial, since even though different aspects do predominate at the beginning, middle, and end of psychotherapy, there is considerable overlapping.

Part I deals with the psychotherapist's early concerns, namely, formulating a diagnosis, conceptualizing a treatment plan, making a contract with the patient, developing an alliance, and observing early transference manifestations. Each of these may have to be considered throughout therapy, however. For example, the diagnosis is just a working hypothesis that has to be continually tested as new data become available. The treatment plan and the contract may have to be modified with increased understanding of the patient or with changes in the patient's circumstances. The alliance with the patient is a dynamic, ever-changing relationship. In successful therapy, the alliance usually grows stronger. At any given time, though, the strength of the alliance can be affected by the patient's defenses or the therapist's interventions. These elements of psychotherapy are discussed after the presentation of the first five therapy sessions.

In Part II the concept of "working through" is demonstrated and discussed. The process of working through begins with the patient's first insight and continues throughout the rest of therapy. With most patients, working through takes center stage for approximately 60–70% of therapy. For the patient presented in this book, working through is the main process in 30 of the 44 sessions.

Part III is concerned with the termination phase, an integral but often neglected aspect of therapy. For the patient whose chief problem is dealing with separations and losses, most of the therapeutic work occurs during an extended termination phase. For other patients termination is a fairly demarcated process occurring near the end of therapy. The termination process for this patient included the last nine sessions.

The therapy sessions are not presented in their entirety. The account of each session is based on notes taken by the psychiatrist during the hour. These notes include the dialogue that illustrates the psychodynamic process, the patient's emotional state, and the patient–therapist interaction. Each of the sessions is followed by a discussion.

By presenting much of the actual verbal interchange between the psychotherapist and the patient, this book demonstrates how the therapist obtains information from the patient and how he uses that information for therapeutic purposes. The main goal of psychotherapy is to decrease the patient's symptoms while increasing his self-understanding, improving his interpersonal relationships, and enhancing his capacity to deal with new problems.

Brief essays on important psychotherapy topics are included in juxtaposition to the sessions that best demonstrate them. The essays are on psychiatric diagnosis, treatment planning and technique, the therapeutic contract, the alliance and transference in psychothereapy, the working through process, and the termination process. Some lay readers may find the essays on the alliance and transference in psychotherapy difficult, since part of it deals with a highly theoretical topic, namely, transference and nontransference aspects of the alliance.

Some readers may experience a sense of greater continuity by passing over the essays on a first reading of the book. I hope the reader will share the excitement of discovery as he joins the patient and therapist on a journey through 44 sessions.

Details such as names, places, and occupations were changed to protect the privacy of the patient. Care was taken so that these changes distorted neither the presentation of the patient's psychodynamics nor the presentation of the psychotherapy.

The psychotherapy demonstrated and discussed in this book is the therapy of a man with a psychoneurosis. Certain principles that apply to the therapy of neurotic patients must be modified in the therapy of psychotic and borderline patients.

Leonard H. Kapelovitz, M.D.

PART I

Beginnings

Chapter 1
Evaluation Sessions

Paul Turner started our first session by saying: "I'm twenty-five, single, a graduate student in sociology, and I'm hurting."

Mr. Turner had called me a week earlier requesting psychotherapy. He explained that several months earlier he had read an article in Life magazine about the use of Dilantin* for the treatment of emotional problems. He felt Dilantin would be useful for his symptoms, "compulsive repetition of words and difficulty urinating in the presence of other people." At that time he saw Dr. Krueger, a Student Health Service psychiatrist, who helped him decide that the main thing bothering him was his difficulty in forming an intimate relationship with a woman. Even though he wanted to continue working with Dr. Krueger, he had to terminate because the Health Service policy limited psychotherapy to twelve sessions.

Dr. Krueger suggested that the patient consider psychoanalysis. Mr. Turner saw a psychoanalyst, for an evaluation, who recommended further psychotherapy and referred him to me. I agreed to meet with Mr. Turner so that he could tell me more about himself and his problems. He expressed concern about whether or not I would accept him for therapy. I replied that if, after we met, we both decided that psychotherapy seemed indicated for him and if we felt that we could work with each other I would be glad to see him in psychotherapy.

*Registered tradename.

Mr. Turner appeared at my office promptly at the designated time. He was a tall, thin, good-looking young man with long black hair and a flowing moustache. He wore a heavy plaid wool shirt, Levis, and hiking boots. In short, he looked like a typical graduate student. As we introduced ourselves he nervously rubbed his moustache and stammered slightly. His handshake was hearty but his palm was covered with perspiration.

Mr. Turner continued our first session by saying, "I'm only working fifteen to twenty hours a week instead of the forty or fifty hours that I would like to be able to work. Also, my relationships with girls are better but I'm still confused. I pretend a lot. I'll pretend that I'm depressed or I will act child-like. I'll pretend that I'm in love immediately. I fabricate emotions. I think that's modeling after my father. My mother was sickly and my father always tried to make it up to her. I look for a potential Cinderella and hope I'll be the prince who can help her."

Recalling the patient's wet palm and observing his anxiety, I asked, "What are your thoughts and feelings about seeking therapy again?"

PATIENT: Mixed. I'm relieved because I think I'll get help, but I feel weak because it means I can't work out my own problems. Dad always told me I could do anything if I tried hard enough, but then he was never satisfied with what I did. I have the story about "The Little Engine That Could" tattooed on my brain.

THERAPIST: Your mixed feelings are very understandable.

PATIENT: Relief, hope, fear, weakness. Your understanding and accepting that makes it a little easier for me. Another concern is that I have a lot of difficulty with emotions. I find it painful being close to people. I can have very strong feelings, though, about characters in books. They're idealized. I don't have to worry about their feelings toward me.

THERAPIST: Will your difficulty in expressing emotions and feeling close to people interfere with your forming a relationship with me in therapy?

PATIENT [with considerable anxiety]:   I really feel threatened by that question. I'm afraid you're going to reject me. You won't accept me into therapy.

THERAPIST: You did have to terminate with Dr. Krueger before you felt that you had completed therapy. Did that seem like a rejection too?

PATIENT: No. Dr. Krueger explained that at our first meeting. I knew we would only have twelve sessions. It was just the Health Service policy. It wasn't anything personal. Dr. Krueger and I were always very business-like. Your style is very different. I've been here for only a few minutes with you and I'm already feeling very emotional.

THERAPIST: How do you feel about that?

PATIENT: I felt safer with Dr. Krueger, but I guess my problems are with emotions, so maybe I'd better learn how to deal with them. I gained a lot from seeing Dr. Krueger, though. I'm still living alone in the mountains in an A-frame but I'm starting to relax a little. I've started to date more and I spend some time just sitting around talking with people. It's fun.

THERAPIST: When you called me you said that you had contacted Dr. Krueger for therapy after reading an article in Life magazine about Dilantin. Was there anything else going on in your life at that time that led you to seek therapy?

PATIENT: I don't think so. In fact, only three days before I called Dr. Krueger I had received notice that I had passed my preliminary examinations. That was good news. It meant that I could continue in the Ph.D. program. My mother had died of cancer several months before I called Dr. Krueger. My Dad remarried while I was seeing Dr. Krueger. It reminded me of Hamlet, where he says the funeral food was not yet cold when the wedding feast began. I was still a little depressed about Mother's death but that didn't come up much during the twelve sessions except in terms of my anger at Dad for remarrying so soon. I felt that Dad had Mother all those years. He could have gone without a woman for a while.

THERAPIST: We will have to explore all that you have mentioned in more detail but now I'd like to hear more about your current situation.

PATIENT: I'm working for my Ph.D. in sociology. I'm working part-time as a teaching assistant. Being a teaching assistant is kind of hard: I don't have time to prepare enough. Sometimes I feel confused. I am proud, though, of being able to handle myself in front of a class. I'm really doing that much better this semester than I had in the past. I like my supervisor this semester, too. He's much more structured than the one I had last semester. Sometimes I feel a little uneasy when I'm teaching because I catch myself having sexual fantasies about some of the girls in the class. I don't think a teacher should do that. Anyway, that's about where I am now.

THERAPIST: Next time we meet I'd like to find out more about how you got to where you are now. From what you've told me so far, I do think that psychotherapy is indicated and that you and I will be able to work together.

PATIENT: I'm really glad you said that. I was thinking the same thing but was afraid to say it. How often will we meet?

THERAPIST: Do you have some ideas about that?

PATIENT: Dr. Krueger and I met once a week. That seemed about right.

THERAPIST: I think once-a-week therapy will be appropriate. If later it seems indicated to either increase or decrease the frequency, we can discuss that. Another thing that you and I will have to decide is what fee you pay. The fee paid by patients seen in this Clinic depends on their income and their expenses.

PATIENT: I was hoping that you would set the fee.

THERAPIST: It would be useful for you and me to work out the fee together.

PATIENT: I'd like to think about it for a while. If I paid so much that it was a burden, I'd resent it. If I didn't pay enough, I'd feel guilty.

THERAPIST: All right, we can discuss it further when we meet next week.

DISCUSSION

The Telephone Contact

Even though I greatly respected the judgment of the psychoanalyst who referred the patient to me, I chose not to make any therapy contract beyond an initial evaluation session when the patient first called. Therapy begins with the initial contact between the therapist and the patient. It is important to teach the patient from the beginning that therapy is a mutual endeavor, with patient and therapist sharing both the decisions about therapy and the work of therapy. Learning, whether in therapy or in general, takes place in many different ways. It can be conscious or unconscious. It can take the form of conditioning, either classical or operant. It can occur through identification, imitation, or incorporation. Insight learning is another form. Finally, learning can be passive or active. That is, the concept can be talked about or experienced. Each of these forms of learning will be discussed as it occurs during therapy.

The learning started during our telephone conversation was active and probably unconscious. Instead of talking about the patient's role in therapy I tried to set the stage for him to experience it. I neither told him that it was important for him to take an active part in therapy and decisions about therapy nor did I explain why that would be useful for him. Instead, I invited him to come for an evaluation during which he would tell me about himself and his problems, and during which he and I would mutually decide whether or not to embark on a course of therapy.

Another practical reason for the therapist not assuring the patient over the telephone that he will treat him is that neither the therapist nor the patient has the information at that time on which to base such a decision. In this case I, and probably the patient, trusted the judgment of the referring psychoanalyst. Nevertheless, I wanted to experience at least one session with the patient before committing myself, in order to rule out any unforeseen contraindications for therapy.

Another telephone issue is whether or not the fee should be discussed when the patient calls requesting an appointment. In this case it was not necessary, since I was seeing the patient in the Clinic, where the fee was determined on a sliding scale depending on the patient's income and expenses. Even if the patient does not ask about the fee, it should be discussed early in one's contact with him. This is especially crucial if there is any question about the cost of therapy being a burden on the patient. To start a patient on a course of psychotherapy which he will not be able to finish because of the cost is contraindicated. It means transferring the patient to a clinic or terminating prematurely. Occasionally a contract made with the patient cannot be completed because the patient suffers an unforeseen financial reversal. In that case a lowering of the fee or arrangement for delayed payments seems indicated. Often, of course, the total cost of therapy cannot be estimated until an evaluation of the patient has determined the frequency and approximate number of sessions that will be indicated.

Another concern involves answering telephone calls from patients who have called when the therapist was not available. Often, when the therapist returns the call, someone other than the patient answers and the patient is not there. What does the therapist say at that point? Generally it is best to leave one's name and telephone number. For example, "This is Dr. Jones returning Mrs. Smith's call. I can be reached at 123–4567 until five today." This may lead to problems if the patient has kept his therapy secret. But not leaving one's name can cause problems, too; e.g., a patient's husband may think it is a boyfriend calling. When a patient keeps his therapy secret, the reasons for the secrecy should be explored. To an adolescent, it may be his way of trying to separate from his family. To a middle-aged man it may be a way of dealing with an affair unknown to his wife. To another patient, therapy may have an unconscious meaning, such as being symbolically equated with masturbation.

When a friend or relative of the patient calls, the therapist should let the caller know that he will feel free to share the telephone conversation with the patient. It is also helpful to ask the caller why he is calling the therapist rather than dealing directly with the patient.

The First Session

After asking the secretary which patient in the waiting room was Mr. Turner, I said, "Mr. Turner, I'm Dr. Kapelovitz. Please come with me to my office." I mention this obvious technique only because a first-year psychiatry resident I was supervising once reported to me the painful results of a different approach he used in the same situation. He merely asked the man in the waiting room to accompany him to his office. The man protested that he was not sick and did not need a doctor. The resident at first thought this was part of the man's psychopathology. It soon became clear, however, that the man was one of the Clinic janitors.

The handshake at the initial meeting of the therapist and patient is diagnostically useful. The heartiness of Mr. Turner's handshake had little significance because most people raised in the Midwest and West are taught to shake hands in that manner. His sweaty palm, however, was indicative of anxiety. There are other characteristic handshakes. For instance, often a masochistic patient lowers his shoulder so that his hand is under the therapist's. An occasional patient will show reluctance to shake hands or even refuse to do so. The meaning of this reluctance has to be explored, since it can reflect anything from shyness to a germ phobia to paranoia. Most therapists do not shake hands with their patients at every session, but ongoing information about the patient can be gained by observing his posture, his gait, and his gestures.

The initial interview is extremely important. Often the tone is set for the entire course of therapy during this session. The information obtained during this session should allow the therapist to make at least a hypothesis about a developmental diagnosis and to start formulating a treatment plan. The forming of a "therapeutic alliance"[1] or a "working alliance"[2] is begun. Usually a partial contract can be made.

To obtain the information I need I keep in mind two basic questions: "How can I be of help to you?" and "How did you become the person you are now with that particular predicament?" Occasionally these two questions are all that need to be asked. The first question generates information about why the patient came to therapy when he did, what he expects from the therapist, and details about his current life. The second question leads to a discussion of his past, including his relationship with important people in his life. Usually these questions have to be supplemented by other inquiries which follow naturally from the material presented by the patient.

It is also useful during the initial interview to discuss with the patient his feelings about therapy and about coming to a therapist. This serves many functions. It is alliance building. It demonstrates to the patient that it is permissible and useful to express his thoughts and feelings about the therapy and the therapist. This patient experienced the usual ambivalent feelings of relief and a blow to his self-esteem combined with hope and anxiety. He also expressed his specific attitude about dealing with problems, where that attitude came from, and something about his relationship with his father. I noted to myself the potential transference implications of his statement about his father, i.e., that it would probably manifest later as his thinking that I was not satisfied with his efforts in therapy. I could also predict that he would have similar concerns about other authority figures in his life.

Freud described his approach as follows.

What the material is with which one starts the treatment is on the whole a matter of indifference—whether it is the patient's life-history or the history of his illness or his recollections of childhood. But in any case the patient must be left to do the talking and must be free to choose at which point he shall begin. We, therefore, say to him, "Before I can say anything to you I must know a great deal about you; please tell me what you know about yourself."[3]

Some therapists prefer a much more structured form of history taking. To a great extent, the form of history taking selected depends more on the personality and communication styles of the individual therapist and patient than on theoretical considerations. From a theoretical standpoint, however, the less structured form allows the patient to talk about what is important to him. It allows for freer associations and for a greater role for the unconscious. The therapist learns from what the patient leaves out as well as from what he says. For instance, one patient spent two sessions telling me about his past without ever mentioning his father. I finally intervened with: "Didn't you have a father?," said in an understanding tone of voice. The patient became aware that he had not mentioned his father, revealed that father died when he was a child, and recognized that he still had unresolved feelings about his father's death. I do not think as much would have been accomplished if number 33 on a long list of inquiries had been: "Tell me about your father."

Each initial interview, of course, has its own specific considerations. My confrontation about whether or not he could tolerate an emotional relationship with me was early but diagnostically helpful. He became anxious but handled the question without withdrawing as a schizophrenic may have or invoking obsessive–compulsive defenses as an obsessive–compulsive neurotic would have done. Both of these diagnoses had to be ruled out. Schizophrenia, latent, was a consideration because of the difficulties he described in object relationships and because of his claim that he fabricated emotions instead of really having them. Obsessive–compulsive neurosis was a consideration because of his initial presenting complaint of "compulsive repetition of words." A third diagnosis which the response to this intervention supported was that of a hysterical success neurosis. He had already described a work phobia and difficulty in becoming intimate with a woman, both of which suggested problems at an Oedipal level. Further support for this diagnosis came later in the interview when he said that he had been notified that he had passed his Ph.D. preliminary examination three days before he requested therapy. Even though he denied it, I was quite certain that this was the real precipitant for his seeking therapy. For this type of patient a success causes anxiety. The patient also experienced concern about his father's remarriage which would be predicted with this diagnosis.

As far as ego strength assessment is concerned, his record of graduating from college, entering graduate school, and passing his preliminary examination all indicated some capacity for achievement. He had sexual fantasies about some of the girls in the class he taught but controlled his impulses. The fact that he berated himself for having these fantasies alerted me to watch for other signs of a strict superego. At the end of the hour my working hypothesis was that the patient's major difficulty was unresolved Oedipal problems manifest as a severe conflict about competition.

The patient's having had previous therapy also colored the initial interview. His relationship with his previous therapist meant that I had two additional chores: I had to determine if he had adequately grieved the loss of his former therapist and, if not, to help him to do so. I also had to help him distinguish between his former therapist and me. Mr. Turner had at least partially resolved the loss by blaming it on Health Service policy. He had also started to compare and contrast me with his other therapist.

We made quite a firm therapy contract near the end of the hour. I felt free to do so this early in our relationship because the diagnosis seemed fairly clear, I was quite certain that psychoanalytically oriented psychotherapy was indicated, and we had already demonstrated that we could work with each other. His having just completed twelve weeks of therapy contributed to our being able to move as quickly as we did. The only other form of therapy I seriously considered for this patient was psychoanalysis. I had not, at this time, ruled out psychoanalysis. I did think, however, that if psychoanalysis turned out to be indicated, then the therapy I did with him would set the groundwork for it.

(One of the issues touched on in this discussion, the forming of an alliance, is discussed in more detail at the end of Part I. Two other issues raised by this session, the frequency of sessions, and whether psychoanalysis or psychotherapy is indicated, will both be discussed in some detail at the end of later "Session" sections.)

Earlier in this discussion I briefly described the circumstances of the patient's referral to me. Some general observations can be made in regard to the referring of patients, the handling of referrals, and the issue of patients currently or previously in therapy with another psychotherapist.

Before the psychoanalyst gave my name and number to the patient, she checked with me to see if I had the time and interest to take this patient into therapy. This is a simple courtesy which is helpful to both the therapist and the patient. It saves the patient the frustration and the feelings of rejection that can occur if he calls a therapist who, for lack of time or some other reason, turns down the patient. A turndown of this type is often enough to tip the balance of an already ambivalent patient toward not making further efforts to seek help. A patient is much more likely to follow through on a referral if the referring person tells him that the therapist has been contacted and is willing to see the patient for evaluation and, if indicated, for therapy. It is also helpful to the therapist in handling the initial telephone call if he has some background about the patient. If the therapist does not hear from the patient in a reasonable amount of time, he should let the referring therapist know.

If the patient does come for an evaluation, a brief letter to the referrer thanking him for the referral and telling him about the disposition is usually appreciated. Most referring physicians prefer this to a phone call both because of the convenience and because they can place the letter in the patient's chart as a reminder the next time they see the patient.

The occasion frequently arises where I receive a call about a possible referral from a non-psychotherapist who does not know other psychotherapists in the community, e.g., from a physician who is not a psychiatrist. If I do not have time to treat the patient, I usually offer the choice of my seeing the patient for evaluation with the explanation that I would then have to refer him on to an appropriate therapist or of giving the referring doctor the name of another therapist who I think will have time.

When a patient contacts me who is currently in therapy with someone else I always inquire as to whether or not he has discussed seeing me with his current therapist. I do so primarily for the benefit of the patient. Often a desire to see another therapist is a resistance and/or an acting out of the transference. If the patient and his therapist can look at the patient's wish to see another therapist, the resistance and/or acting out can often be resolved with a resulting disappearance of the desire to see someone else. If exploration of the wish does not lead to its disappearance, then the therapist should welcome his patient having a consultation with another therapist, even if the eventual recommendation is a change of therapists. If the therapist becomes aware of reaching an impasse with a patient it behooves him to refer the patient for consultation or to seek supervision from a professional colleague. When a patient who has terminated therapy with another therapist in the same city calls me, I inquire into the patient's reasons for not returning to the same therapist. Unless the reason for starting with a new therapist is straightforward, I explain the advantages of returning to the former therapist.

SESSION 2, MARCH 8   **THE FIRST DREAM**

PATIENT: Let me tell you about a dream I had last night. Early in the dream I seduced a girl somehow. It was a jovial, happy feeling, but there really wasn't any affection involved. This is a girl I have had sexual intercourse with, but no other relationship with in real life. In the middle of the dream I realized that I should be at an Air Force Reserve meeting that is coming up this weekend. I started rushing around. The Air Force Reserve building reminded me of where I teach. It's a complicated building. I was running around the building looking for a sergeant to tell him an excuse for my being late. When I got to the office the sergeant wasn't there but an officer, like a captain, was there. He just said it was okay. I didn't need an excuse. I discussed the dream with a friend to figure out what it meant. I concluded that I hate the Air Force and I don't want to go but since the building was like the one I teach in, we thought it might relate to responsibility in general. Deviousness also reminded me of Dr. Krueger showing me that I can't form a straightforward relationship. There's always something devious about it.

THERAPIST: I wonder why you had that particular dream last night?

PATIENT: I think it was because I had been thinking about the Air Force Reserve meeting this weekend. Having to deal with the sergeants and the officers does make me anxious.

THERAPIST: In the dream there was a bad sergeant, good captain.

PATIENT: Yeah. The good captain excused me. I expected this one sergeant who really is an asshole. He resents college students. I had to be excused because if I missed more than once I would be fired. I knew this sergeant wouldn't excuse me but an officer may. Do you know the story about the key, the cup, the wall, and the bear? The key is supposed to equal knowledge; the cup equals love; the wall is supposed to be an obstacle; but I fantasied it as having an open door so I could get away from the frightening bear. The dream was the same as that story. I found a way out.

THERAPIST: The dream started as an enjoyable sexual experience with a woman. It then became something frightening in the Air Force where you feared punishment, but it had a pleasant ending with the good captain.

PATIENT: My idea about gentlemanly, grown-up acting is not compatible with the way I act sexually.

THERAPIST: What is your idea about grown-up sexual behavior?

PATIENT: I have trouble with sex. I have to justify it by pretending I'm in love. I have to feel that I need her and she needs me, that it's not just desire.

THERAPIST: Where did that idea about sexuality come from?

PATIENT: I'm not sure. I think it's the way my parents, like my Dad, thought about sex. Carrying that around in my head does interfere with my satisfying my desires.

THERAPIST: Do you think the dream was also related to the therapy relationship?

PATIENT: I never thought of that. I do have the fear that therapy may prevent me from fulfilling my desires, that it will make me conventional.

THERAPIST: You do have some ambivalence about therapy.

PATIENT: That happened to me before too. Like I justified seeing Dr.

Krueger with that article on Dilantin. I didn't think that I wanted any extended therapy but then I realized I was just fooling myself. I didn't have a physical glandular problem. I have a problem relating with people. Pills aren't the answer. Sometimes I think I should have taken LSD. That might radically change my ideas. I may still take it. One girl I know said it made her like herself better but she also said that she got more out of a marathon group therapy. This therapy is threatening to me. I don't realize it until I get here. Then I think I'm going to have to give up my infantile ways of doing things. I had the same feelings about Dr. Krueger, but actually in therapy with him he was like the officer, even though I was afraid he would be like the sergeant.

THERAPIST: What are your ideas about therapy making you conventional?

PATIENT: I don't really understand that myself. Through all my dealings with my relatives, they used to compare me with that kid in the comic strips, Dennis the Menace. They told me to keep quiet. Dad would just tell me to "shut up." But the relatives gave me more attention. But the thing I got attention for was not mature, conventional stuff. Since I enjoyed that I'm afraid to give it up. I may view you more like my father.

THERAPIST: What do *you* want out of therapy?

PATIENT: I want to feel better, to attain things that I want; but that's vague.

THERAPIST: It sounds like you want to be able to get the kind of gratification that is appropriate for someone your age: good relationships with people and the ability to function well in your studies.

PATIENT: Do you see me as an adult? It's like I have two sides. I want to drop out, go to Canada, live in a commune, but I also want to be an important scientist. I feel I have to make a choice, be one of these kinds of persons. I don't know what I want to be.

THERAPIST: That sounds like a legitimate task.

PATIENT: Yeah. It seems like another part of some one big problem.

THERAPIST: What is the one big problem?

PATIENT: I'm not sure. I guess it's relationships with people and how I feel about myself.

THERAPIST: What about your relationships with other people and with yourself?

PATIENT: I've never been close to my parents, my brother, or anyone until the last couple of years. Now I do have three close friendships at school. For the first time I started to care about what would happen to others. I feel good if something good happens to them.

THERAPIST: You said earlier that you may view me as being more like your father than like your other relatives. What was it like with Dad as you were growing up?

PATIENT: I've talked with people about this so much and never get anywhere. All I get is emotional confusion. I feel I hate my Dad but at other times I feel he did good things for me. I can talk about him but I can't really talk about my relationship with him. He was very concerned about being proficient. He never cared if he and I were close, just about teaching me things like tennis. Being good at tennis helped him in the business world. He considers himself an expert tennis player, the best car driver in the world, and so on. He really is proficient. I feel I'm an extension of him, not existing in parallel when I'm with him. When I was home for his wedding people would ask me what I was doing and he would answer for me, but he really doesn't want to know what I actually do. He just wants to know what my position is. Last summer he was vulnerable because my mother died. I'd tell him something and he'd say, "Tell me something I don't know." He got married six months after Mother died. I didn't know what to make of that. The night before the wedding they had a dinner. He needled people, supposedly in fun, but if anyone needles back he really strikes out. I'm just beginning to realize that he's a pretty defensive guy himself. Somehow I make the connection between that and my feeling at times that if someone with me is turned on by something and I'm not, I have to respond anyway. In seminars I'm hesitant about speaking up. I'm afraid someone will respond like my father does. You know, say, "Tell me something I don't know." A lot of my confusion is caused by my even turning thoughts off to avoid this. Sometimes it has even generated a sort of paranoia.

THERAPIST: What do you mean by paranoia?

PATIENT: I become overly self-conscious. I will say things that I hope will elicit a favorable response. I try so hard I ignore what I feel myself.

THERAPIST: I'm sure that will sometimes happen in therapy, too, even though you know that what I'm most interested in is what you are feeling and thinking.

PATIENT: I just don't know how I feel about people or things. I vacillate to extremes about the same person. Oh, before we run out of time today, I want to tell you that I have been thinking about the fee but I haven't really reached a conclusion.

THERAPIST: How do you feel about my asking you to take part in setting the fee?

PATIENT: I'm not being devious about the fee, but I am so often that I feel guilty anyway.

THERAPIST: It would be easier for you if I set the fee.

PATIENT: Yes, it would. Often my father would ask my opinion and not take it. Also, I don't want the responsibility. Okay, I did come up with a figure. I think five dollars a session but that scares me. [He then detailed his income and expenses; five dollars per session did seem like a reasonable fee for him within the guidelines of the Clinic fee schedule]. It's not much money. Is this a problem for me because my father was always concerned about money? Or, are there other reasons that I'm having so much trouble with it?

THERAPIST: Father was an important person in your life, but it probably means many things to you.

PATIENT: That frightens me. It frightens me that how I feel depends partly on what I pay. Also, I'm afraid to ask people for things.

THERAPIST: Time is up for today. I will charge you five dollars for the last session and for this one but we can still leave it open for discussion if you want.

DISCUSSION

The first session generated many questions in my mind which I noted for further exploration. I wanted to obtain more history about his past. I was especially interested in his relationships, both his early ones with his family as well as later ones during latency, adolescence, and early adulthood. A knowledge of a patient's relationships is an essential part of any diagnostic evaluation. Since difficulty with relationships was his presenting complaint, early exploration of this issue was indicated. I was also interested in further exploring his thoughts and feelings about leaving therapy with Dr. Krueger and starting with someone new. I wondered if the anxiety he had during the first session with me was a continuation of feelings he had during sessions with Dr. Krueger, or if it was indeed something new, as he suggested.

Although I was tempted to start the second interview by raising some of these questions with the patient, I did not. Instead, I followed the old dictum of allowing the patient to start each session. As usual, doing so proved to be very useful. If I had started with questions I may have never heard the dream that he reported. The dream and the discussion of it which followed answered many of the questions that I had in my mind in more depth than I would have ever obtained by direct history taking. This session also illustrates that there is not a sharp demarcation between evaluative sessions and therapy sessions. Instead, the two merge. Very often the form taken by the early evaluation sessions is predictive of how the "therapy" sessions will go as well. In this case we saw that the patient was able to do a great deal of the therapy work himself.

In this session Paul presented his first dream in therapy. I will discuss this particular dream, initial dreams in therapy, and dreams in general from the standpoints of theory and technique.

As often happens, the first dream in therapy contained the patient's central conflict, namely castration anxiety, his expectations and ambivalence about therapy, and some clues about the kind of transference relationship that was likely to develop. In this case, one could predict that the ambivalence about his father that came out in both the dream and the subsequent associations would also be relived in a new edition in the therapy. The therapist has many alternatives in handling an initial dream in therapy. He can listen without commenting, or he may express an interest in dreams, or ask about the day's residue, or see how much work the patient is capable of doing with the dream without undue anxiety and increased defensiveness. I certainly listened in such a way that the patient was aware of my interest. I started working with the dream by asking him why he had had that particular dream that night; in other words, I inquired about the day's residue. This is always useful. It seems especially useful in introducing to a patient a way of working with dreams. Most patients are used to thinking that something in their current life situation has brought on a dream. A patient can explore this without excessive anxiety.

The next steps that I took—namely, examining some of the individual elements of the dream, interpreting the dynamic line, and exploring some of the transference implications—are not steps that I usually take when a patient presents his first dream. The reason for not going this far is that, with most patients, doing so would just increase defensiveness. One of the main goals with the dream at this stage of therapy is merely to help the patient see that it could be useful to bring dreams into the therapy session and express interest, so that the patient will indeed continue to remember and report dreams. To start to interpret unconscious, latent elements of the dream is often so frightening to a patient early in therapy that it actually can lead to repression of dreams for many months after. I tried to gauge this as I went along during the session. Perhaps because the patient had had some previous therapy he seemed to be able to deal with the dream in this way without becoming too anxious or defensive.

The way to determine whether or not this was too much, too fast, is to watch what happens to his reporting of dreams in subsequent sessions. If he either stops reporting dreams or reports dreams that are much more disguised and censored, one can be quite certain that his defenses were increased by the work that was done with that initial dream. If, on the other hand, he continues to report dreams which are as clear and understandable as this first dream, we can assume that he was able to make use of the work done on this initial dream.

Had this been a less psychologically sophisticated patient, I definitely would have begun much more cautiously. For instance, I could have said, "That is an interesting dream. What do you know about dreams?" In this way I could have found out what the person's attitude, superstitions, and previous uses of dreams had been. This patient answered that question without my asking it. He told me that he had discussed the dream with a friend to try to figure out what it meant. He then also told me what he thought the meaning of the dream was. This does bring up another point: His discussing the dream with someone else does lead to some contamination. I did not know which were his associations and which were his friend's. I made a note to myself to watch for any other signs that the patient was diluting the material in the sessions by discussing it with other people first. If this continued to be a problem, I planned to bring it up for discussion with the patient.

There is one main exception to the statement I made earlier about the first dream reflecting the patient's conflict, whole personality, and relationship to the therapy and therapist. The exception is when a person comes to therapy because of an external trauma. In this case, not only the first dream reported but many dreams that the patient has may be dreams which serve to attempt mastery over the trauma.

There are at least six ways to begin the analysis of a dream. One can begin by asking for the day's residue, which is the way I began in this session. Historically, Freud, in analyzing his own dreams, which he wrote up in his great book, *The Interpretation of Dreams,*[4] began with the first element of the dream and got associations to each element step by step. At that time the emphasis was on id-oriented interpretations of dreams. A third way to begin is to focus on the major affect in the dream. For instance, in the dream for this session the early affect was one of joy and happiness; later the affect turned to fear and finally to relief. A fourth way is to avoid any intervention at all. Instead, one can wait for the patient to bring forth his own associations. Another method that is often very useful is asking the patient to repeat the dream. Almost invariably the patient will remember some additional fragment of the dream that he had forgotten, that is, repressed in the first telling. The newly remembered fragment is usually very significant. Finally, a sixth way to begin is to ask the patient why the dream came to mind at that particular time in the session. This really was not relevant in this session, since the patient started the session with the dream. When a patient does recall a dream in the course of a session, everything that he says both before and after the recall can be considered associations to the dream.

If one does focus on the individual elements of the dream, he should be thinking about what the elements represent. It is useful to think about whether the elements represent id, ego, or superego productions. For example, actual dialogue in the dream often turns out to be superego material. One should also consider where each element fits in terms of transference implications, genetic–historical material, and the patient's current life situation. Everything that I have said in this paragraph about examining dreams is also relevant to the therapist's examination of any communication from the patient. Anna Freud, in her book *The Ego and its Mechanisms of Defense,*[5] suggests that the analyst should be hovering equidistant between the id, ego, and superego as he listens to material. Anna Freud was focusing on the intrapsychic aspects of the patient, to which I would also add self and object-representation. In psychotherapy, in contrast to psychoanalysis, there is also more attention paid to the patient's current external realities.

One cannot take either the individual elements or the affect at face value—often in the dream one has to consider that they represent the opposite as well. One must always keep in mind the polarities. For example, when the patient talks about the wish to do something in the dream, the therapist must also think about the patient's wish to have something done to him. When the patient talks about activity the therapist should also think about passivity. Some of the other polarities to keep in mind are: yes and no; heterosexual and homosexual; many and few; and large and small.

It is often useful to ask for additional details. For example, one patient reported that in a dream he went to a large building. I asked him which building and with whom he went to the building. He then remembered that it was with his mother and that it was a medical building. It turned out that this was the medical building that his mother did indeed take him to as a child. He then had many associations to early experiences with doctors.

The therapy situation may be represented in many different ways in the dream. Such things as time, money, offices, buildings, people in a building, or even the therapist himself will appear in the dream as parts of the therapy situation. Frequently the patient will report dreaming about a journey. This is often the patient's way in the dream of representing the therapy process. For instance, he may describe the journey as uncharted, or rough, or smooth, or pleasant, or terrifying, all of which refer to his current thoughts and feelings about the therapy situation.

The interpreting of dream symbols has become a popular pastime. There are even books available listing hundreds of symbols and their supposed meanings. This really misses the point. It is not just the anatomical id material represented by the symbols that is important, but also the ego experiences associated with that symbol. For example, a patient might describe a very phallic snake in one of his dreams. It is very easy but not very useful to say that that snake represents a penis. One can find out much more about the patient and help the patient much more by asking him a question such as, "What has been your experience with snakes?" A question of that type will often lead to associations from early childhood, which helps both the therapist and the patient to understand some of the latent meanings of the dream.

Internal conflicts are often represented in dreams as external struggles. For example, the struggle between an id impulse and the superego might be represented as a fight between the patient and some wild beast.

The therapist should also pay attention to the particular wording. Puns are often used to disguise meaning in the dream. Patients in Denver will frequently report dreams about C.U. (the University of Colorado). Analysis of this often leads to the meaning of C.U. equals "see you." The name of the therapist will often appear in a dream in a slightly disguised manner. One of my patients reported a dream about the son of her previous therapist, Dr. Kapel. My name, Kapelovitz, translates into son of Kapel.

In addition to content, which I have been focusing on, one should also look at the form and the function that the dream serves for the patient. Does the telling of the dream take up the whole hour, thus acting as a resistance to looking at other material? Is the dream told in an entertaining way as a gift to the therapist? Questions such as those help the therapist to understand why the patient is telling that particular dream at that particular time.

Dreams are also useful prognostically and diagnostically. A young woman in therapy reported a dream in which she had a sex-change operation which turned her from a man into a woman. She was very happy in the dream with the results. Prior to this dream the patient had been complaining about being a woman and expressing wishes to be a man. Diagnostically I wondered if the dream represented a change in her sexual identity conflicts. Prognostically I wondered if this was a turning point in the therapy, namely that she now was going to seek fulfillment as a woman, which up to that point had been frightening to her. Up until then her wish to be a man had been a defense against her fear of being an adult sexual woman. Finally the dream confirmed for me that the patient saw the necessary changes that had to come about as changes within her intrapsychically, rather than external environmental changes. All of these considerations turned out to be true as the therapy progressed.

Freud[6] has discussed the relationship between the latent dream and the manifest dream on a number of occasions. One of his clearest discussions of this relationship is in Chapter 11 of *Introductory Lectures on Psychoanalysis*. He calls the process by which the latent dream is transformed into the manifest dream "the dream work." The dream work functions to obscure the latent wishes and to put the wishes into dream form. He describes four main types of dream work: condensation, displacement, regression to image and secondary elaboration. *Condensation* is accomplished by omitting some latent elements, by allowing only fragments of others to pass over into manifest content, and by putting together many latent elements into one by their shared common characteristic. He describes two ways in which *displacement* commonly takes place. Either the latent element is replaced by something else or the emphasis is displaced from an important latent element to an unimportant one. *Regression to image* involves the process of changing the thought or wish into a visual image. Occasionally, as mentioned before, conversation will also appear in the dream. By *secondary elaboration* Freud was referring to the work that the person does upon awakening which involves taking the primary process content of the dream and putting it into secondary process; that is, into a logical, coherent form. Although in therapy one often deals largely with the manifest content, it is often useful to try to understand the latent content as well. The process by which the dream work is reversed is, on the patient's part, association, and on the therapist's part, interpretation. These two activities help lead from the manifest content back to the latent wishes and impulses.

Freud saw all dreams, with the possible exception of those brought on by a traumatic neurosis, as being wish fulfillments. Although the manifest content may appear to be the opposite of what one would wish, analysis of the latent content invariably leads to the dream being a fulfillment of a wish. One example that Freud used to illustrate this was the common occurrence of examination dreams. This type of dream usually occurs the night before an important examination. Often there is much anxiety in the dream. The manifest content is about failing an examination. The interesting thing, however, is that usually it is an examination on a subject that the dreamer has previously taken and passed. The wish, of course, is that he were taking the examination again that he had passed rather than one which he is fearful of failing.

Modern dream and sleep research has shown that people dream every night and usually three to four times per night. Some people, however, are capable of repressing all of their dreams. A patient of mine early in therapy claimed that he had never had a dream in his life. During the fifth session he told me with great excitement that he was now able to report remembering a dream for the first time in his life. That first dream heralded an increasing ability on the patient's part to be in touch with his unconscious. Other people remember one or more dreams every night.

Because of the important use that can be made of dreams in psychotherapy, I have discussed the patient's dream, and dreams in general, in some detail. There are some other aspects of the second hour that deserve examination. For instance, how was I processing the material that led me to ask him about his relationship with his father? From the dream and his associations to it it was clear that he was ambivalent about therapy, about me, and about his father. It was also clear from some of the things that he said that he had entered therapy with a ready-made father transference to me. For these reasons I thought it was important to find out in some detail what kind of father transference could be expected to develop. The patient was wondering whether I would make him conventional or help him be independent and obtain his own goals. He was afraid that I would say, "Tell me something that I don't already know," like his father so frequently did. It was clear, though, that he had also started separating and individuating from his father.

He saw his father as a very proficient man, but was also able to recognize some of his weaknesses.

During the session I said that I was interested in his thoughts and feelings. At the time I thought that would provide a bit of education about the therapy relationship. In retrospect I wonder if it was a counterproductive statement in that it was reassuring him that I would be different than the father who said, "Tell me something I don't already know." Giving him that reassurance led to a closure of that conflict instead of allowing us to further elaborate it.

The last topic from this second session that I wish to address is that of fees. The patient nicely illustrated how intimately intertwined the setting of the fee is with his own intrapsychic concerns and conflicts, his past experiences with people, and his expectations of his relationship with the therapist. Financial matters are often more difficult to discuss for many patients and therapists than the most intimate sexual material. Looking at sex and money in the broadest way, it is not surprising that they are both of such great importance to people. Sex in this sense provides for the survival of the human species, while in our society money, to a great extent, provides for the survival of the individual.

Considerable time was spent in the first two sessions setting the fee, but there was no discussion of how the billing and payment would take place or of whether or not there would be a charge for missed sessions. Now I usually say something such as, "I will give you a bill the first session of the month for the previous month's sessions. Usually I expect payment by the next session." Some patients will find this an agreeable arrangement; others will suggest alternatives. For instance, a patient may say that he is paid on the tenth of the month and would prefer to pay the bill after that. Another patient might suggest that he will pay his share of the bill on that arrangement, but would like to pay the insurance part of the bill when he receives payment from the insurance company. What arrangement is made is less important than that some arrangement be agreed upon so that deviations from that arrangement can be explored and understood.

For similar reasons I have also moved in the direction of setting up prearrangement for dealing with a missed appointment. In the past I would deal with each individual missed session with the patient to try to determine whether or not it was resistance or an unavoidable reality. Although this has some advantages, it has the disadvantage of putting the therapist in the role of the judge. It also leads to greater potentiality for countertransference coming into play. Some therapists take the position that the patient is responsible for payment for all scheduled sessions regardless of the reason he might miss. Some other therapists set up time requirements; for example, a session cancelled twenty-four hours in advance or a week in advance is not charged for. Still other therapists will not charge if the patient misses for certain agreed-upon reasons, such as severe physical illness or extreme weather conditions. The particular policy that the therapist works out with his patients has to be an individual matter. Having an agreed-upon policy, however, seems to be very useful.

Although I have emphasized how the arrangement or policy is used in the therapy, I do not mean to suggest that there is nothing to choose between various possible arrangements. Consider the issue of third party payment, e.g., insurance. The therapist should emphasize that the financial arrangement is between him and the patient—not between him and the insurance company. This means that the therapist will bill the patient and expect payment directly from the patient. It is up to the patient to obtain reimbursement from the insurance company. Even the arrangement with the patient paying his share immediately and the balance when he receives payment from the insurance company is usually contraindicated because of the potential it provides for acting out. For instance, a patient who is angry at his therapist can delay applying for reimbursement instead of dealing with the anger in the therapy. Interference in the therapy by third party payment is kept to a minimum if the therapist limits his interaction with the third party to filling out the therapist's part of the required forms. Even then the role of the third party often has to be analyzed. Eissler's[7] recent paper on the payment of fees provides an excellent detailed overview of the topic.

Beginning therapists often wonder what to call their patients. During the first session I addressed this patient as Mr. Turner, and the usual textbook dictum is to continue to use the patient's title and surname throughout therapy. However, I have found in actual practice that many young patients in the West are more comfortable being called by their first names. The patient and therapist must both understand what the form of address means to the patient. Early in therapy this issue was dealt with and I began calling the patient Paul. He continued to call me Dr. Kapelovitz.

SESSION 3, MARCH 15th   **PARTIAL INTERPRETATIONS**

PATIENT: This was the best week that I can recall.
THERAPIST: What was special about this week?
PATIENT: I had a funny conflict with a girl. I resolved it in favor of not asking her out any more. I would ask her out late and she would say, "I have work to do." I didn't know what she was saying; whether she really had work she had to do or if she just didn't want to go out with me. So, I asked her in advance. She said she was going bike riding. So I asked if she was telling me not to call her anymore. She just said, "The world is ambiguous." I decided

the hell with it. I don't have to beg her. It makes me angry when someone doesn't respond to me. I still like her but I'm going to leave it alone unless I get some positive indications from her. Anyway, that's part of why I felt better.

The other part is that I got a different job in the Reserves. I got a job in the psychiatric section. I'll be called a psychiatric technician. The woman social worker who is in charge of all the psych techs put us all in a sensitivity group where we give each other feedback about our personalities and behavior. I may even start looking forward to the meetings. My training in the Air Force has been in the medical field. After basic training I had a twelve-week on-the-job training course in a dispensary. I took blood pressures and did simple lab tests. I was in a six-month deal, but only had to stay in 4½ months. Then I was discharged to the Reserves for six years. I have four years left in that. I've really been promoted fast. I'm a buck sergeant now. That means that I have the second highest rank in the group assigned to be psychiatric technicians. I'm a lot more comfortable now. No one is giving me orders all the time. I was scared to death just before I started the military.

THERAPIST: What was frightening to you about the prospect of starting in the military?

PATIENT: I don't know. It was like when I first started jobs. The first job I had was as a paper boy. I had to get up at 5:00 AM. That's one reason I hate getting up early now. I have to go to the Reserves at 6:30 AM, which means getting up at 4:30 AM, Dad always thought that working hard in bad conditions was good for me. I remember working for a manufacturing company when I was a teenager. They told us to clean some things. I really worked hard. I tried to make it spic and span. I tried to get every bit of dirt off. Now I realize that they just wanted the main gook off.

THERAPIST: Was that typical of you when you were younger?

PATIENT: Yeah. I was just frightened something bad would happen to me if I didn't do everything just right. My father...[pause] There are two ways to treat kids: If they do something good, just say, "That's good." Or, you can criticize them. Tell them how to do what they did better. The latter was what my Dad always did with me. I began to develop the expectation that I'd always screw up. Now I resist doing things because I'm afraid I'll mess up. It makes me look lazy but it really isn't laziness. It's fear.

THERAPIST: You started the session talking about your relationship with the woman. Then you went on to talk about what was happening in the Reserves, then about your fears about the military and about jobs in general, and finally about your relationship with your father.

PATIENT: Maybe I hate the military because I hate my father. My father is so damn business-like. He could put love on a ledger basis.

THERAPIST: You talked about your fear of your father. In your dream last week you talked about the fear of the bad sergeant. But there also seems to be some unknown fear that something terrible is going to happen to you.

PATIENT: Oh, boy. It's that unknown fear that really gets me. Even though I know it's irrational. Like in the Reserves. I've made 34 out of 34 meetings, but as soon as I start to get any reprimand I start sweating and then I get afraid and then I get angry.

THERAPIST: It sounds like you try to handle your fear and anxiety by becoming angry.

PATIENT: I'm much more comfortable with anger. I'm handling school authority better and even the Reserves but not my father. I've never been able to say to him, "Don't do that to me," but I'm going to have to someday.

THERAPIST: Someday you're going to have to realize that you are no longer a little boy, that you are an adult, too.

PATIENT: I once had a plan of doing just that, of relating to my Dad like two adults. I've never been able to say anything to him when he made me angry but I was going to do it when I went to his wedding. It didn't seem right, though, when I was just seeing him for that one day.

THERAPIST: Do you feel you have to have a confrontation with your father?

PATIENT: I feel I'd like to. I don't quite believe I have to. I've never been able to exert my individuality with him. I feel that if I could do that with him, I could do it with anyone.

THERAPIST: You've had this kind of relationship with your father for a long time.

PATIENT: That reminds me. Once when I was a senior in high school I borrowed my Dad's car. I drank a pint of vodka in about a half an hour. Then I smashed the car into the garage and passed out. My father asked me the next day if I did it because of something he had done to me or if there was something that he could change. I don't think he really could have changed, but he may have said that I was misinterpreting his actions. I couldn't tell him what I felt then. I just said, "You and Mom are really great parents," but really I felt that they were too strict because they felt that I couldn't handle myself in what they considered a dirty, dangerous world. But they had always said, "We have a good family; we do things right; we never fight." As a 17-year-old I didn't know what was right. Anyway, that was an example of their inviting a complaint, and even when they invited it, I couldn't make it. I think my father could have taken a complaint but my mother would have made me feel, "How could you say that to me after all the pain I went through for you?"

THERAPIST: Did she really ever say anything like that?

PATIENT: No, but she gave me that feeling. Once in high school in Nebraska my girlfriend decided to go to Aspen. I decided to follow her. I tried to kiss my mother when I was ready to leave. She wouldn't let me because I was leaving her. I don't think she worried about my leaving. She just implied that I was doing it to hurt her somehow. That made me angry. In June last year we found out that my mother had lung cancer. I went home to see her. The first thing she said was, "Are you still smoking?" I felt she was saying, "It's your fault that I have lung cancer." That is a strange reaction on my part.

THERAPIST: You have some doubt about that interpretation of what she said.

PATIENT: Yeah. Yet I felt I was being blamed. Whether she meant it or not, the important thing is that I took it that way.

THERAPIST: Yes; it could have been meant in a positive way, too.

PATIENT: Yes; like "Stop smoking so you don't get cancer yourself." But there always was a discrepancy between what she said and what I felt she was telling me. Mother had an endocrine problem. For years I thought that was my fault. I'd see pictures of her before I was born. She was really beautiful but in the pictures after I was born she had this moon face and heavy body with skinny arms and legs. Her face would break out and her skin would get blotchy [*crying*].

THERAPIST: I think you miss your mother.

PATIENT: I do. Very much. Even though I complained about her, I loved her very much, too [*continues crying*].

THERAPIST: We have to stop for today.

PATIENT: I told you that I wasn't an emotional person, but I really get emotional about some of the things we discuss here.

DISCUSSION

The patient's initial statement in this session "This was the best week I can recall," immediately raised many questions in my mind. Had therapy up to this time been so anxiety-laden that the patient was resorting to a "flight into health"? In other words, was he going to tell me that he was now cured and no longer needed therapy? Alternatively, I wondered if I and/or the therapeutic process had filled some important need of his. If this was the case I wondered at what developmental level this need was occurring. Was I the mother at an early symbiotic level, allowing him to lean on me for ego strength? Was I a mother who was fostering trust and autonomy? Was I the parent encouraging separation and individuation, which would allow him to go on to age-appropriate behavior and interests? Another possibility was that the patient had indentified with his conceptualization of me. All of these considerations, of course, implied some internal change in the patient. It also occurred to me, but I thought it less likely, that some external circumstance over which the patient had no control led to his having a very good week.

The best way to find answers to these questions was to explore with the patient what he meant by it having been the best week he could recall. He started out by explaining that he had confronted a conflict with a girl in such a way that it raised his self-esteem. In the past he would have been more passive in a similar situation. He then described his change in jobs with the Air Force Reserves from medical technician to psychiatric technician. This allowed for more direct identification with me. Since the patient did not seem to have even a preconscious awareness of that identification, I thought it was premature for me to interpret it to him. Later in the session he had many associations to his relationship to his parents. Although he tended to focus on the negative aspects, it was also clear that he had many positive things going in his relationship with both of them. It appeared that at this stage of therapy, he was imbuing me with many of those positive aspects of his ambivalent feelings about his parents. I think one can conclude that the answer to my initial question about why he had such a good week is that all of the above considerations played some role, although some more importantly than others.

The patient showed that he understood the concept that earlier experiences affect current feelings and behavior. He talked about his father's earlier criticism of him developing "the expectation that I would always screw up; now I resist doing things." I then gave him a resume of the hour up to that point, wondering if he was able to see that what he talked about in the session was not random but rather flowed in association to previous material. He responded by trying to make a connection between two of the elements: namely, his hating the military and his hating his father. I then went a step further, trying to show him that there were also connections between the fear of the father in this session and the fear of the sergeant in the dream from the previous session. I took this a step further, suggesting to him that there was also an unknown fear that caused him anxiety. I was thinking of castration anxiety, but did not mention that to him at this point. He confirmed the correctness of this partial interpretation by responding with a great deal of affect and additional associations. His observing ego was also able to see the rational aspect of his anxiety.

I then tried to help him see the connection for him between anxiety and anger. Anger is often a secondary emotion which replaces a more painful emotion such as anxiety or humiliation. While emotions such as anxiety and humiliation are often experienced as passive, that is, caused by others, anger has a more active feeling. An angry person starts thinking about ways of responding to the cause of his hurt.

Throughout this session, but especially in the latter half of it, the patient provided a great deal of information about his relationship with his parents without any direct questioning about it. This is an example of the process of associative anamnesis, that is, the undirected recalling of past history.

As almost inevitably happens, historical material that comes out in the context of the patient's current concerns is more relevant and meaningful than material elicited by a series of questions. We learned about the patient's early work pattern, we saw some of the workings of his ego and superego, and we saw that his parents probably were not really as bad as he wanted to picture them. For instance, when he described some actual situations, it became clear that his parents did try to respond to him. When the patient got drunk and smashed the family car, his father didn't punish him; instead, his father asked if there was something that he or the patient's mother could do to help the patient. Some of my interventions were early attempts at trying to help him correct his distorted object representation of his parents.

There were real problems with his parents, though. For instance, in his vignette about leaving home to follow his girlfriend to Aspen, he described his mother's difficulty in allowing him to separate and individuate. It also appears that father did have difficulty giving the patient credit for a job well done.

Some confirmation of the hypothesis made in the initial interview about the harshness of his superego was obtained in this session. He interpreted his mother's question, "Are you still smoking?" as meaning, "It's your fault that I have lung cancer." Clearly this was a superego projection; that is, he himself felt guilt for his mother's cancer but then switched it around so that he understood her to blame him for it. My intervention at that point was an attempt to help his ego look at the distortion. His associations led to similar guilt feelings that he had experienced in childhood. He blamed himself for his mother's endocrine problem, which apparently was some form of Cushing's disease. I speculated to myself that this had grown out of some wishes in the negative Oedipus. During the course of normal development in the little boy there is not only the wish to have Mother and to be rid of Father, but sometimes the wish to have Father and to be rid of Mother. If this was an important factor in the patient's development, it probably would not come out in the therapy in the transference until the termination phase. Often a male patient with a male therapist who has unresoslved conflicts in the negative Oedipus will express these during the termination phase as he is about to lose the therapist. The old passive longings for the father are then revived and repeated in the transference.

His memories about his mother reactivated the mourning process. That was probably the first crying he had done in relation to the loss of his mother since the period immediately after her death.

The patient had still reported almost nothing about his only sibling, a brother. I was confident that he would describe his relationship with his brother when the material in the sessions made it appropriate.

He did not report a dream in this session. I was unable to conclude whether or not that was a defense against over-active intervention on my part when he presented his initial dream. Had he not presented the dream and also been defensive in other ways during this hour, I would have assumed that he was responding to overactive interpretation. Since the hour as a whole seemed to be very productive and relatively free of resistance, I anticipated that he would report dreams once again in later sessions.

SESSION 4, MARCH 22   "I FEEL SMALL"—CASTRATION ANXIETY

PATIENT: Last week we talked about conventionality. That's related to my relationship with the opposite sex, too. I've been attracted the last few years to bizarre women. I got screwed up by a girl with a bad reputation. She had some escapades with a football player when she was 14 and everyone knew about it. That's one reason I was attracted to her. I feel that if people aren't eccentric they're shallow, but that quality turns me off too. If they are that eccentric they have problems which will interfere with our relationship.

THERAPIST: What draws you to eccentric women?

PATIENT: In junior high a couple times I tried to hustle the girls considered popular. Once I thought I was madly in love with the most popular girl in school. I tried to get involved with her but I couldn't. Even back in grade school with puppy love, with no sex on my mind, I always wanted the most popular girl. But I would always feel I wasn't quite good enough so I'd choose the opposite. Maybe I saw the opposite as the only alternative for me. Some of my friends are bizarre, too. They live in the mountains like I do. Like hippies, but they are in graduate school. There's one student of mine that I am really attracted to, but I'm afraid my friends won't think she's cool because she's so straight. She's very smart. I don't know if I'm hesitant because I'll be turned off or because my friends will be.

THERAPIST: What's important to you?

PATIENT: Right. I have to figure out my own feelings. As independent as I appear, I'm really not. I'd like to be. I want intimacy but I'm afraid. I want to hustle a girl but I'm afraid I don't know how to structure it.

THERAPIST: I don't understand what you mean by "structure it."

PATIENT: As if everything has to come off just right. I want to be delicate; like the way my father had to treat my mother. They never screamed at each other. They always pretended that everything was rosy.

THERAPIST: He had to treat her like that?

PATIENT: There's a funny kind of hostility in my mother's family. She and her sister were always disgusted, not angry. When you did something wrong they got disgusted. You can't fight disgust.

THERAPIST: How would it make you feel when they got disgusted?

PATIENT: I would feel guilty. Mother was always quiet and I'd blame my father for everything. Only recently do I realize that Father at least tried to be affectionate once in awhile. Mother never was.

THERAPIST: Like when you wanted to go to Aspen.

PATIENT: Yeah. For some reason I can't think of examples before I was 15 years old. I can recall some humiliating things from earlier, but not with my family. Like when I was eight a kid called me "Weak Turner." Was it really confusing to me or won't I let myself recall?

THERAPIST: Perhaps both. It wasn't always clear what your parents' feelings were and you do prevent yourself from recalling.

PATIENT: It's the same now with girls. No matter what they say, I'm not sure what they mean. It's a projection of my own uncertainties about how I feel.

THERAPIST: Have you had relationships where the other person was clear about his thoughts and feelings?

PATIENT: I think Dr. Krueger was, but I was unsure about my feelings with him.

THERAPIST: How did you feel when the twelve sessions were up?

PATIENT: I think I was angry, but I have trouble with thinking about feelings. I'm not really sure I had feelings about it. Maybe I just accepted it as fact. I got along with him pretty well.

THERAPIST: I wonder why "angry" was the first feeling that came to your mind?

PATIENT: That's a possible reaction. It's really not an appropriate one because he had explained to me in advance. Did he have any idea what I felt? [pause] I don't know what it was.

THERAPIST: Are you aware of feelings as you talk with me?

PATIENT: [pause] When I try to think about feelings, it seems like I'm fabricating something. Really I'm just concerned about whether I'm getting somewhere. That's not true. I think it's just too uncomfortable for me to think about my feelings towards you. I don't think there is much about you as a person—I can say you are alert, concerned, but I just don't know whether I like you, don't like you. I think I judge that on the basis of whether or not I'm getting something from someone and vice versa.

THERAPIST: Is this a continuation of what you had with Dr. Krueger or is it different?

PATIENT: I try to make it the same. I try to figure things out in an analytical way instead of being emotional. I was pretty emotional the first time I came here but I haven't been so much since, except the end of the last session. Emotions are confusing to me. I feel I have to create them, pretend that I love or hate.

THERAPIST: It sounds to me as if you think you will be found wanting if we look at your ability to feel. That's a feeling in itself: It's a feeling of inadequacy. But I see no lack of feelings in you and you are already starting to define them more sharply.

PATIENT: That makes sense. That makes me feel a lot better about myself. Maybe I have feelings that I don't want to recognize like there is something bubbling away underneath that I want to keep hidden. Do you have any matches?

THERAPIST: No I don't. How do you feel about not being able to smoke?

PATIENT: It's a way to pretend that I'm doing something.

THERAPIST: Do you recall what you were experiencing when you had the urge to smoke?

PATIENT: We were talking about emotions and I got anxious. Hey! A thought just popped into my mind. I lived one summer in San Francisco with the girl I wanted to follow to Aspen. I was afraid that we'd be caught. It reminds me of my fear of being caught masturbating by my parents. I was always afraid of my parents. Like when we used to steal apples in junior high school. I was afraid of my parents catching me, not the police.

THERAPIST: What if they had caught you masturbating?

PATIENT: There is no fear that anything special would happen. It's just that something terrible would happen. Maybe Mother did catch me and I don't recall. It reminds me of my father bawling me out in Cub Scouts for holding my penis. It's unusual that I can't recall anything before about age seven or eight.

THERAPIST: How old were you when you started masturbating?

PATIENT: About eleven or twelve. Some older guy in the neighborhood showed me how to do it.

THERAPIST: Was there mutual masturbation or some other homosexual play between you and the older boy?

PATIENT: I recall homosexual business taking part way up in a tree and another time at the foot of the tree. Somehow this makes the connection for me with the in group vs the not-in group. Like I was in between. The guys in the tree, there were three or four, were in and the guy at the foot of the tree wasn't. I think I had two experiences. I don't know. Maybe more. I don't know if I was seven or twelve. The guy at the foot of the tree said, "You've got a small one, too." That bothered me. That put me in the uncool group.

THERAPIST: Does that still bother you?

PATIENT: Yeah. The size of my penis was a hangup for years. I was a late developer for pubic hair and penis size. I feel small.

THERAPIST: Do you have a small penis?

PATIENT: Not really, but I feel that I do. It still makes me nervous thinking about it. That reminds me. I had a dream last night. In the dream a friend and I were sitting in my house talking very rationally. Suddenly two rowdies came by. I loaded a shotgun with extra shells from my pocket. Then the dream cut to two people being shot. Then suddenly two law officers in blue appeared. Next there was a policeman holding a large revolver. He said to me, "Do you have a hand gun permit?" I said, "I don't own a hand gun. It must belong to one of the rowdies." Then the dream faded into a desolate landscape.

THERAPIST: That's a very interesting dream, but it's almost the end of the hour, so we will not have much time to work on it. What brought the dream to your mind now?

PATIENT: When we were talking about small penises I thought of the hand gun and then I remembered the whole dream.

THERAPIST: In the dream there were rational people and rowdies and law officers.

PATIENT: Do you think those could all represent different parts of me?

THERAPIST: Does that make sense to you?

PATIENT: It makes a lot of sense to me but I hadn't thought about it until you pointed out the three types of people in the dream.

DISCUSSION

How to determine the frequency of psychotherapy sessions is an important problem for which very little rationale has been developed. Psychoanalysis is usually carried on four to five times a week. This frequency was determined as being optimal for developing a controlled regression and an intense transference neurosis. Insight psychotherapy most frequently is carried on at a frequency of once to twice per week. The frequency in supportive psychotherapy varies widely. At one extreme is the chronic schizophrenic, who may be seen only once a month with the goals of periodically enhancing his ability to reality test and of evaluating the effectiveness of the medication he is taking. At the other extreme would be the patient in supportive therapy during an extreme crisis who might be seen daily. Even in insight psychotherapy the frequency may occasionally be increased during a period of crisis. For instance, a man who I was treating whose basic psychopathology was that of a narcissistic personality disorder, as described by Kohut,[5] was on the verge of decompensating into a psychotic depression during a period of extreme stress in his life. For a period of about two weeks I had a daily psychotherapy session with him each morning before he went to work. This provided an alternative to hospitalization which allowed the patient to continue working, and also avoided what would have been, for him, an extreme blow to his self-esteem.

I raise the issue of frequency of sessions at this time because the beginning of this session provided some evidence that once-a-week psychotherapy was probably the frequency of choice for this patient. He began the session by referring back to a topic, conventionality, that he had raised in a previous session. This was evidence that with once-a-week psychotherapy this patient was able to maintain continuity from one session to another. In addition to the ability to maintain continuity, it was clear that he had also been doing some work on his own in between sessions. He not only returned to the topic of conventionality, but reported that in thinking about it he began to realize that it also applied to his relationships with women. Another important consideration relates to the effect of frequency on the balance between transference and non-transference material and between the patient's emphasis on internal versus external reality. The more frequent the sessions, the more likely that the focus will be on transference material and on the patient's internal reality, and less about his relationship with other people and what is going on in his external life. In short, frequency should be determined by the goals, the patient's psychopathology, the patient's ego strengths, and the particular situation or level of crisis.

As the patient continued, he made it clear that his problems were with identity and intimacy. In Erikson's[9] epigenetic theory of ego development, finding one's identity is a life task appropriate to adolescence and developing intimacy is the task appropriate to young adult life. His conflict about his identity came up in the earlier session, in which he discussed conventionality. At that time he described his fantasy of either leading a counter-culture type of life or leading the life of the creative businessman–scientist. In an earlier session he had also talked about his fears that psychotherapy would make him conventional and that he would then no longer be creative. He shows more of this "either/or" kind of thinking in this session when he described his conflict about dating girls who are either "straight" or "hippie" types. At a later point in the session I tried to help him get beyond this "either/or" type of thinking into a thinking that accepts concepts such as "both/and."

The specific phrasing of interventions is very important. Consider my intervention in this session after he has been talking about his attraction to eccentric women. My intervention was, "What draws you to eccentric women?" Contrast that phrasing with the following alternative: "Why are you drawn to that kind of person?" The phrasing that I did use made use of his own words, "eccentric women." By using the word "what" instead of "why," the intervention avoids sounding judgmental. For most people a "why" question reminds them of childhood interrogation about why they did something wrong. Perhaps an even better intervention would have been to avoid asking any question at all. Instead, I could have made a comment such as, "There are probably many reasons for your attraction to eccentric women." This still invites him to employ his analyzing ego to understand his attraction without asking him a question. The argument in favor of not asking questions is that to some extent the world is divided into those people who can ask questions and those people who have to answer questions. Some patients experience being asked questions as infantilizing. For them it is a repeat of parent/child or teacher/student roles. Not all patients respond this way but it is worth keeping in mind for the occasional patient who has this negative reaction.

The patient went on to state a theme that one can predict will be prominent throughout the therapy, considering what we know about his level of development and his psychodynamics. The theme is that he is not big enough or, more specifically, that his equipment is not big enough or good enough. He not only has the feeling now but recalls how it manifested in early adolescence and latency. As the session continued, his concerns were reported in increasingly specific ways. His associations went from being caught masturbating, to his father reprimanding him for holding his penis, to two childhood homosexual experiences, and finally to the very specific concern about the size of his penis. At that point I tried to do some reality testing by asking, "Do you have a small penis?" His response indicated that intellectually he knew that his penis was not small but that he felt that it was. The internal representation that he had of his penis was that it was a small one.

As I listened to him describe his fear of being caught masturbating, it became clear to me that what he feared most was being embarrassed and humiliated. His fear was that his parents would see his masturbation as an inadequate attempt at being an adult sexual man. Little boys during the Oedipal struggles go through a series of fantasies about their relationship with their parents. The little boy goes through the following series of rationalizations in regard to his fantasy that he could satisfy his mother in the same way that his father does. First he says, "I could if she would." Then he has to rationalize why she will not by saying, "She would if he (Father) would let her." What the little boy avoids is the extreme narcissistic humiliation of recognizing that even if mother would and even if father would let her, there is no way that he could sexually satisfy her with his five-year-old sexual equipment. This patient is still fearing that narcissistic humiliation and trying to avoid it. Of course, it was far too early in the therapy to try to make an interpretation to the patient on that topic. The related fantasy that the little boy has during the Oedipal period is that the father will castrate him in retaliation for the little boy's wish to have mother and to get rid of father. There was evidence of castration anxiety in this session too, but, again, it was too early to make an interpretation.

Once again in this session we saw some evidence that the patient was starting to bring some balance to his concept of his father. The patient recognized that "I blame my father for everything; only recently do I realize that Father at least tried to be affectionate." Almost invariably in successful insight psychotherapy, the patient develops a less distorted and more balanced representation of both his parents.

Some of the patient's psychological mechanisms that were in evidence in this hour are worth pointing out. Several times he noted his repression by complaining that he had difficulty remembering childhood experiences. He also demonstrated that he had an observing ego that was capable of making a defense interpretation of his own material. Consider for example his statement, "Was it really confusing to me or wouldn't I let myself recall?" I took that a step further by suggesting to him that maybe both were operating and that it wasn't an either/or situation. He then talked about "projection of my own uncertainties about how I feel" onto women. That was interesting, since in the previous session I had pointed out his projection to him. Now he was able to see it himself.

When the opportunity arose during the session to discuss further his relationship with his former therapist, I did so for two reasons: First, I wanted the patient to be able to express any unresolved feelings he had about the termination with the former therapist; second, I wanted him to compare and contrast me and our work together with his former therapist and their work together, in order to help him differentiate us. With some patients no therapy can take place until this differentiation is clearly made. The most extreme case in my own practice was a young woman who came to me for therapy after two years of twice-a-week therapy with another therapist. She and her former therapist had together physically acted out many of her sexual fantasies about him instead of trying to analyze them. Before we were able to do any therapeutic work on her conflicts, she had to be clear in her own mind that my goal, unlike her former therapist's, was going to be psychological understanding rather than mutual sexual gratification.

When patients eat or smoke during a session, it is usually a sign that they are either not satisfied with what they are receiving from the therapist or that they characteristically handle anxiety with oral gratification. A useful way to deal with this is to ask the patient what he was experiencing at the time he decided to either eat or smoke in the session. In this session the patient's urge to smoke was frustrated by a lack of matches. I still handled the urge in a similar way. This approach has weaned many of my patients from smoking during the sessions. Some of them, as they gained more understanding about the anxiety that led to their smoking, have also been able to completely discontinue smoking.

The patient presented another dream, but near the end of the session. The technical question at that point was how to make best use of the dream with only a few minutes left. I chose to first point out the defensive aspect of not bringing up the dream until there was almost no time to work on it. Unlike the first dream which he brought up at the very beginning of the session, this one came to mind in the course of the session in association with something else. My next statement, "What brought it to mind now?" was an attempt to make use of this to help the patient think in terms of psychic causality; that is, thoughts do not occur randomly but in association to previous thought. I used the remaining minutes to help him discover that the dream represented his ego, id, and superego, in the forms of the rational people, the rowdies, and the law officers respectively. I did not try to explore with him the deeper id aspects of the dream, for instance, his wish to have a loaded shotgun, which represented a big penis. Combined with the wish was the fear that his impulses would leap out of control if he did have the loaded shotgun, that he would kill someone or do something else dangerous; nor did I have time to point out the displacement in the dream where in effect the ego was saying to the superego, "Don't blame me; blame the id." This is represented in the dream by the patient saying, "I don't even own a handgun. It must belong to the rowdies."

SESSION 5, MARCH 29   **PSYCHOTHERAPY OR**
                                                  PSYCHOANALYSIS?

PATIENT: Were we talking about emotion?

THERAPIST: Uh-huh.

PATIENT: I went out with a new girl Saturday night.

THERAPIST: What was her name?

PATIENT: Julie. We bought a couple bottles of wine and went for a long drive. When we got back we made out for a while. I felt good because I really felt like making out and wasn't just doing it because I felt it was appropriate. Julie was a student of mine last semester. It was our first date. In the past the hangup with girls has been that I didn't act on my feelings. I was just acting before; it wasn't spontaneous.

THERAPIST: Do you prefer to be spontaneous?

PATIENT: Yes. Yet I'm restless around people who try to be spontaneous. It's something you just have to allow to happen. I'm getting much better at it, but I'm still lacking.

THERAPIST: What inhibits your spontaneity?

PATIENT: Fear. I could do it with this girl because the conversation just flowed. She encouraged it. She made me feel relaxed. Julie should be more threatening than other girls because she's smarter; but it's the other kind who threaten me.

THERAPIST: You don't have any fear that you'll be found lacking in the intellectual area.

PATIENT: That's true. My fear with girls is that I'll act and they won't respond. Like the girl I lived with for a summer in San Francisco. That fall she quit writing. She wouldn't let me know how she felt. I felt like killing myself; really, I wanted to kill her. It made me physically sick for days: I threw up, I couldn't eat. I can't take an un-answer. I think it's related to my mother.

THERAPIST: How's that?

PATIENT: Often I'd come to her and ask questions or assert myself with her or ask for help, but I would get no response. She would just make me feel there was something wrong with me. I'm too self-centered.

THERAPIST: How so?

PATIENT: If someone treats me nice I feel good, but not because it was nice for them to do it, but because it made me feel comfortable. I want to feel good about myself. I refer everything back to myself. Whatever another person does, I wonder how it refers back to me. Emotional things make me turn inward. Then I become less responsive.

THERAPIST: What about Saturday night?

PATIENT: That was more spontaneous. It really felt good. We just fooled around. We pretended that we were Bonnie and Clyde, things like that. I do become more spontaneous when I'm drunk. I get more impulsive. I act out my feelings instead of just thinking about them.

THERAPIST: What keeps you from doing the same thing when you're not drunk?

PATIENT: I'm not sure, but I'll give you an example. When I'm sober, if I see a girl I know and I want to talk to her, instead of doing it I just keep thinking about it, and then I get afraid.

THERAPIST: What comes to mind?

PATIENT: I start thinking, "I'll soon try to get her to bed," so I'm not treating her right. I have devious motives.

THERAPIST: I don't understand.

PATIENT: I think about status. First I think, "I'm way above her," then I feel she's way above me.

THERAPIST: Did you grow up with the idea, "Good girls don't screw"?

PATIENT: No—just if they are way above me they're for someone else, not for me.

THERAPIST: Who is the someone else?

PATIENT: Just about anyone. If it's a typical college girl, then it's some athlete. If it's a hippie, then it's some groovy, LSD-head. It almost never turns out that I think a more intellectual person would be the someone. That's because I don't see intelligence as sexual. Also, I'm pretty good at intellectual things.

THERAPIST: Earlier you related your inaction to your relationship to your mother.

PATIENT: Yeah. It was just a vague feeling. I keep thinking of the time I went to Aspen and when mother was dying and wouldn't let me get close.

THERAPIST: Are you afraid now that women won't let you get close?

PATIENT: Yes. Fear of that and also the opposite. If they get too attracted to me, I get uncomfortable. I guess I make some girls uncomfortable because it is so important to me that I get to them fast. Then they have to answer my demands for closeness. I'm like the neurotic housewife who keeps asking her husband, "Do you love me?." One girl told me I was a pest. I don't ask them for verbal confirmation, but I keep wanting physical signs that they love me. I think I need that so badly because I never got it from my mother. I keep trying to get it from other women.

THERAPIST: What's the future in that?

PATIENT: None. You really can't get it. I know that now. For the last few weeks I've felt strong enough so that I don't even need it.

THERAPIST: But the old yearnings are still there.

PATIENT: Yeah. Actually I'd probably be repulsed if someone did treat me like a five-year-old kid and smother me with love. It's funny. I'm getting less sexual activity since I've been feeling more comfortable with myself. I used to be infantile about sex; always trying to prove my masculinity. I used it like a narcotic instead of letting it be a relaxed, enjoyable thing.

THERAPIST: What do you mean when you say you were infantile about sex?

PATIENT: I always worried about my capacity and about the capacity of the woman to make me really comfortable. I get the feeling I want to shrink into a little kid again and be nursed. Adult sexuality just isn't that way.

THERAPIST: Are you a breast man?

PATIENT: Yeah, yeah [*starts laughing*].

THERAPIST: Something made you laugh.

PATIENT: It occurred to me that I still am a breast man. Of course, it's a cultural thing too. I'm preoccupied with breasts. I want youthful, taut breasts. I wonder if those are projections of my wanting an erect penis? But, I like big, soft breasts too. They're comfortable and good. I really don't have a preference now but in the past I liked the big, soft breasts best. I think that's still slightly my preference. When I was about thirteen or fourteen I used to have a lot of fantasies about just lying on a girl's chest with my head between her breasts. I'm getting embarrassed. I'm embarrassed to tell you but I used to see pictures of girls and masturbate, thinking my penis was pressed between their breasts instead of having intercourse.

THERAPIST: I wonder what causes your embarrassment?

PATIENT: It's wrong to have fantasies like that.

THERAPIST: Apparently you have some feeling that it's wrong.

PATIENT: I feel that way about a lot of sexual desires that I have.

THERAPIST: We can continue with this next week.

PATIENT: Good. I've been preoccupied with these problems for years but I've never been able to talk about them to friends or anyone. I've always been too embarrassed.

I noted that the patient did not smoke this session, but since neither of us brought it up, I did not find out why. Perhaps it was some combination of our having talked about it the previous session, his having forgotten his matches again, or a decreased level of anxiety during this session.

DISCUSSION

This discussion of Session # 5 will be divided into four main parts. First I will discuss aspects of the session itself. Next I will try to assess the therapy thus far, including diagnostic considerations, the developing alliance, and early transference manifestations. In the third part I will compare and contrast insight psychotherapy and psychoanalysis. I will include a discussion of indications for each and of analysability. Finally, I will use the second and third parts of the discussion to help explain why insight psychotherapy seemed to be the treatment of choice for this patient.

Aspects of the Session

When Paul told me that he had gone out with a "new girl", I asked for her name. The technical reason for requesting names is to help the patient keep from distancing. Otherwise, this patient probably would have gone on for many sessions referring to "the girl I told you about" instead of calling her Julie. Another reason for obtaining names is that it facilitates communication between therapist and patient. He reported being more comfortable and more spontaneous with Julie than he had with most women in the past. Further exploration suggested that this was due to a combination of his feeling somewhat better about himself and some particular characteristics of Julie.

Later in the session he reported his difficulty in dealing with anger. When the girl from San Francisco quit writing him he became furious. He wanted to kill her but found that fantasy unacceptable. Instead, he turned it inward and started having thoughts about killing himself. Then he somaticized the anger, becoming physically ill. One can predict with a fair amount of certainty that if something infuriates him in the future, he will react with the same psychosomatic symptoms, namely vomiting and decreased appetite. I was impressed with Paul's ability to connect his anger at the girl in San Francisco with the lack of responsiveness of his mother.

After that nice piece of work, however, he started to intellectualize, talking about how "emotional things make me turn inward," and so on. When the patient becomes defensive in psychotherapy, the therapist has a number of choices: He can stick with the content, deal directly with the defense, or circumvent the defense. In psychoanalysis I would have definitely dealt directly with the defense. The goal at this stage would have been to help the patient develop an observing, analyzing ego, which would eventually enable him to deal with some of his defenses himself. That may have been the most useful approach at this point in psychotherapy also. However, by deciding to make the intervention, "What about Saturday night?" I chose to circumvent the defense instead. In once-a-week psychotherapy there is some pressure to circumvent defenses and to bring the patient back to the material at hand.

The patient was then able to elaborate on his Saturday night date and to give a third reason for his spontaneity, namely, that he had been drinking. Freud once defined the superego as that part of the mental apparatus that is soluble in alcohol.

Examination of his superego quickly led to his bringing up Oedipal derivatives. By this I am referring to his need to turn his relationships with women into triangular relationships by bringing a man into the picture: ". . . they are for someone else, not for me." He not only postulates another man, he also sees a competitive situation with the man in which he himself is the loser. He even verbalizes that in his relationships with women. He hopes to obtain what he wanted from mother but never received, a confirmation that he is lovable.

When the patient started to regress, I first tried to get across the idea that the wish to regress is normal and understandable, but that there is no future in it. My goal was to promote maturity. But it immediately became clear that I had made a premature intervention. As soon as I realized the patient's need to work through some of his struggles about his wish to regress and the repulsion caused by it, I stopped interfering with the regression. When I asked him, "Are you a breast man?" he answered, "Yes," and then laughed. Laughter is often the way the unconscious says "yes." The laughter was comfirming that he was not only a breast man when he was an infant but that he still is. This question also led to his sharing with me many of his sexual fantasies that

in the past he had been too embarrassed to share with anyone. When he
labeled his fantasies as being "wrong," I again made an intervention that had
the goal of altering his superego in the direction of less harshness. I ended the
session by suggesting that we continue talking about his sexual fantasies the
following meeting. My goal in doing this was to let him know that I was
comfortable talking about these fantasies, to give him some reinforcement for
having done something that he found difficult and embarrassing, and to promote continuity from one session to the next.

Assessment of the Therapy

After completing five sessions, we have reached a point where we can
profitably try to consolidate the assessments made so far. Diagnostically we
can now, with some assurrance, place him in the category of psychoneurosis.
His ego has developed adequately along the major developmental lines. Reality testing is intact, self-representation and object-representation have been
fairly well differentiated. There is evidence of the development of an ego
ideal and of a superego. His ego ideal is still somewhat in flux. At times he
thinks he should strive for the almost impossible goal of becoming a Nobel
Prize-winning scientist. At other times he thinks it would be very glamorous
to be a drop-out from society; he could lead a carefree life relatively free of
responsibility. His superego is, at times, overly harsh and prohibitive, leading
to inhibitions of some of his thoughts, feelings, impulses, and behavior.
There is also some evidence that his superego hasn't been totally internalized.
Often his behavior is inhibited by fear of punishment by some external agent
rather than by an internal conviction that what he wants to do is wrong. To a
large extent, his sexual and aggressive drives have been neutralized in the
service of functioning for the ego. His most prominent defense mechanism is
repression; however, he uses other defenses such as intellectualization, undoing, projection, and reaction-formation. His main psychopathology grows out
of deficiencies in certain lines of development. The patient experiences his
psychopathology as inhibition in the areas of work, sex, and play, combined
with an internal discomfort, most of which is anxiety.

Within the broad category of psychoneurosis, the specific diagnosis
which best fits this patient is hysterical neurosis. Most of his object relationships are triangular. Even those which start out as dyadic relationships he
turns into triangles. Recall, for example, his first dream. At the beginning he
was having a sexual relationship with a woman. He quickly brought in a man
whom he split into two parts, the bad sergeant and the good captain. In his
fantasies, whenever he sees a woman he wants, he imagines that she already

has a man whom she prefers to him. The particular way he arranges these triangular object relationships is typical of the Oedipal level. Also typical of Oedipal level conflicts are his inhibitions. In his mind, success at love or work or play can only come about as a result of competition with another man. We have already heard some evidence through his dreams and fantasies and, as one can predict, we will hear much more, that he thinks that any success comes at a cost to another man who will then try to punish him. He prominently uses hysterical defenses such as repression and displacement, although he also uses a number of obsessional defenses as well. There has been evidence that castration anxiety is a prominent symptom.

We can consider the patient in terms of some of the major developmental lines that are discussed in the section on developmental diagnosis at the end of Part I. In terms of the self object developmental line, the patient has clearly reached the stage of triadic relationships which usher in the Oedipal period. He has not yet, however, resolved the Oedipus in such a way that he can have a relationship with a woman of his own without fearing retaliation from a man. One form that this is taking with the patient in early adulthood is his difficulty in forming intimate relationships with women. There is also some indication that the separation–individuation phase was adequate but not optimal. Although we haven't heard material directly from that period prior to about age three, we have seen some derivative suggestions that there were problems. An example is his story about his mother's difficulty in letting him go when he wanted to follow a girlfriend to Aspen. His inability to master the adolescent task of forming a firm identity is also evidence of some problem in the earlier separation–individuation phase. This should be qualified, however, to point out that the separation–individuation process continues throughout one's lifetime.

A related subject is the patient's dealing with the death of his mother. In spite of some denial, he has been going through a fairly adequate mourning process. Although I presented it in a greatly condensed fashion, he has done a significant amount of mourning during these early sessions as well. This indicates some capacity to deal with separation in a healthy way. The self-object developmental line can be seen as a continuum with egocentrism at one end and altruism at the other. Egocentrism implies qualities such as selfishness and immaturity. Altruism suggests the opposite. The person who is very far towards the side of egocentrism is unable to empathize with others, while the altruistic person is able to put himself in another person's place and see the world through that person's eyes. Mature love is altruistic. An altruistic person not only obtains direct pleasure from his relationship with another person, he also obtains satisfaction from sharing the other person's pleasure and from providing the other person with pleasure. Although our evidence is still scanty, it appears that this patient has moved toward the level of altruism, but has not yet completely reached it.

Next consider the anxiety developmental line for this patient. There are still remnants of fear of annihilation, of stranger anxiety, and of separation anxiety, but these are minimal. The patient has, in reality, experienced a loss of a parent, but has been dealing with that loss. There is considerable evidence that firm object constancy has developed. He certainly makes use of signal anxiety. Both the fear of castration and the fear of superego punishment are prominent.

A functioning, working alliance has developed rapidly with this patient. This provides evidence that Paul developed firm basic trust early in life and went quite far in the self-object developmental line. The patient cathected me and our work together with a fair amount of psychic energy. He quickly identified with my way of working in the therapy and started making use of it himself.

One goal of psychotherapy is to help the patient develop a new structure in his ego, what I will call the therapeutic function. By this I mean the ability to carry out confrontation, clarification, interpretation, and working through. In the early stage of treatment the therapist provides his own ego as a kind of auxiliary to that of the patient. Gradually the patient learns to assume some of the therapeutic functions himself. In Paul's case he was able to interpret one of his defenses in the same way I had interpreted it in a previous session. His ability to do therapeutic work on his own between sessions is also strong evidence that he has been developing good therapeutic function.

There has not yet been much intense transference development. There have been, however, many clues as to the transference we can anticipate. He has both bad and good representations of each parent. It is likely that in the course of therapy he will at times see me as the belittling father and at other times as the father who tried to show him some affection. He will also see me at times as the rejecting mother and at other times as the mother he dearly loved. One of the goals in therapy will be to help him integrate the disparate views he has of his parents. This is one of the tasks of the early separation–individuation phase, but one that often has to be reworked at later stages in a person's life. Probably as the patient works through his relationship with me he will also be able to integrate his relationships with his parents.

Insight Psychotherapy and Psychoanalysis

The patient has been discussed with regard to psychiatric diagnosis, the alliance, and transference. The therapeutic contract was discussed as it developed.* The time has come to formalize a treatment plan. Because of the patient's psychopathology and the way that it is interfering with his life, some therapy is clearly indicated. The question is, what kind of therapy? Based on what I knew about him diagnostically the question is my mind was still whether insight psychotherapy or psychoanalysis would be the treatment of choice. In order to make this decision, I had to compare and contrast the two modalities in my mind, including indications for each and analyzability.

Insight psychotherapy and psychoanalysis form a continuum which is clearly distinguishable at the two extremes. Psychoanalysis is a specialized form of insight psychotherapy. It is more extensive and intensive than the usual insight psychotherapy. Free association is used to explore and to make conscious the dynamic, genetic, and transference aspects of the patient's personality and behavior. The development and use of the regressive transference neurosis will be described later. Insight psychotherapy is less extensive, less intensive, and does not make use of free association. More emphasis is placed on making conscious the psychodynamic (the cross-sectional functional equilibrium of the personality) and less on the psychogenetic (the infantile and childhood sources of the adult personality) and transference elements. Where the treatment falls on the continuum depends on factors related to both the therapist and the patient.

In terms of the therapist, my own experience can be used as an illustration. As I progressed in my education as a psychoanalyst and in my experience doing psychoanalysis, both the psychotherapy and the psychoanalysis that I did changed. With those patients I was seeing in once- or twice-a-week psychotherapy, who could benefit from or were capable of more analytic type work, the therapy moved in that direction. The case presented in this book was done the year I was Chief Resident in Psychiatry at the University of Colorado Medical Center. It is an example of the type of psychotherapy I was doing near the completion of my psychiatric residency but before I had started training at the Denver Psychoanalytic Institute. Early in my first psychoanalytic cases, I carried over many of my psychotherapeutic techniques. As I developed more as an analyst, I was able to do more classical psychoanalysis with these patients.

Where the treatment falls on the continuum also depends on the patient. There are patients in psychotherapy whose psychological-mindedness, ego strength, ability to regress in the service of the ego, to work with unconscious material, and to work in the transference allow them to have therapy which approaches psychoanalysis while they are sitting up face-to-face once or twice a week. Patients without those attributes, who are in four to five times a week,

*Technical essays on these subjects appear at the end of this Part.

on-the-couch psychoanalysis cannot be analyzed by classical technique alone. Instead, the analyst has to introduce parameters[10] and other modifications of technique.[11]

OVERALL PLAN, GOALS, AND TECHNIQUES OF PSYCHOANALYSIS

The overall plan in psychoanalysis involves the development of a regressive transference neurosis, which is then worked through and resolved. This allows the patient to re-experience and/or remember the formerly unconscious infantile and early childhood conflicts, impulses, wishes, and solutions. With the help of the analyst, the patient can then use his adult ego and experience to find more adaptive solutions. Resolution of these formerly unconscious early conflicts leads to changes in the patient's symptoms and character. Concomitantly the psychic energy formerly used to defend against conscious awareness is freed up for creative and adaptive uses.

Several techniques facilitate the achievement of this overall plan. Frequent sessions tend to increase the intensity of the transference and to keep the material focused on the patient's intrapsychic life. Use of the couch further enhances regression and fantasy. The reclining position is associated with regressed states in everyday life, such as sleeping, where psychological defenses are at a minimum. The relative immobilization along with the agreement that fantasies will be verbalized but not acted upon frees the patient's ability to fantasize and free associate. The analyst's being out of the patient's sight also facilitates the patient's free associations and his projections onto the analyst in the regressive transsference neurosis. The patient is not inhibited by the analyst's physical characteristics or reactions. The analyst's main functions are to be a transference object and to interpret.

The overall plan of psychoanalysis also affects the development of the alliance. In both psychoanalysis and psychotherapy the alliance is an adult form of early healthy relationships. Basic trust, symbiosis, and identification are all involved. In the symbiotic phase of childhood development the parent, in the role of an auxiliary self, provides the functions for the child that the child cannot yet perform himself. Gradually, by use of several processes including identification, the child takes over these functions. In psychoanalysis the analyst provides a special auxiliary ego, with an analyzing function. The goal is for the patient to develop a new ego structure which allows him to take over the analyzing function for himself.

In supportive therapy the therapist never gets beyond the level of being an auxiliary ego because a working alliance is not developed where the patient takes over the therapeutic function. In insight psychotherapy the patient does develop the therapeutic function but it is different from the analyzing function. The difference between the therapeutic and the analyzing function should become clear from the overall discussion and from the section on treatment planning and technique later in this book.

In order to be analyzed a patient must be capable of developing a working alliance and an analyzable transference neurosis. The transference neurosis is analyzable only if it is observable by both the patient and the analyst. Without the capacity to form a working alliance, the patient lacks the capacity to develop an observing ego and an analyzable transference neurosis. Nunberg[12] described a patient who could not be analyzed because she expected literally to find her father in the analyst. She was not capable of stepping back and observing that she was experiencing the analyst in the analytic situation *as if* he were her father. Without the *as if* distinction, the patient develops a transference psychosis. Analyzability is determined by evaluating the patient's ego structure. Good clues as to the patient's ability to develop an alliance and a transference neurosis come from obtaining a history of the patient's relationships and of his ability to work.

In psychoanalysis defenses are dealt with more vigorously than they are in psychotherapy. First the defenses and then what is being defended against are interpreted. This grows out of the overall plan of uncovering as much defended against material as possible. The goal is to bring what was unconscious into the patient's consciousness.

OVERALL PLAN, GOALS AND TECHNIQUES OF INSIGHT PSYCHOTHERAPY

The transference neurosis, a sine qua non of psychoanalysis, is not part of the plan for psychotherapy. A regressive transference neurosis is of no value unless it can be resolved. Instead, the therapist facilitates the development of a less intense transference relationship, which is used in the four ways described in the section on alliance and transference. Most of the therapeutic work is done with latency, adolescent and adult derivatives of infantile and early childhood conflicts. Many patients in insight psychotherapy, including the patient described in this book, are arrested at some point in their development. The goal, then, is to help the patient through that stage of development so that he can go on to the next stage. The plan with this patient is to deal with him for the most part at the stages of development where he is arrested, late adolescence and early adulthood. The reasons for his problems now do go back to childhood (an inadequate solution of the Oedipal conflict and faulty self and object-representation), but significant changes in his symptoms, his character, his development, and his understanding can come about without a reliving of the Oedipus in the therapy situation. Since most of the work will be done in stages later than early childhood, there will be very little exploration of his primary process thinking. Even in dreams where the primary process thinking is apparent to the therapist, most of the dream interpretation to the patient will be at a secondary process level.

Primary process thinking is characteristic of infancy, dreams, and psychotic states and is approximated in free association. The restrictions of logic, reality, time, and space are abandoned. Secondary process thinking is the ordinary conscious thinking of adults, is under mature ego control, and is characterized by the usual rules of logic, syntax, and reality.

Again, the techniques follow from the overall plan. The sessions are frequent enough to insure continuity, to achieve a desired balance between focusing on intrapsychic processes and current external reality, and to titrate the level of regression in the sessions. For similar reasons, psychotherapy is usually conducted face-to-face. Sitting provides some of the same advantage of partial immobilization without the strong regressive pull of lying down. The patient is asked to speak freely, in other words, not to consciously withhold, but his verbalization usually is kept firmly in secondary process.

Both the psychotherapist and the analyst are very active in their mental and emotional processing of the patient's material, but the therapist usually makes more frequent interventions. The analyst, especially during the middle phase of analysis, tries to foster the maximum elaboration of fantasies and development of the transference. Premature interventions lead to premature closure. The therapist, however, has different goals. He intervenes earlier because he wants to help the patient see connections and patterns without developing a transference neurosis. As mentioned in the discussion of an earlier session, defenses in psychotherapy are sometimes circumvented rather than interpreted.

Before the therapist obtains any specific information about a patient he already knows a great deal about him based on the therapist's knowledge of psychological development and of human beings in general. As the diagnostic process continues, the therapist is able to make fairly specific hypotheses about the patient.

Because of the severe time limitations of psychotherapy, the therapist may share some of this thinking with the patient to show him a new way of looking at psychological problems. The patient in psychotherapy just does not have enough time to discover on his own how to work in therapy. The therapist's thinking aloud acts as a stepping stone for further exploration no matter whether the patient agrees, disagrees, understands, does not understand, or further elaborates. When imparting this kind of information to a patient the therapist guards against encouraging intellectualization and against appearing all-knowing by making clear the provisional nature of these communications.

Why Insight Psychotherapy was Chosen

Using the knowledge obtained about the patient thus far and keeping the above discussion in mind, how do we decide whether to continue with psychotherapy or to recommend psychoanalysis? The patient meets all the criteria for analyzability. Based on my evaluation and the way he had worked in the first five sessions, I was confident that he was capable of developing a working alliance and an observable transference neurosis. In addition, he was motivated by the discomfort he was experiencing and by his curiosity about his own mental and emotional functioning.

Once it is determined that a patient appears to be analyzable, the next question is: Is psychoanalysis the treatment of choice or is there treatment available to achieve the patient's goals with less time, effort, and money? I decided that insight psychotherapy was indicated for this patient. Chronologically he was in his mid-twenties, but fortunately he still had the psychological flexibility of a late adolescent. This meant that he was still in the process of an adolescent reworking of the Oedipus. The fact that he was stuck in the process did not matter. As long as an adolescent solution to the Oedipus had not been solidified, there was still room for psychotherapeutic intervention without the need for reworking in a regressive transference neurosis.

In contrast, a few months after I started seeing Mr. Turner I was referred a 27-year-old married history instructor with one child. His presenting complaints were similar. His promotion was being held up because of his inability to publish and his relationship with his wife was not satisfying. His dynamics and ego structure were similar to Mr. Turner's, except that he had rigidified a faulty adolescent solution to the Oedipus. Since reopening the issue in a meaningful way required the development of a transference neurosis, I recommended that he seek psychoanalysis.

REFERENCES

1. Zetzel ER: Current concepts of transference. Int J Psycho-Anal 37:369–376, 1956.
2. Greenson RR: The working alliance and the transference neurosis. Psychoanal Q 34:155–181, 1965.
3. Freud S: The Standard Edition of the Complete Psychological Works of Sigmund Freud, Volume XII: On Beginning the Treatment, Strachey J et al. (eds). London, Hogarth Press, 1958.
4. Freud S: The Standard Edition of the Complete Psychological Works of Sigmund Freud, Volume IV: The Interpretation of Dreams, Strachey J et al. (eds). London, Hogarth Press, 1962.

5. Freud A: The Writings of Anna Freud, Volume II: The Ego and the Mechanisms of Defense. New York, International Universities Press, 1966.
6. Freud S: The Standard Edition of the Complete Psychological Works of Sigmund Freud, Volume XV: Introductory Lectures on Psychoanalysis. London, Hogarth Press, 1963.
7. Eissler KR: On some theoretical problems regarding the payment of fees for psychoanalytic treatment. Int Rev Psycho-Anal 1:73–101, 1974.
8. Kohut H: The Analysis of the Self. New York, International Universities Press, 1971.
9. Erikson EH: Childhood and Society. Norton, New York, 1963, 2nd ed., Chap. 7.
10. Eissler KR: The effect of the structure of the ego on psychoanalytic technique. J Am Psychoanal Assoc 1:104–43, 1953.
11. Little M: Transference in borderline states. Int J Psychoanal 47:476–85, 1966.
12. Nunberg H: Transference and reality. Int J Psychoanal 32(Part I): 1–9, 1951.

Essays

PSYCHIATRIC DIAGNOSIS

A psychiatric diagnostic label is useful in several ways. A diagnosis is a form of shorthand which allows patients to be classified according to disease type, and which enhances communication about patients. For example, if a patient is diagnosed as suffering from a hysterical neurosis, the therapist can apply all his knowledge about what people with that disorder have in common. Two trained people can communicate a great deal to each other in one or two words. Unfortunately, a diagnostic label is an imperfect form of shorthand, since it conveys different things depending on who made the diagnosis and who heard the diagnosis. Furthermore, no two "hysterics" or "obsessive–compulsives" are exactly alike. The specifics of each person's history and development must be known in order for the therapist to make useful therapeutic interventions.

Another use of a diagnosis is in treatment planning. If a psychotherapist makes a diagnosis of psychoneurosis he may recommend psychotherapy. If the diagnosis is schizophrenia a combination of medication and psychotherapy may be indicated. If the diagnosis is in the general category of organic disorders, however, he may refer the patient to a physician with a different medical specialty. (Treatment planning will be discussed in more detail in the next section.)

A diagnosis can also be used to form hypotheses about the patient. The therapist then uses the hypotheses to make predictions about the patient's prognosis, the course of therapy, the kinds of psychological defenses that the patient will use, the kinds of transference that will develop, and the kinds of interventions that will be useful. The predictions that are correct support the hypotheses about the patient, but it is equally useful to watch for the surprises that will necessitate the modifications of the hypotheses.

49

Several different types of diagnoses are made by psychotherapists. The two most common are descriptive diagnoses and developmental diagnoses. The descriptive diagnosis is based on observable traits and symptoms of the patient. The developmental diagnosis depends on a psychodynamic theory of psychopathology and personality development. Beginning therapists usually make descriptive diagnoses. As their training progresses, especially if it is psychoanalytically oriented, they start to make a developmental diagnosis which takes into account the genetic, dynamic, characterologic, and developmental findings as well.

Let me illustrate: If a first-year psychiatry resident just beginning his training labels a patient a hysteric, I assume he is talking about an overly made-up, flamboyant, flirtatious, seductive young woman who wildly overreacts and has several dramatic symptoms. In short, his patient fits the stereotyped description of a "hysterical woman."

If a fully trained, psychoanalytically oriented psychotherapist makes the same diagnosis, I assume he has taken into consideration the patient's early life experiences (genetic), has observed triangular object relationships and Oedipal-level dynamic conflicts (dynamic), has observed characteristic hysterical defenses such as repression and displacement (characterologic), and has seen castration anxiety as a prominent symptom. For this therapist all of the descriptive findings observed by the beginning therapist could be absent and he would still make the diagnosis as long as the genetic, dynamic, characterologic findings were present.

One of the psychotherapist's main diagnostic goals is to discover the patient's central conflict. This is a repetitive conflict which occurred in the patient's past, is occurring in his present, and will occur in his future unless there is a therapeutic intervention. This central conflict may be either some maladaptive behavior or an emotional state with genetic–dynamic roots. The eventual purpose of most of the therapist's interventions will be to help the patient understand and deal with his central conflict, thus enhancing the patient's development.

Another dimension of developmental diagnosis is the assessment of ego strength. As conceptualized in psychoanalytic structural theory, the ego has two major executive functions. The first is to deal with the reality of the outside world. The other is to mediate between the id impulses and the superego demands, usually by using one or more defense mechanisms.

By obtaining answers to the following questions, the therapist can fairly accurately evaluate how well the ego is functioning. How well does the patient deal with the external world? How mature are his relationships with other people? Is he in touch with reality? In spite of unresolved conflicts, is there evidence of his achieving in school or work or social situations? Can he deal in a reasonable way with stress?

Another series of questions helps to evaluate the ego's capacity to deal with the patient's internal world. Has the patient handled his drives and conflicts by acting them out in destructive ways or has he partially sublimated them? What are his main ego defenses? How does the patient deal with his superego? Does he let guilt incapacitate him or does he use his superego as a guide? Does he have an ego ideal which is so impossible to achieve that he becomes depressed or is he able to put it in perspective?

Based on an assessment of a person's ego development, the following major diagnostic categories can be distinguished: psychoneurosis, character neurosis, borderline, and psychosis.

The ego of the psychoneurotic and character neurotic has matured adequately along the major developmental lines. Reality testing is intact. Self-representation and object representation have been differentiated. There is evidence of the development of internalized structures for guidance (ego ideal) and self-appraisal (superego). Sexual and aggressive drives have been largely neutralized so that they are functioning in the service of the ego. A number of sophisticated defense mechanisms have developed, e.g., repression in the hysteric or intellectualization in the obsessive. Both the psychoneurotic and character neurotic have a similar psychopathology; they repetitively use their maladaptive childhood solutions to conflicts. The ego's assessment of the psychopathology distinguishes the two diagnostic groups. For the psychoneurotic the pathology is unacceptable (ego-dystonic). He seeks therapy when his internal discomfort becomes intolerable. The ego of the character neurotic finds his pathology acceptable (ego-syntonic) and only seeks therapy when his pathology interferes with his relationships, job, or something else external.

The borderline has a mixture of an intact and a psychotic ego. Although he may have developed adequately in a few of the important developmental lines, he will demonstrate significant inadequacies in several others. He can handle a relatively stress-free situation but decompensates much more easily than the neurotic under stress. An amount of anxiety which the neurotic would interpret as a signal to mobilize his psychological defenses may be overwhelming to the borderline patient. People with problems along the narcissistic lines of development are also placed in this category by some authors.

The psychotic has gross ego deficiencies. These may be constitutional defects, lacks in development, or severe regressions from a previously attained higher level of development. The person with the constitutional defect has the poorest prognosis. Except when the regression is caused by organic brain damage, the person who regressed from a previously attained higher level of development has the best prognosis.

A developmental diagnosis changes throughout the course of therapy.

As the therapist learns more about the patient's developmental lines he can make a more accurate and more complete diagnosis. The diagnosis also changes if the therapy is successful.

Although the growth during therapy is usually in individual developmental lines where there were deficiencies, there can also be changes in the major categories of diagnosis. As an example, consider a patient who enters therapy as an obsessive character neurotic (obsessive–compulsive personality).

An early goal of therapy may be to convert his behavior pattern from ego-syntonic to ego-dystonic. (Although this will initially increase his discomfort it will enhance his desire to work in therapy and his chances of changing his maladaptive pattern of behavior.) Once his behavior becomes ego-dystonic, his diagnosis changes from a character neurosis to a psychoneurosis by definition. With further therapy, his diagnosis may change from obsessive–compulsive neurosis to hysterical neurosis. This change is not surprising if psychopathology is understood dynamically and developmentally. Both the hysteric and the obsessive are defending against the Oedipal conflict. The hysteric is functioning at an Oedipal level of psychosexual development but defends against the sexual and aggressive wishes of that period, primarily by means of repression. As a result of unconsciously projecting his aggressive wishes to kill the parent of the same sex onto that parent and then displacing the wish, the hysteric often fears being harmed and develops phobias. The obsessive either never reached the Oedipal level of development or, in most cases, regressed back to the anal stage because the mechanisms of repression, projection, and displacement did not adequately deal with his anxiety. He then utilizes anal–level defenses such as intellectualization, isolation of affect, reaction formation, and undoing. Unlike the hysteric, who often fears being hurt, the obsessive often fears hurting someone else. This is the original aggressive wish toward the parent which has not been disguised by projection and displacement or totally repressed. To deal with his fear of hurting someone else, the obsessive often develops compulsions which may vary from a one-word thought to complex rituals. Often during the course of therapy, as anxiety decreases with increased understanding and verbalization, the patient ceases his regression and gives up his obsessive defenses and symptoms. Repression becomes his major defense. The patient then is a classical hysterical neurotic until the completion of the working through and re-solving* of the Oedipal conflict. By the end of successful therapy the highest level defenses, neutralization and sublimation, should be playing a larger role.

Developmental lines have been referred to, but so far not discussed. An

---

*Fleming and Benedek[1] introduced this spelling of the word resolution to emphasize that the patient brings the conflict under greater ego control by solving it in a new way but the conflict does not resolve, dissolve or disappear.

examination of two important developmental lines should suffice for a working understanding. Figure 1 provides a graphic illustration of the normal self-object developmental line up to about age six, and a summary of the anxiety line. The corresponding psychosexual stages are included as reference points.

Self–Object Developmental Line

During the *autistic phase* the infant cannot distinguish between self and non-self. He and the world are one. During the *symbiotic stage* the infant begins to develop a blurred concept of difference between himself and the parenting figure. In contrast to the autistic stage, during which the infant thought he was omnipotent, he now sees the parent as omnipotent. Arrests at these early stages can lead to severe psychopathology, such as that seen in the autistic child. During the *separation–individuation phase,* the child develops fairly clear boundaries between himself and the parenting figure. In the *diadic phase* the child realizes that he has a relationship with the father and a relationship with the mother, but does not yet comprehend the relationship the parents have with each other. He continues to develop his self-representation as well as object representations of the parents. By the end of this stage the child should have developed gender identity and attained object constancy. The onset of *triadic relationships* ushers in the Oedipal period. The child now realizes that the parents have a relationship with each other that influences each parent's relationship with him.

This discussion of the self-object developmental line is, of course, greatly simplified. For instance, there are invariably other children and adults in the child's life that have to be represented and understood in his self-object conceptualization. The two-way arrows in Fig. 1 point out the possibility of both regression and of further development. In addition each developmental stage effects subsequent developmental stages.

Several inferences about how a patient went through these stages can be made even during an initial interview. For instance, if every time a male patient describes a relationship with a woman he also talks about a real or imagined man in her life, one can hypothesize that he reached, but did not adequately resolve, the triadic level. An adequate solution would have been his having identified with his father, and having realized that he too would be an adult man someday and that he could then have a woman of his own. If, in addition, the patient is 30 years old, has never left home, and is reluctant to leave the therapist at the end of the session, one can suspect that separation–individuation was not mastered either. During the course of therapy, however, both of these phases may be mastered and the developmental diagnosis would change.

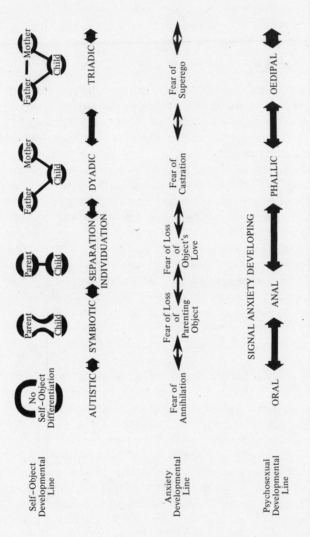

Fig. 1. Three developmental lines.

Anxiety Developmental Line

During the autistic period, it is postulated that anxiety takes the form of *fear of annihilation*. *Stranger anxiety* and *separation anxiety* are early signs that the infant has developed an object representation of the parent that differs from his representation of other adults. Anxiety now begins to take the form of *fear of the loss of the parenting object*. As object constancy develops, anxiety starts to be a *fear of loss of the object's love* or fear of the object's condemnation. By this time, however, anxiety becomes less overwhelming because *signal anxiety* has been developing. Now the onset of anxiety is seen as a warning that the drives and wishes have to be defended against in order to prevent greater anxiety. Whatever psychological defense mechanisms the child has developed up to that point are called upon to defend against the drives and wishes. When triadic relationships develop, anxiety starts to take the form of *fear of castration*. As the solving of the triadic phase takes place, the child starts to internalize his perception of the parents' moral code, leading to development of a superego. Anxiety now becomes played out on an internal stage between the ego and the superego. Out of *fear of superego* punishment, the ego either defends against the id impulses or works out a compromise between the id and the superego.

With many patients there is one further diagnostic task. Although most patients come to a therapist with a specific presenting complaint, many merely speak of a vague discomfort. In the latter case, the therapist often has to help the patient diagnose his specific reasons for seeking therapy.

(For further discussion of developmental diagnosis I recommend Blanck and Blanck.[2] A. Freud [3] is largely responsible for the concept of developmental lines. A recent paper by Mahler[4] provides a good starting point for the study of symbiosis, separation, and individuation.)

TREATMENT PLANNING AND TECHNIQUE

A thorough diagnostic approach as described above is a very useful aid in answering the questions one has to ask when planning treatment: Is treatment indicated at all? If so, what kind of treatment? This second question is very complex. It depends on the patient, the therapist, and the external situation. What are the patient's wants and needs? What kind of therapeutic work is this particular patient capable of doing? What kind of help is the therapist capable of providing? What would be the ideal kind of therapeutic help? What is actually available? These questions were discussed in detail with regard to Paul Turner at the end of sessions 1 and 5.

There are many ways of classifying therapy. A common dichotomy is "insight psychotherapy" vs "supportive therapy." An old dictum is: "Do supportive therapy when necessary and insight psychotherapy when possi-ble." This, of course, implies that insight is better than support. Actually, the important consideration is: What is most useful for a particular patient at that particular moment in his life in the context of the total therapy picture? For instance, the therapist should not be overly supportive just to provide tempor-ary relief if the long range goal of therapy is insight. Usually, the greater the patient's ego strength the more likely it is that the therapist will do insight psychotherapy.

Supportive Therapy

What is being supported in supportive therapy? This again depends on the patient. In general, one supports the patient's assets as a way of building self-esteem. For the most part the therapist supports the patient's ego func-tions. These include dealing with the external world, dealing with the de-mands of the superego and the id, and providing psychological defenses. For a schizophrenic or borderline patient the major tasks of therapy are often to support repression and to "loan him the therapist's ego" to help him deal with external problems he cannot solve himself. With other patients the therapist may support id drives. The ascetic adolescent often needs support for his sexual drives. The middle-aged man or woman with ulcers may need support for expression of his aggression and dependency. The patient with poor impulse control, on the other hand, may need external support for his superego. Other supportive procedures include medication, reassurance, ad-vice, substitute activities, and even some forms of transference gratification.

It should be noted that most of these procedures actually interfere with insight psychotherapy. As an example, consider transference gratification. As a child, the patient may have wanted approval without any demands from his mother. In therapy he wants the same from the therapist. If the therapist gratifies this wish it will be almost impossible for him and the patient to understand it as a distortion from the past. There are times, however, even in insight psychotherapy when one has to use one or more of these supportive measures. Obviously, to do first-rate supportive therapy the therapist has to have good insight into the patient and the patient's problems.

Insight psychotherapy, although a different process with different goals, is at times appropriate for the same patient receiving supportive therapy. For example, a schizophrenic comes to a session complaining that his nose has started to grow flatter and will soon disappear. His next association is that his wife has been rejecting him the past week. The therapist could respond "supportively" by assuring the patient that his nose is exactly the same size it was in all the previous sessions. It may be more helpful for the therapist to make an insightful comment such as, "Ever since your wife started 'snubbing' you, you have believed your nose was growing flatter.'' The converse is also true. Even in psychoanalysis, where the patient and the psychoanalyst have agreed to pursue insight in dealing with all of the patient's behavior and material, it is sometimes necessary for the analyst to be supportive. If a patient calls to cancel the next several appointments because he has just received word that his father died, most analysts would immediately respond in a supportive way.

Interventions Common to Both Supportive and Insight Therapy

In between those interventions that are used predominantly in supportive therapy and those used predominantly in insight psychotherapy is a group of activities often found in both supportive and insight psychotherapy. These activities include suggestion, reinforcement, abreaction, and what Alexander[5] has called the "corrective emotional experience" or "emotional training."

SUGGESTION

Suggestion as used in supportive therapy is very similar to the giving of advice. It is a suggestion as to what one might do with regard to his life situation. Suggestion in insight psychotherapy is more equivalent to education. The therapist educates the patient as to the patient's role in psychotherapy. For instance, early in psychoanalysis the analyst will usually suggest to a naive patient that he follow the fundamental rule of analysis. That is, he will suggest to the patient that he freely associate, saying whatever comes to mind even though it seems irrelevant or embarrassing. Similarly, in insight psychotherapy the psychotherapist may suggest to the patient that he try to communicate freely. Another example is the therapist's suggestion to the patient that it is important for the patient rather than the therapist to begin each hour.

REINFORCEMENT

Reinforcement is also used in both supportive and insight psychotherapy. As defined by operant conditioning theory, reinforcement is anything which leads to an increase in a desired behavior. In practice, it is used more directly in supportive therapy and more subtly in insight psychotherapy. In supportive therapy, if a patient accomplishes some goal the therapist may say something like, "You must be pleased with yourself for having accomplished that. I'm certainly pleased that you did." That is very direct reinforcement of the patient's behavior. A similar thing occurs in insight psychotherapy. For example, if a patient tells the therapist about a dream the insight psychotherapist may express interest in it and work very hard with the patient to understand its meaning. This, too, is reinforcing, and will probably increase the number of dreams that the patient brings to therapy.

ABREACTION

Abreaction is the emotional reliving of central conflict experiences from the past. Unlike the activities previously mentioned, abreaction is something done by the patient rather than by the therapist. The therapist can only facilitate or discourage abreaction. Abreaction in the sense of emotional discharge is used in supportive therapy to provide temporary relief. The use of abreaction in psychoanalysis or insight psychotherapy is quite different. Bibring[6] summarizes this latter use by pointing out that originally abreaction was considered a curative agent. Later it was thought of as offering evidence to the patient that he really has repressed impulses. With this understanding, abreaction became the first step in acquiring insight through interpretation.

CORRECTIVE EMOTIONAL EXPERIENCE

The *corrective emotional experience* is brought about by the psychotherapist deliberately providing an experience with an authority figure different from experiences that the patient had with early authority figures, such as parents. Of course, the early experiences that the patient recalls may be either real or imagined. Often, early in therapy the patient recalls one or both of his parents as being very punitive and tyrannical. As therapy continues, the patient will often recognize that this is a distortion of the true situation. It is then useful to work with the patient to determine why he distorted actuality at that time and why through transference he continues to distort it in the present. If the patient did have punitive parents and has generalized that all authorities are punitive, the therapist might be able to provide an emotional experience which would "correct" the distortion that all authorities are punitive. Unfortunately, the force of the patient's compulsive repetition of his neurotic distortion is so great that a new experience not coupled with insight usually has very little effect on it. This technique, at best, temporarily helps to build an alliance between the therapist and the patient.

Insight Psychotherapy

Insight psychotherapy utilizes predominantly five kinds of interventions, all of which have the goal of increasing the patient's insight about himself. These interventions are utilized in the following order: acknowledgment, confrontation, clarification, interpretation, and working through.

ACKNOWLEDGMENT

This is the process by which the therapist lets the patient know that the emotions that he is experiencing are recognized, and that what he is saying is understood. It is the sharing of the therapist's empathy with the patient. Acknowledgment serves two main purposes: It is the first step in forming an alliance because it communicates to the patient that the therapist is working with him. Secondly, acknowledgment increases the patient's self understanding because often he is neither aware of his own emotional state nor completely cognizant of what he is saying. To some extent acknowledgment objectifies what the patient is saying because he then hears it from someone else.

The therapist obtains the necessary understanding by listening, and through empathy. Brief bursts of identification with the patient, i.e., intense empathy, greatly enhance one's understanding of a patient. The therapist's understanding can be communicated to the patient in many ways. Sometimes a nod of the head or one word suffices. At other times a direct statement is needed; for example, "This is very painful for you." Occasionally the most effective communication is a gesture, such as offering a box of facial tissues to a patient the first time he cries.

CONFRONTATION

This is the pointing out to the patient his behavior, reaction, emotion, or problem. The goal is to make him aware of these processes. Confrontation is, of course, a necessary step without which none of the following procedures could be used. Early in therapy confrontations are almost always made by the therapist. Later in therapy the patient is able to recognize, on his own, neurotic behavior previously pointed out by the therapist. Eventually the patient is able to confront himself even when faced with new material.

CLARIFICATION

This is an elaboration of confrontation. It involves collecting examples of the process being discussed. The therapist then uses the examples to illustrate to the patient the pattern and variations of this particular process. Whenever a patient describes something about himself in abstract generalities the therapist should ask for specific examples. Specific examples not only enable the therapist to make a clarification, but also help him to go on to the next step, interpretation. In psychotherapy the therapist clarifies much more than he interprets.

These concepts can be illustrated by a clinical example of acknowledgment, confrontation, and clarification. With moderate anxiety, a very bright young man described a chess game that he had played the day before his therapy session. He was much more skilled than his opponent but took over seventy moves to win the game. Early in his description I acknowledged his anxiety. When I confronted him with the fact that he could have won the game with far fewer moves he at first denied it. As he thought more about the game he conceded that he had several chances to win earlier. He then recalled many other chess matches in which he allowed a much weaker opponent to almost but not quite win. This pattern was further clarified by my pointing out with examples that the patient held back in most competitive endeavors against less gifted opponents.

The next session the patient reported, "I was about to make a move in a chess game Tuesday when I thought about our last session. I realized I was repeating my old pattern. I reconsidered and made a different move which allowed me to win in just three more moves. I felt good about changing what I now realize is a maladaptive pattern, but I also felt a little uneasy about defeating the other fellow so quickly."

It is clear from this material that the patient was able to make use of the confrontation and clarification but that further work was needed to allow him to change his behavior without feeling anxious.

INTERPRETATION

The above leads to the next step, *interpretation*. In general terms, interpretation is an intervention which brings into the patient's consciousness something that was previously unconscious. A complete interpretation would examine the material from a topographic, dynamic, economic, genetic, structural, and adaptive point of view. Topography refers to Freud's early description of the psychic apparatus which divided it into the conscious, the preconscious, and the unconscious. The dynamic view refers to the interplay of mental phenomena. Economic in this context refers to the understanding of psychic energy. Genetic, as used in psychoanalytic theory, refers to constitutional factors and early life experiences which contribute to the development of the phenomenon in question. The structural theory which adds to the topographical theory is a later conceptualization of Freud's which divides the psychic apparatus into ego, id, and superego. Adaptive refers to the way in which a psychic phenomenon relates to the environment; for example, secondary gain from a symptom.

It should be noted that a complete interpretation is made infrequently in psychoanalysis and almost never in psychotherapy. A complete interpretation, when made, is presented as a series of partial interpretations. For the chess playing patient described above, a genetic, a structural, and an adaptive interpretation were necessary to help him understand the anxiety he experienced when he was victorious too easily. This patient has a younger brother who was less intelligent and less talented than the patient. When the patient defeated his brother in competition his parents made remarks such as, "You should be ashamed of taking advantage of your little brother" (genetic). These judgments of his parents became incorporated into his developing superego (structural). He developed a solution which originally appeared adaptive. He won but only by a little bit. His parents, his brother and his superego could all tolerate this symptomatic compromise (adaptive). Unfortunately, what was adaptive when he was a child was now maladaptive. By holding back he frequently failed when he could have succeeded. Topographic, dynamic, and economic interpretations could have been made from the material presented by the patient, but they were not necessary for the patient to deal adequately with the problem facing him.

Working through will be discussed in Part II.

Short-Term and Long-Term Therapy

Another classification of psychotherapy based on desired goals is short-term vs long-term therapy. *Crisis intervention therapy* is an example of short-term therapy with two main goals. The first goal is to help the patient deal with the precipitating crisis. The second goal is to help him develop the tools to deal with that or a similar crisis in the future. Once those two goals are accomplished the therapist and the patient may terminate or they may negotiate a new contract with new goals. For instance, they may decide to enter into long-term therapy with the goal of working out a long-standing characterological or neurotic problem.

The Therapy Matrix

A further consideration is whether the patient should be treated individually or in a group. Individual psychotherapy includes such therapies as psychoanalysis, psychoanalytic therapy, client-centered psychotherapy, behavior therapy, and hypnosis. Group therapy involves various kinds of group psychotherapy, combined individual and group psychotherapy, family therapy, and psychodrama. For each kind of therapy one can find indications and contraindications. Often the training and interests of the therapist determine which therapy matrix is used. There are, however, a few general guidelines that one can use to make an appropriate choice. Although intrapsychic problems can be treated in a group situation, individual therapy seems better suited to deal with them in depth. Conversely, interpersonal problems can be dealt with in individual therapy, especially since there is usually an underlying intrapsychic etiology. Group therapy does, however, have some special advantages in trying to deal with interpersonal problems in that they can be observed directly in the therapy, not only between patient and therapist but between the patient and other patients.

Group therapy is also indicated with a patient who develops an overly intense transference which is detrimental to the therapy. For example, a severe hysteric who tends to sexualize every interaction and to develop such a strong erotic transference to the therapist that she cannot tolerate remaining in therapy might be much better treated in a group, where the transference is more diffuse.

The total make-up of a group is also important. While one or two severe hysterics may do well in a group, a group made up of only severe hysterics would probably not function for more than a few sessions. There have been several reports of successful groups made up entirely of patients with sociopathic disorders. This last type of group is helpful to the group members if they are willing to examine each other's conscious evasions and unconscious defenses, but very destructive if they merely support each other's pathological behavior.

Marital therapy is often the best approach when patients describe marital difficulties as their primary problem. This is especially true if both husband and wife acknowledge that they both contribute to the marital problem. Later, if either or both of them wish to work on a long-term neurotic or characterological problem, a new contract can be negotiated, as was discussed above in relation to crisis therapy. Similar considerations apply to family therapy.

Other Forms of Therapy

For the sake of completeness I will mention, but not discuss, organic therapies and milieu therapy. The organic therapies include the use of medications such as tranquilizers, antidepressants, and sedatives. Also included in organic therapy are the convulsive therapies, insulin coma therapy, and psychosurgery. Milieu therapy usually refers to hospital or day-care therapy, or some specific aspect of hospital or day-care treatment such as occupational or recreational therapy. There are also multiple combinations of two or more of the therapies mentioned above.

A complete catalogue of psychotherapies would have to begin with the various forms of analysis and end with Z-therapy.

THE THERAPEUTIC CONTRACT

The word "contract" has traditionally been used to describe the agreement or relationship between the therapist and the patient. Because of the legal connotations of the word "contract" which do not exist in the agreement between the patient and the therapist it is somewhat of a misnomer. The agreement worked out between therapist and patient is more analogous to what develops during a blind date than to a legal contract. It is very complex and is developed gradually.

Usually the patient obtains a psychiatrist's name from a friend or physician whose judgment he trusts. The patient calls the psychiatrist, introduces himself, and expresses the desire to see him. Either on his own or in response to the psychiatrist's questions, he reveals how he obtained the psychiatrist's name and why he wants to see him. The person who referred the patient to the psychiatrist may or may not have contacted the psychiatrist in advance to let him know that he could expect a call.

The psychiatrist, like the person being asked for a date, now has to answer some questions: Is there a time in his schedule to see another patient? If so, does this patient have a problem which is appropriate for him to treat? If his schedule is full he will probably refer the patient to another therapist. If he has openings but the patient has a psychiatric problem which he is not prepared to handle, he may refer the patient to a psychiatric colleague. For instance, a psychiatrist who does only outpatient psychotherapy is not going to accept a patient with a severe psychotic depression who will require hospitalization. On other occasions, it will become clear from the telephone call that the problem is not psychiatric and that another medical specialist is indicated.

If the patient and therapist do agree to meet, it is usually understood that this appointment is for evaluation. It is really a two-way evaluation. The psychiatrist is thinking in terms of a diagnosis and treatment plan as described above. The patient has probably been very anxious since calling the psychiatrist. He has been wondering what the psychiatrist is like and what kind of impression he will make on the psychiatrist. He wonders if the psychiatrist will understand him, will be able to help him, and will accept him as a patient. The patient's expectations will depend on past experiences, cultural prejudices, and inner resistances.

On the day of the appointment they meet in the waiting room, introduce themselves, and go into the psychiatrist's office. The psychiatrist tries to understand the patient and his problems. Often during the first or second interview the patient will ask the psychiatrist to answer questions about himself. This raises a problem of technique. If a patient asks during the first few interviews a question such as, "Where did you receive your training?," a straightforward answer is usually indicated. The answer to that question will help the patient make some assessment of the therapist's professional qualifications. If the patient asks the same question during the middle of therapy, the therapist may still answer it, but only after exploring with him why he asks that particular question at that particular time. Another question frequently asked by the patient in the first interview is: "Can you cure my problem?" This is a complex question which cannot really be understood or answered until one knows the patient very well. Even when the therapist has successfully treated similar patients many times before, the most reassurance that he can give is: "Other people with similar problems have been helped by psychotherapy." Questions of a personal nature about the therapist's life are a different matter in insight psychotherapy. These are usually neither answered nor discouraged. Instead the meaning of the question to the patient and the patient's fantasies about possible answers are explored. Knowledge about the therapist's personal life interferes with the development of a transference and with the patient's ability to project his own attitudes and impulses onto the therapist.

By the end of the first session most experienced psychiatrists have a fairly good idea about the patient, his problem, whether or not he can benefit from therapy, and whether or not they can work together. Some therapists will come to a decision with the patient after the first session to either terminate or embark on a course of therapy. Many therapists prefer to arrange further appointments for evaluation to obtain more information about the patient, including how they work in therapy over a period of several sessions. These decisions, of course, have to be made mutually by both patient and therapist.

If, at the end of the evaluative sessions the patient and therapist agree to continue, they should reach agreement on fee, payment of fee, length of sessions, time of sessions, frequency of sessions, and meeting place. Either as part of the initial contract or when the situation arises, they should also agree on what happens if either patient or therapist comes late or if either misses a session. Although these issues sound almost mechanical every one of them has important meanings to the patient.

The general structure of therapy is sometimes explicitly discussed but often it is just implicitly understood. What is permissible behavior for the therapist and for the patient? What limits do each have to observe? Similar questions are asked on a blind date but the answers are not the same. For the most part talking, understanding, and having fantasies are permissible in therapy, but acting is not. Usually psychotherapy takes place with both the therapist and the patient sitting down. One reason for this is to inhibit physical action during therapy. There is also a restriction on socializing between the therapist and the patient. The relationship is professional, not social.

In addition, and often this is not verbalized, a style should have at least started to develop with regard to what the therapist does in therapy and what the patient does. The therapist's style will depend on his own personality and training as well as on the particular patient. The patient will, at least initially, respond as he usually does in a relationship with an authority figure.

From the above discussion of the therapy contract it should be clear that even though efforts are made to make it explicit, much remains hidden. For instance, the therapist tries to understand the patient's hopes and expectations of the therapist and therapy and the patient tries to explain these to the therapist but only gradually do they become clear to both. As goals change the contract has to be renegotiated, often several times.

The blind date that may or may not develop into an ever-changing, long-term, mutually beneficial relationship seems still to be quite analogous to the therapy contract. There is one major difference. On occasion the blind date develops into a marriage contract which is often a lifelong relationship. The psychotherapist, on the other hand, has as one of his goals to help the patient reach the point where their relationship is no longer necessary.

THE ALLIANCE AND TRANSFERENCE IN PSYCHOTHERAPY

The alliance is that part of the relationship between patient and therapist that allows them to work together and allows therapy to take place. There are two main tasks for the patient in developing the alliance: The first includes the patient developing a trust in the therapist and investing emotional energy in the relationship with the therapist. The patient's trust that the therapist has the patient's best interest in mind and the emotional investment in the relationship, explain why a patient is willing to remain in psychotherapy in spite of the frequent hard work and emotional discomfort experienced. This first task has many transference elements.

The second task for the patient is relatively transference-free. The patient identifies generally with the therapist's way of doing therapy and specifically with the therapist's rational, observing, understanding ego. Outside of a psychotherapeutic situation, most people do not expend much effort reality testing, observing, and trying to understand what they experience or do.

Traditionally, alliance has been considered a form of transference. Fenichel[7] spoke of the "rational tranference" and Stone[8] of the "mature transference." Zetzel called this relationship "the therapeutic alliance," but wrote about it in a paper entitled, "Current Concepts of Transference."[9] Greenson, emphasizing the patient's ability to work in the therapy situation, speaks of "the working alliance" but discusses it in a chapter entitled, "Transference."[10] Unlike the authors quoted above, I distinguish between transference alliance and nontransference alliance. In order to make this distinction clear, I will first discuss transference and countertransference in relation to the alliance and then the nontransference alliance.

Transference and the Alliance

Transference is the inappropriate repetition in the present of a relationship that was important in a person's childhood. This simple definition emphasizes four of the important aspects of transference:

1. Transference is a displacement of aspects of a past relationship into the present.

2. The original relationship, which is displaced into the present, was with someone important in the person's childhood.

3. The displacement is always a distortion in terms of the time and often also a distortion in terms of the person and/or situation.

4. The displacement is repetitive.

Fenichel[11] succinctly described tranference as "the patient misunderstands the present in terms of the past."

Transference is often a resistance to psychotherapy. At other times, especially early in the course of psychotherapy, transference contributes to the alliance and increases the amount of work that can be accomplished. For example, one of my patients had a history of gaining an expression of maternal love by working hard. In therapy the patient wanted an expression of love from me. The unconscious script that the patient wrote was, "the therapist is [like] my mother. If I work hard in therapy the therapist will express love for me the way my mother did."

Initially the positive side of this transference strengthened the alliance. However, this transference phenomenon, like most others, was ambivalent. The positive side of the transference was that the mother (therapist) rewarded hard work with an expression of love. The negative side of the transference was a resentment that the mother (therapist) required hard work before she would express her love. The patient's resentment in therapy increased because I did not follow this script. Even when he worked hard, I did not gratify his transference desire for an expression of love. As long as the transference contributed to the alliance I had no reason to interpret it. When the resentment and frustration growing out of the transference started to interfere with the alliance, interpretation became necessary.

In this case, I pointed out that the patient had displaced his old relationship with his mother onto me and the therapeutic situation. I further pointed out that his hard work was rewarded by the progress that we had made in therapy. He was dissatisfied, however, because he expected his hard work to result in a maternal expression of love in addition to progress in therapy. The patient was then able to give examples of dissatisfaction with school and work growing out of the same transference reaction. He wanted maternal expressions of love from his teachers and employers in addition to the usual rewards of school and work. Our alliance was restored and he learned how transference interfered with his obtaining satisfaction not only from therapy, but also from other aspects of his life.

Transference plays a much lesser role in psychotherapy than it does in psychoanalysis. In psychoanalysis, transference is facilitated by the therapist's being less of a real object than he is in psychotherapy. This is promoted by the psychoanalyst's encouraging the patient to free associate, by the frequency of the sessions, by the regression in the sessions, by the psychoanalyst's frustrating the patient's desire for a real object relationship, and by the use of the couch. Eventually a very intense transference becomes a central issue in the patient's life. Much of his waking and sleeping time is spent in fantasies about the psychoanalyst. During the sessions, the patient regresses, reliving old relationships and experiences. With the help of the psychoanalyst, the patient uses his own mature, rational ego to find healthy solutions to these old problems. The analysis of the transference neurosis accounts for the most significant changes in the patient that occur during psychoanalysis.

In psychotherapy, transference is rarely that intense and time considerations do not permit as thorough an exploration. Unlike the transference neurosis, which is promoted by the psychoanalytic situation and is directed toward the analyst, transference phenomena can be directed toward anyone. It is important for the psychotherapist to be aware of both actual and potential transference, but usually not necessary for him to interpret it to the patient. For instance, a woman in psychotherapy had a twin sister with whom she had shared all her possessions and relationships. Along with other problems, she was having marital difficulties. I considered seeing her husband for an evaluation, but decided not to when I realized that she had transferred to her husband the old sibling rivalry with her twin sister. This meant that I was potentially the object of an intense negative parent transference. She would have interpreted my seeing her husband as her once again having to share her parents' attention. At that point in therapy it was important for the alliance for her to see me as *her* therapist.

In the example above, the therapist used his understanding of the patient's actual and potential transference to himself and to others to guide his therapy planning and decisions, but did not discuss this understanding with the patient. Often the understanding the therapist gains from observing the transference relationship is shared with the patient. This does not involve deep interpretation of the early core relationships, but rather a demonstration of how the transference relationship reflects the patient's current relationships with people outside of therapy. The therapist is able to observe the therapy situation first hand in its totality. Provided that he has maintained therapeutic neutrality, he can also be certain of the patient's defensive distortions in the patient's understanding of the situation. Since inevitably the therapy situation mirrors other relationships, the therapist is then in an excellent position to help the patient see to what extent he contributed to and controls his current life situations. The patient, having recognized his repetitive patterns, can then find new solutions to the old conflicts if he so chooses.

This use of the transference relationship should not be misunderstood to be a justification for sharing with the patient the therapist's emotional reactions. If the therapist experiences either positive or negative feelings toward the patient, he should use that as a signal to try to understand how and why the patient is provoking that response at that particular time. For instance, if a patient repeatedly reports that people in his current life situation get angry with him, a repetition in the therapy situation should help the therapist understand and explain to the patient how he elicits responses of anger from others.

There are, though, at least three reasons for directly interpreting transference in psychotherapy:

1. When the transference interferes directly with the alliance and prevents therapy from progressing. Freud[12] stated, "So long as the patient's communications and ideas run on without obstruction, the theme of transference should be left untouched."

Both negative and positive transference phenomena can obstruct therapy. An extreme example of negative transference interfering with the alliance would be a patient whose transference reaction involved so much anger that he was unable to work with the therapist until the transference was interpreted. Although a positive transference often facilitates psychotherapy, it too can prevent therapy from taking place. An example was a young woman who missed a scheduled appointment. Review of the previous session revealed that she had developed a strong, positive father transference to the therapist with many warm, loving feelings and sexual fantasies. This was so frightening to her that she was unable to return for the next appointment. A direct interpretation of what she was experiencing reduced the intensity of the transference to a level she could tolerate. Therapy was resumed.

2. The patient's desire for transference gratification frequently has to be interpreted. If the therapist gratifies the wish, he precludes any chance of understanding it. On the other hand, if he frustrates the wish without explanation or interpretation, he may involve himself in a stalemate with the patient. This was illustrated by a case a resident presented in a psychotherapy conference. The young woman he was treating had been sexually molested at five. She recalled enjoying the experience, but denied any responsibility for its occurrence. In adolescence she was "raped" by a boyfriend. She came for psychotherapy because her marriage was threatened. She could only have intercourse with her husband if he pretended to rape her. In therapy she wanted the resident to "solve my problems, pull the answers out of me."

The resident tried first frustrating and then gratifying her wish to have him do all the work in therapy. There was absolutely no therapeutic progress. He then explored the problem with the patient. He pointed out the pattern in her sexual history and related it to the expectation she had of therapy. Following this clarification, the therapist was able to interpret the genetic roots of this pattern, namely, her unconscious childhood wish to possess her father without being responsible. By seeking insight rather than providing gratification, the alliance was strengthened and a great deal of therapeutic work was accomplished.

3. It is often useful to interpret transference in order to help a patient see an event as intrapsychic, rather than interpersonal. For example, a college student whom I was treating had just completed the rough draft of an honors thesis. He reported that he had felt very good about his work until he started thinking about describing it to me. He decided that I would tell him that the thesis was not original and that it added nothing to what was already known about the subject. He added, "I'm afraid to speak up in classes because I'm afraid the professor will think my ideas are worthless." His next association was that he had always been afraid to tell his father his ideas for fear that his father would belittle them. He saw all three of these examples as interpersonal problems: between him and me, between him and his professors, and between him and his father. I pointed out that it was his severe conscience at work in each instance, to help him see that the problem was his intrapsychic conflict instead of the interpersonal relationships. Eventually the patient realized that he was not only transferring to the therapist the response he would expect from his father, but also that he had incorporated into his own superego what he had perceived to be his father's values. This carries the process a step further than the more general use of the transference relationship to demonstrate to the patient that it is a reflection of his relationships with others.

Countertransference and the Alliance

Countertransference is the therapist's inappropriate repetition in the therapy situation of a relationship that was important in his childhood. Macalpine[13] states: "While the analysand has to experience the past and observe the present, the analyst has to experience the present and observe the past; he must resist any regressive trend in himself. If he falls victim to his own technique, and experiences the past instead of observing it, he is subject to counter resistance." The phenomenon of countertransference may be best described by paraphrasing Fenichel's simile: the analyst misunderstands the past in terms of the present. Countertransference is usually harmful to the alliance and unless recognized, inevitably results in a therapeutic impasse. Controlled, observed regression on the part of the therapist, however, is often useful, e.g., the use of free-floating attention.

The therapist should continually watch for signs of countertransference in his behavior, thoughts, and feelings. Karl Menninger[14] lists twenty-two "common ways in which countertransference makes its appearance." Some of the manifestations of countertransference that he lists are: inability to understand certain kinds of material, depressed or uneasy feelings during or after hours, carelessness in regard to arrangements, persistent drowsiness, trying to impress the patient, arguing with the patient, premature reassurances, and dreaming about the patient. Detection is the first step in the correction of countertransference. Other steps that Menninger suggests include a personal analysis, analyzing countertransference manifestations "in the light of one's personal self-knowledge," and discussing the problem with a trusted colleague.

The therapist can also make use of countertransference. Whenever a therapist detects a manifestation of countertransference he should ask himself: (1) What does it mean? (2) What provoked the countertransference? (3) What does it reveal about the patient? The answers to these three questions will provide information about the patient and about the patient–therapist relationship.

As indicated by the content of this section thus far, I do agree that transference and countertransference can play a role in the alliance between patient and therapist. I even agree that at times the alliance is mostly a form of transference. Sometimes, however, a good alliance can be nearly free of transference. Probably no relationship between any two people can ever be completely free of transference. The transference alliance can and does facilitate the work of therapy, but it is always contaminated by other motivations as well.

Nontransference Alliance

The *nontransference alliance*, in contrast, is characterized by the patient and therapist both having the sole goal of carrying out the therapeutic work as efficiently as possible. Greenson[15] says, "The working alliance is a relatively rational, desexualized, and deaggressified transference phenomenon." I would suggest that the working alliance is, to some extent, transference free, and that this is increasingly true towards the end of a successful insight therapy. It is this transference-free element that makes it possible for the patient to look at the transference elements in the working alliance.

The patient's role in the transference-free part of the alliance consists of using his rational observing ego and of identifying with the therapist's therapeutic behavior. The patient's rational observing ego evaluates his behavior both in and out of the therapy situation to determine its therapeutic productiveness or counterproductiveness. He then makes a decision to do what is productive. An example in therapy would be a decision on the patient's part not to suppress material once he realizes that saying what is on his mind is therapeutically useful. An example of behavior outside of therapy would be acting out in the transference. If there is a good alliance, the patient will stop his acting out once he realizes that acting out a conflict interferes with attempts to understand the conflict.

Dealing with acting out in the transference can be used to illustrate both transference alliance and nontransference alliance. A patient may stop acting out if the therapist states the behavior is interfering with therapy, even if the patient does not understand why the behavior is interfering. For instance, a young man, during the first few months of psychotherapy, reported during each session on the number of women he had seduced. I made several unsuccessful attempts to help him to understand what was motivating his behavior. Then I said, "We will not be able to understand your need to add to your collection of women whom you have seduced until you stop seducing indiscriminately." He said, "You are probably right." He then decreased the amount of time and energy he was putting into seducing women. Instead, he directed his efforts toward working out the problem. The motivation for his agreeing to my statement grew out of a transference alliance. He translated a childhood feeling that "father knows best" into "the therapist knows best."

Another patient responded quite differently to my making the same statement in a similar situation. He said, "I don't know why I try to be a Don Juan. I don't enjoy the sex, but it decreases my anxiety. Maybe if I quit being a Don Juan, I'll be able to understand what causes my anxiety. In the long run that will be more useful." The second patient came to the same decision as the first, but it grew out of a nontransference alliance. His decision was based on an assessment of the situation by his rational observing ego and on identification with the way I worked in a therapy situation. One can illustrate the relative importance of transference in the alliance as therapy progresses. (see Fig. 2). In short, transference plays a varying role in the alliance throughout therapy, being relatively more important early in psychotherapy. This graph would, of course, differ somewhat for each patient and therapist combination.

Facilitating the Alliance

This all leads to a frequently asked question: "How can the therapist facilitate the development of the alliance?"

Freud[16] said that the first aim of therapy was to develop rapport with the patient. To do this, Freud said that one needed only to have adequate time, to show a serious sympathetic understanding, and to clear away the resistances that crop up. Sterba[17] pointed out that the patient identifies with the therapist's

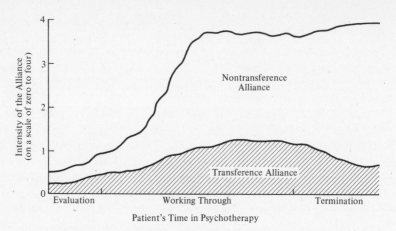

Fig. 2.   The relative contribution of transference and nontransference forms of the alliance over the course of psychotherapy.

working style. With most patients, the therapist can best facilitate the alliance by rolling up his sleeves, getting to work, and doing therapy. The therapist must recognize the high priority that should be given to developing the alliance early in the therapy.

Of the five kinds of insight psychotherapy interventions described earlier, acknowledgment most directly facilitates the development of trust and emotional involvement in the therapy. By communicating his empathy with and understanding of the patient, the therapist shows that he is working with the patient. In the first few sessions this is most commonly done by taking an empathic history. Also appropriate in the first session is exploring and acknowledging the patient's feelings about coming to a therapist. Almost invariably, there are ambivalent feelings. The patient is relieved because there is the possibility of obtaining help, but he also experiences anxiety and narcissistic pain. Many people are brought up with a "do it yourself" ethic. For them, going to a therapist means being inadequate. When the patient realizes that the therapist understands and accepts his ambivalence about starting therapy, a major step in alliance forming has taken place.

Other actions on the part of the therapist that contribute to forming the trust and involvement aspect of the alliance are displaying a non-judgmental attitude about the patient's thoughts and feelings, making painful interpretations with as much tact as possible, remembering what the patient said from session to session, and demonstrating that the therapy is primarily for the benefit of the patient. In regard to the last, the only reward that the patient is obligated to provide the therapist is the agreed fee.

The therapist can also facilitate the other aspect of the alliance: identifying with his way of doing therapy and with his rational observing ego. This is best done by making tactful, properly dosed, and correct confrontations, clarifications, and interpretations. Once the patient has gained some insights, the alliance is further facilitated by helping the patient with the working-through process.

With the occasional patient who does not form a good alliance under these conditions, special attention must be given to the alliance. The therapist may have to explain to the patient how they can best work together or why they are not working well together. Certain patients, such as those described by Fleming[18], who are suffering from childhood object deprivation, cannot form an adequate alliance unless the therapist responds to their level of object need. Very rarely, there will be unavoidable reasons for a particular patient and therapist not being able to work together. For example, if a patient developed an intense negative mother transference to a woman therapist before an alliance developed, a switch to a man therapist would be indicated. The patient would eventually develop a negative mother transference to the male therapist, too, but by that time an adequate alliance should have developed.

The ideal alliance culminates in the patient's being able to do the work of therapy without the therapist. Many patients are eventually able, without the help of the therapist, to carry out the process of psychotherapy, including confrontation, clarification, and even interpretation and working through. When a patient develops that ability, he is usually ready to terminate.

The Real Relationship

The nontransference alliance should not be confused with the "real relationship" as described by Greenson[19]. The real relationship does not depend on displacement from childhood relationships or on the therapy situation. The patient becomes aware of certain traits and characteristics of the therapist. He would also become aware of these if his only contact with the therapist were a social one.

Transference phenomena, transference forms of the alliance, and non-transference forms of the alliance all differ from the real relationship. Transference phenomena, although genuinely felt, do depend on displacement from childhood relationships and, to some extent, on the therapy situation. The alliance, even more than transference, depends on the therapy situation for its existence. Transference forms of the alliance depend also on displacement from childhood relationships. Nontransference forms of the alliance do not depend on displacement from childhood relationships. If they are related to childhood at all, it is in being adult, developed, neutralized forms of earlier healthy interpersonal relationships.

One can illustrate the real relationship, the transference, and the alliance by showing how a characteristic of the therapist, such as consistently running behind schedule, can affect all three relationships. The therapist should of course, try to understand why he is consistently late. In terms of the real relationship, the patient will probably be justifiably annoyed. The transference may manifest as a fantasy of the patient that the therapist prefers the patient he sees before her (e.g., just as she thought her mother always preferred her older brother). If the alliance is strong, however, the patient will be able to continue working in therapy in spite of this characteristic of the therapist. If the alliance is weak, the patient may terminate.

In short, the alliance is an integral part of psychotherapy. A good alliance allows the rest of psychotherapy to take place.

The Course of Therapy

One can illustrate the course of therapy, including the relative importance of transference, the alliance, and the real relationship, in the form of graphs (see Fig. 3 and 4). As was true of Fig. 2, the curves are not precise contours. They would vary somewhat with each patient–therapist combination. Note that in psychotherapy the three parameters follow the same general pattern over time as they do in psychoanalysis. The transference, however, is less intense and the real relationship more distinct in psychotherapy than in psychoanalysis. Both the psychotherapist and the psychoanalyst should strive for maximum involvement in the alliance and minimal countertransference interference throughout the therapy. Both can permit more expression of the real relationship early in the evaluation phase and toward the end of termination.

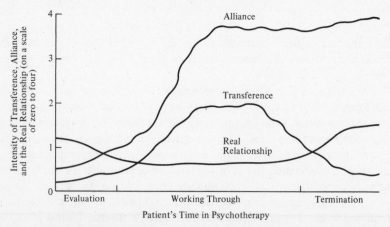

Fig. 3.   The relative importance of transference, alliance, and real relationship during the course of psychotherapy.

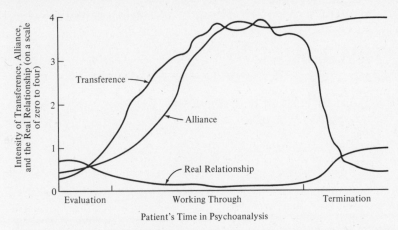

Fig. 4. The relative importance of transference, alliance, and real relationship during the course of psychoanalysis.

Resistance

Earlier it was noted that transference reactions can act as resistance and interfere with therapy. The same is true of the alliance and the real relationship. Frequently in psychotherapy a patient will describe dreams in such detail that no time is left in the session to work on understanding them. The patient may consciously congratulate himself for his ability to recall the dream in detail, but actually that is just a form of resistance masquerading as working in the alliance.

The real relationship can also be used as a resistance. One of my patients had the fantasy that if he were too successful I would be killed. He then assured me that I would not really be killed if he were successful at his work. He then fled to the real relationship and said, "But, of course, you already know that without my assuring you." Although his last statement was true of our real relationship, it was still a flight into reality in order to keep from examining his fantasy and the assurance that followed it.

REFERENCES

1. Fleming J, Benedek T: Psychoanalytic Supervision. New York, Grune & Stratton, 1966, Chap. 7.
2. Blanck G, Blanck R: Ego Psychology: Theory and Practice. New York, Columbia University Press, 1974, Chap. 7, pp. 91–118.
3. Freud A: The Writings of Anna Freud, Volume VI: Normality and Pathology in Childhood: Assessments of Development. New York, International Universities Press, 1965.

4. Mahler MS: Symbiosis and individuation. Psychoanal Stud Child 29:89–106, 1974.
5. Alexander F, French TM: Psychoanalytic Therapy: Principles and Application. New York, Ronald Press, 1946.
6. Bibring E: Psychoanalysis and the dynamic psychotherapies. J Am Psychoanal Assoc 2:745–770, 1954.
7. Fenichel O: Problems of Psychoanalytic Technique. Albany, NY, The Psychoanalytic Quarterly, Inc., 1941.
8. Stone L: The Psychoanalytic Situation. New York, International Universities Press, 1961.
9. Zetzel ER: Current concepts of transference. Int J Psycho-Anal 37:369–376, 1956.
10. Greenson RR: The Technique and Practice of Psychoanalysis. New York, International Universities Press, 1967, Chap. XXX, pp. 190–209.
11. Fenichel O: The Psychoanalytic Theory of Neurosis. New York, Norton, 1945, p. 29.
12. Freud S: On beginning the treatment, 1913. In The Standard Edition of the Complete Psychological Works of Sigmund Freud, Strachey J (ed). London, Hogarth Press, 1953, Vol. 12, pp. 121–144.
13. Macalpine I: The development of the transference. Psychoanal Q 19(4): 501–539, 1946.
14. Menninger K: Transference and countertransference. In Theory of Psychoanalytic Technique. New York, Basic Books, 1958.
15. Greenson RR: The Technique and Practice of Psychoanalysis. New York, International Universities Press, 1967, Chap. XXX, p. 207.
16. Freud S: On beginning the treatment, 1913. The Standard Edition of the Complete Psychological Works of Sigmund Freud, Strachey J (ed). London, Hogarth Press, 1953, vol. 12, p. 139.
17. Sterba RF: The dynamics of the dissolution of the transference resistance. Psychoanal Q 9:363–379, 1940.
18 Fleming J: Early object deprivation and transference phenomena: the working alliance. Psychoanal Q 41(1):23–49, 1972.
19. Greenson RR: Transference. In The Technique and Practice of Psychoanalysis. New York, International Universities Press, 1967, pp. 216–224.

PART II

Working Through

A Brief Essay on the Working Through Process

Freud[1] stated, "Anyone who hopes to learn the noble game of chess from books will soon discover that only the opening and end games admit of an exhaustive systematic presentation and that the infinite variety of moves that develop after the opening defy any such description. The gap in instruction can only be filled by a diligent study of games fought out by masters." Nevertheless, I will attempt a "systematic presentation" of the middle phase of therapy followed by thirty therapy hours, not "fought out by masters," but struggled through by me and one of my patients.

Relatively little has been written on the very important topic of working through because of its complexity. In a 1965 article, Greenson[2] provides an excellent starting point for looking at the problem of working through. His contribution begins with a survey of the literature. As he points out, Freud first introduced the concept of working through in his paper, "Remembering, Repeating, and Working-Through,"[3] written in 1914. Greenson sums up Freud's concept by saying, "working through is necessary in order to overcome the resistances of the id, the psychic inertia, adhesiveness of the libido, and the repetition compulsion." Many authors (e.g., Lewin, Fenichel, and Kris) have been credited with pointing out the parallel between the work of mourning and working through.

Greenson defines working through as "the analysis of those resistances and other factors which prevent insight from leading to significant and lasting changes in the patient." He states as a goal of working through "to make insight effective, i.e., to make significant and lasting changes in the patient." By insight Greenson means: making conscious for the patient what was previously unconscious or preconscious. Greenson,[4] in his book, adds to the definition of working through: "... the psychological work which occurs after an insight has been given and which leads to a stable change in behavior or attitude." Later in the same book, he adds: "... the repetitive, progressive and elaborate explorations of the resistances which prevent an insight from leading to change." For Greenson the essential procedures in working through are repetitions and elaborations of certain steps in the analysis of resistance combined with reconstruction. The procedures that he lists for the analysis of resistance are

(1) Recognize the resistance
(2) Demonstrate the resistance to the patient
(3) Clarify the motives and mode of resistance
(4) Interpret the resistance
    (a) Discover what fantasies or memories are causing the affects and impulses behind the resistance
    (b) Pursue the history and unconscious purposes of the affects, impulses, or events in and outside of the analysis, and in the past
(5) Interpret the mode of resistance
    (a) Pursue this and similar modes of activity in and outside of the analysis
    (b) Trace the history and unconscious purposes of this activity in the patient's present and past.

Those procedures in the analysis of resistance which Greenson would put under the process of working through would be repetitions and elaborations of steps 4a,b and 5a,b. In addition, he would add the procedures of historical reconstruction and reconstructions of the self-image and the identity as working through procedures. Finally, for the patient's part, Greenson would say that working through could only take place if the patient developed a regressive transference neurosis and simultaneously a working alliance with the analyst. "In working through the patient must be willing to try to assimilate and integrate the insights gained from the analysis and to do some of the analytic work outside of the hour."

Resistance is a manifestation in the therapy of the patient's defenses. Since defense is mainly an ego function, it follows that working through also operates through the ego. The main motives of resistance are to avoid both pain and change. Given the strength of resistances, it is not surprising that a single interpretation or abreactive recall of a trauma rarely leads to lasting change, in spite of movies and novels to the contrary. An understanding of resistance and working through provides an answer to the question: Why does therapy take so long? An understanding of resistance and working through even goes a step further. It raises the question: Why doesn't therapy take longer?

Often a theme that is just barely hinted at when it first comes up is elaborated, expanded, and further understood from many different directions in subsequent sessions. An analogous process takes place in a symphony. Usually a symphony only contains a few major themes which are stated and restated in a variety of ways. The richness of the symphony comes from elaborating these themes in different keys, different time signatures, played by different combinations of instruments, and juxtaposed in different ways onto other themes.

All material from the patient can be heard in terms of its implications for the patient's current life, the patient's past, and the therapy situation, including the transference. Exploring all three of these aspects with the patient is part of the working through process.

Working through should be distinguished from the "broken record response." If a patient deals with the same material in the same way repeatedly, it is probably a form of resistance. If, each time the material comes up, the patient is able to see it more clearly or is able to expand it and, in addition, he has some affect as he is talking about it, the material is being worked through. Visually, the broken record response can be illustrated by a circle with a dot on it. The dot comes up repeatedly but is always in the same place. Working through would be illustrated by a helix, where the dot repeatedly appears at a higher and higher level of organization.

The forces that oppose working through can also be discussed less abstractly. One of the most potent is the reluctance of a person to give up a mode of functioning, no matter how neurotic or maladaptive, that was once a solution to a conflict. It should be remembered that all symptoms and neurotic patterns were originally solutions. Unfortunately, they were childhood solutions that have persisted into adulthood. Most people live by the adage, "better the devil you know than the devil you don't know." People are more comfortable with what is familiar than with what is strange. People are especially reluctant to give up something until they have something to take its place. The *primary gain* provided by symptoms and neurotic patterns is the relief of inner emotional conflict. There may also be *secondary gains* from an illness, such as sympathy, attention, decreased responsibility, and monetary benefits.

Often there is tremendous pressure from a patient's environment against his changing. A patient's family and friends have expectations about the patient's behavior and reactions. When he varies from these expectations he tends to meet resistance from his family and friends. The therapist, too, has to make sure that his own resistance to change is not interfering with the patient's progress.

There are also many forces that promote working through. Most patients seek therapy because they are hurting and are at least consciously motivated to change. Natural growth and development are on the side of finding more adaptive patterns of behavior. A patient's environment, which can oppose working through, also often promotes it. External reality usually reinforces more mature and adaptive behavior. Finally, the therapist has, as his major goal, to help the patient work through his problems and bring about positive changes. When there is a good working alliance, a reciprocal process is set in motion. Each time a therapist makes a correct interpretation the patient makes use of it by associating to additional material. This new material, in turn, enables the therapist to make additional interpretations. This reciprocal process leads to greater and greater understanding and elaboration of the problem.

There are a number of developmental considerations related to the process of working through. The therapy situation allows the patient to resume ego development in his new relationship with the therapist. The therapist helps this relationship differ from others that the patient has experienced by helping the patient to consciously examine the relationship. This allows for a reworking of many developmental stages which the patient had formerly worked out with the important people in his life, such as his parents. Even with a patient whose problems are mainly Oedipal, there will be pre-Oedipal areas of development that were not optimal which affect the particular form of the Oedipus for that person. Pre-Oedipal regressions are not only defenses against examining Oedipal material, but also problems to be worked through per se. The therapist can also help the patient work through fantasies at various levels of development, for example, the sexual and aggressive fantasies of the Oedipal period.

All children have traumatic experiences, even in the average expectable environment. Two common traumatic experiences that all children undergo are separations and the realization of their smallness in comparison with adults. A working through of these early traumas allows a patient to come up with an adult solution to replace his childhood solution.

Many patients, some much more clearly than others, do work through their problems in an orderly developmental sequence. An adult in psychotherapy may, during the working through phase of therapy, examine his earliest memories about childhood problems for several weeks. This will be followed by a transition to problems during the latency period, which bring to mind additional early childhood problems. Next there will be a switch of focus to adolescent problems, but still with additional new material related to childhood and latency. This type of patient is often ready to begin termination when he has worked through all the developmental stages up to and including his current life situation. The working through process continues after successful therapy as the patient further explores his past, as well as his new life experiences.

REFERENCES

1. Freud S: On beginning the treatment. *In* the Standard Edition of the Complete Psychological Works of Sigmund Freud. Hogarth Press, London, 1958, Vol. 12.
2. Greenson RR: The problem of working through. *In* Schur M (ed), Drives, Affects, Behavior, Vol. 2. International University Press, New York, 1965.
3. Freud S: Remembering, Repeating, and Working-Through. *In* the Standard Edition of the Complete Psychological Works of Sigmund Freud. Hogarth Press, London, 1958, Vol. 12.
4. Greenson RR: The Technique and Practice of Psychoanalysis. New York, International University Press, 1967.

Chapter 2
Starting to Deal with Competition

PATIENT: We decided to continue talking about masturbation and homosexual stuff.

THERAPIST: All right.

PATIENT: Did I mention that masturbation made me feel potent? I'd indulge not for the pleasure but for the idea that having an erection confirmed something. Sex has served that purpose, too. It seems okay to confirm one's masculinity, but I often feel I'm overdoing it. When I was living with Patricia in San Francisco, that was part of it. I was hung up with her because I was trying so hard to show that I was a big stud. I don't feel like talking about it. I don't know if I'm uncomfortable or if it's because I don't see it as a problem any more. I used to be preoccupied by that problem. I'd feel weak and sweaty. I'd feel relieved after sex. Sex proved something to me and was a release of tension. Last week I went out with a woman and I went to bed with her but I didn't feel that I had to prove anything. She's divorced and has a couple of kids. We just had a good time.

THERAPIST: You used to have to prove that you weren't castrated.

PATIENT: Yes. That really rings a bell. What comes to my mind is that my mother had polio. It left her with a deformed leg. Her calf was almost gone and she seemed to have deformed eyes. She had that endocrine disease. I thought I'd caused it all. The other thing that keeps coming to my mind after you said that is that I was slow to develop sexually. Even now I'm conscious of not having much body hair. That really bothered me when I was younger. I

85

did occasionally wonder too about my penis being bent when it was erect. I wondered if it was because I had masturbated, but then I saw that other guys were built that way, too. Mainly I dwelled on the small size. I also worried about my broad hips and small shoulders. I felt like I was built in a feminine way.

THERAPIST: Just in the past?

PATIENT: There is still a little bit of it, but it's not as conscious as it used to be.

THERAPIST: Did you talk to your father about these things?

PATIENT: No. He's bothered by them too. I recall, though, that father told me that he had a bigger penis than I did. He tended to make that kind of comment to other people, too. Like, once my uncle had to piss over the side of the boat. My dad said, "You need a microscope to see your prick." He used to make me and my brother feel that even when we grew up we wouldn't be as good and as big as him. Even in his family and my mother's family he is financially the most successful and looked up to.

THERAPIST: It sounds like it was hard to compete with Dad.

PATIENT: Now I've decided not to let myself get into a subordinate position to him. He likes to be on top. He likes to be an expert. It reminds me of last summer. He wanted me to come with him on business calls and I did. He would introduce me to secretaries as "this is our youngest."

THERAPIST: What were your thoughts and feelings when he did that?

PATIENT: It embarrassed me. It made me special in a way I didn't want to be special. It reminds me that I'd feel uncomfortable eating out because Dad used to be overly familiar with waitresses, yet I realize now he was a little nervous about it too. He'd try to get me involved in sort of an intimate way with the waitress. He'd seem friendlier there than at home. It embarrassed me.

THERAPIST: What was the embarrassment about?

PATIENT: It drew attention to me. I didn't know how to handle it. I don't want him to have anything to do with my life.

THERAPIST: You seem to feel very strongly about that.

PATIENT: I'm tired of being known as Bobby Turner's son. It was a real opening around the golf circuit but somehow it became a hangup. I'm very uncomfortable around him. He always attacks and argues. I feel more mature now than he is. He's a great producer, a great worker, but he's not a great person. He used to make me think people would like me on the basis of my skill. Now I realize that's not very important. Now I look for people I can enjoy talking with. Dad was a big phony with people. He always had an act going.

THERAPIST: That's a concern of yours, too.

PATIENT: Yes, it is sometimes. Like with the emotion business. But it's growing less so. Now I'm really enjoying having concern for others but I worry. Am I really opening up with emotions or just practicing? I don't know if I have full-grown, full-blown emotions.

THERAPIST: Full-grown, full-blown?

PATIENT: Fellatio, blowing up, losing control. Grown equals mature. Having friends.

THERAPIST: You are tying a lot of things together. Growth, emotions, friendships, sex.

PATIENT: Right. That didn't just happen. I forced myself to grow. I have a very optimistic, long-term outlook. Since I've been in therapy with you I've felt less tied to my dad.

THERAPIST: Now you are able to see your father as a man with some weaknesses and also as a man who is successful, but in a different way than you want to be successful.

PATIENT: Yes. It sounds almost trivial now. It used to be he was either my model or someone to rebel against. Somehow my work attitude is related to him, too. When I'd finish a job he would come around like an inspector. He would show me how to do it better. Even now I get bogged down in details. I do it to myself now. When I have problems to do I feel pressure to get them done. It's like Dad will be home at four o'clock and I won't have finished the lawn to his specifications. Oh, before we stop, I have to go to Air Force Reserve Camp from June fifteenth through June twenty-ninth. I thought you would like to know ahead of time for your planning.

DISCUSSION

The patient did not talk much about masturbation and homosexuality, the topics with which he introduced the session, but he certainly talked about related content. The material is flowing well. Themes, such as competition, castration anxiety, and identity problems which were introduced in earlier sessions were elaborated upon in this session. The working through process seems to have begun even though the history is still scant. In many ways Paul started this therapy as if it were already in progress. I made the decision to continue the process and collect historical material as it developed.

In this session Paul recognized how he uses masturbation and sexual relationships to convince himself that he is not castrated. He also recognized that he is moving toward using sexuality to enrich and enhance his relationship with a woman.

That all this material was very close to consciousness was borne out by his response to my interpretation, "You used to have to prove that you were not castrated." His associations to that interpretation were first to his mother's deformities, which he equated with castration, then to his own concerns about what he thought was the slow development of his secondary sexual characteristics, and finally to his concern about the shape and size of his penis. When I asked him if he had been able to discuss his concerns with his father, Paul recalled some interesting interactions with his father. Paul recalled that his father belittled the size of his penis and that his father did that with other men as well. As an adult Paul was able to see that this reflected his father's own uncertainty, but as a child it just confirmed his own concerns about himself. The negative effects of the kind of responses that Paul received from his father can be highlighted by contrasting them with a conversation between a more empathic father and his three-year-old son.

    SON: Why are you so much bigger than I am?

    FATHER: You'll be as big or bigger than I am some day.

    SON: I didn't know that!

The father in this example is able to empathize with his son's need to straighten out his confusing perceptions of himself and others. This father gave his son permission to not only equal but to exceed him some day. The son's response indicated a great deal of relief. Reality testing was involved. He became aware of a need to wait, but also gained hope of change coming about some day. That little boy should grow up with better self-representation and less conflict with his father than is the case with our patient.

    Paul spent much of the rest of the session discussing his image of himself and his father and their relationship with each other. Most of my interventions were aimed at helping him to develop a more realistic view of himself and his father and to differentiate himself from his father. This led us into the adolescent identity issues with which the patient is still struggling. Toward the end of the session the patient recognized for the first time that not only his social and sexual inhibitions, but also his work inhibitions are related to his unresolved problems of competition with his father.

    Paul announced his planned two-week absence two months in advance because he thought I would like to know for my planning. This was another indication to me that a good working alliance was developing. Paul was sensitive to the therapy being a partnership in which it was helpful to keep the other person informed of any changes. The discussion following the next session examines announcements by the therapist about vacations.

SESSION 7, APRIL 12   EFFECTS OF COMPETITION ANXIETY

    I departed from my usual practice of allowing the patient to begin the session in order to tell him that I planned to take a two-week vacation in May. Paul's first response was to say that he had planned to ask me if he could miss next week's session so that he could go camping with Julie.

THERAPIST: You seem to be experiencing a lot of anxiety as you tell me about wanting to miss our next session.

PATIENT: I had a lot of trouble telling you that. I'm not sure I would have been able to if you hadn't announced that you were going to take a vacation. I wondered what you were thinking of me. Somehow I think enjoyment is wrong fror me. Since you are planning a vacation, it made it a little easier for me to say that I wanted one too. I've read enough about psychoanalysis to know that when a patient misses a session, it may mean that he is trying to avoid something.

THERAPIST: Do you think that you are?

PATIENT: I've thought about that ever since Julie and I decided we wanted to go camping. I couldn't think of anything that I am consciously trying to avoid. It seems more like I'm able to go camping with a woman because of the work that we have been doing in therapy.

THERAPIST: I think that your concern about what I will think of you for wanting to go camping with Julie is a carry-over from your general concern about what men will think if you have an enjoyable relationship with a woman.

PATIENT: That really fits. I'm having an enjoyable relationship with Julie. She's bright and fun to be with, but I still feel some anxiety about it. For the most part, though, it's the most comfortable relationship I've ever had. Julie is planning to leave this summer.

THERAPIST: Is that why it's so comfortable?

PATIENT: That may be part of it. I'm trying to imagine how I'd feel if I knew she were going to stay around. I'm physically attracted to her and really like her company. I've been thinking about living with her this summer if she decides to stay in Colorado. But I'm really conflicted between long and short term commitments. I often act too quickly.

THERAPIST: Are you now?

PATIENT: I'm trying not to push things but I'm not going out with anyone else. I don't want to appear too eager to her but one part of me [*grits his teeth*] really is eager and anxious. I don't enjoy the drive, I just enjoy arriving at the destination. Everything seems to be a race for me. Going out with a girl always involves competition in my mind, real or imagined. I feel really threatened. I've never liked competitive situations. Like golf. I was good but I could never win.

THERAPIST: What would happen if you did win?

PATIENT: That's interesting. My first reaction is some kind of vague fear. I can't take praise either, but that doesn't involve beating anyone. I think part of the problem is that I want to beat people so badly that I feel uneasy about the aggression. Almost everything I do is somehow geared to getting

women. Like I thought passing my prelims would make me desirable to
women. I want to possess them but I don't admire people who can be domi-
nated easily. In a movie that I saw recently there is a fantasy scene. It
represents hell. There is a slave master with a whip hurting all the women
around. I really liked that.

THERAPIST: What appealed to you?

PATIENT: I identified with him. I wanted to be in his position. You
once asked me what fantasies I have when I masturbate. It used to always be
power things where I had complete control over the woman. I would fantasize
greatly stimulating her, giving her great orgasms. Even in real life I was more
concerned with giving the girl pleasure. That's the only way I could get
pleasure myself.

THERAPIST: You used the past tense.

PATIENT: Except for the episode I told you about last week, I hadn't
gone to bed with a girl for almost a year.

THERAPIST: You didn't actually say it, but somehow you gave me the
impression that you had been screwing a lot recently.

PATIENT: I may have because it means masculinity to me. In my
teenage peer group getting girls and being strong were very important. Occasionally I felt I was most competent, but usually felt least competent. Really I
always felt least competent, but I would try to fool myself. If a girl gave me a
positive response, I magnified it. If I didn't get a response I felt rejected. I
thought in all or none terms. I came up with a different conclusion talking
with you than with other people. With you this all seems to relate to the
competitiveness and feeling inferior. When I talk to others it seems like
hundreds of little problems instead of one big problem. I have to admit that
psychiatrists do understand more than the amateur analysts on campus. I think
some of what is going on at the campus is forced spontaneity, like the frantic
behavior at the singles' bars. It's like with the other girl I told you about
where I never knew where I stood. I think that was related. She enjoyed
contentless experiences, LSD, peyote, psychedelic art. That makes me nervous, because I may say it is beautiful but I don't mean it. Julie has more
traditional values, like I do. Like, with smoking grass. We both would rather
heighten regular experiences than have bizarre ones. Grass makes me uneasy.
Sometimes it gives me happy feelings. Just as often it makes me anxious or
depressed. I enjoy alcohol more because it allows me to be more expressive
and less inhibited. Grass makes me more inhibited. Alcohol makes me more
outgoing, while grass makes me more passive. I'm confused enough as it is
and grass makes me more so. When I'm in a bad mood and take grass I get very
frightened of being caught. I get almost paranoid, and then I get anxious.

THERAPIST: We have to stop now. Have fun on your trip with Julie.

DISCUSSION

The first question raised by this session is when to make administrative announcements about such things as vacations and changes in scheduling. One method is to make the announcement at the very beginning of the session, as I did in this case. The arguments favoring that approach are that the therapist doesn't interfere with material that the patient is already presenting and it allows the patient the rest of the session to respond to the announcement if he chooses to do so. To me the second argument is more persuasive than the first. Even though the patient hasn't yet said anything, the therapist, by making the announcement, is still changing what otherwise would have been the flow of material. A more artistic, but sometimes more difficult approach, is to let the patient begin the session. The therapist then makes his announcement when there is something related to it in the patient's material. For instance, the therapist would make an announcement about a vacation when the patient brings up material about such things as change or separation. Again, the therapist has to make his announcement early enough in the session to allow the patient to respond to it. Some therapists choose to make such announcements at the end of the session. That approach has several disadvantages. It means that in once-a-week therapy the patient has to wait a whole week before he can share his responses with the therapist. It is also a covert message to the patient that the announcement is not open for discussion in the therapy. Actually, such administrative issues as vacations play a very important role in the therapy, especially for patients who have problems with separation or who suffered an early loss. Some of the most significant therapeutic work is done around the therapist's vacations.

The other question related to announcing vacations is how far in advance to make the announcement. If I have any planned vacations I will usually announce those to the patient in the course of the first few sessions. I will then mention my vacation again at least twice the number of sessions ahead of the vacation as the number of sessions that I will be away. For instance, if I'm going to be away two sessions, I will announce that at least four sessions before the vacation. For those patients for whom I know my vacation will be an important issue, I will announce it even further in advance. In addition to those patients for whom a therapist's vacation causes separation anxiety, there are patients who experience it as a narcissistic wound and patients in whom it causes a great deal of hostility and aggression. The patient for whom it is a narcissistic wound has such thoughts as, "If you loved me, you wouldn't leave me" and "I must be a bad person to be driving you away." The patient for whom the therapist's vacation stimulates hostility often has fantasies that the therapist will die on his vacation. Some patients defend against anxiety, pain, and hostility by assuming that the therapist is going to a professional meeting that he has to attend rather than voluntarily leaving the patient.

Many patients will ask the therapist where he is going on his vacation. The degree to which this question is answered depends on the patient's level of development of object constancy. For the patient who can easily evoke the memory of the therapist, the question need never be answered. Instead, the patient's fantasies about the therapist's absence can be usefully explored. Under optimal conditions, object constancy is attained in early childhood. For instance, when a five-year-old boy's best friend went away on vacation, I asked him, "Do you miss him?" The little boy responded, "I don't miss him because I remember him." Patients who have not developed an adequate level of object constancy often need the help of being able to place the therapist in a geographical location in order to be able to sustain a memory of him. Potentially suicidal patients should have a way of reaching the therapist.

It is useful to establish a regular schedule of vacations and observed holidays. This not only allows for a stable relationship with a minimum number of surprises, but also allows the patient to plan his vacation schedule to coincide with the therapist's.

Often around the time of vacations the patient's resistance greatly increases. Sometimes this takes the form of a decrease in the flow of material in the few sessions immediately after the vacation. At other times it leads to threats of terminating therapy. Unless the therapist acknowledges and can work with the anxiety, humiliation, and hostility that have been stimulated by the vacation, the threat to terminate may well be carried out. Terminating is the patient's desperate attempt to force the therapist to understand what the patient was experiencing by making the therapist experience being left.

In this session we also had the issue of a trip planned by the patient. My acknowledging the anxiety he was experiencing in telling me about his planned camping trip was a pre-transference interpretation. I merely pointed out the anxiety and the situation in which it occurred without interpreting any of the unconscious transference causes. Had I wanted to pursue that more directly the next step would have been to ask him what he had in mind when he was wondering what I would think of him. Eventually he would have come to the current triangle involving the patient, Julie, and me, and then to the original Oedipal triangle. He probably would have been able to describe his fear of competition with me and his fear that I would retaliate in some way. In once-a-week therapy, especially in the early sessions, that kind of transference work causes more anxiety than most patients are willing to tolerate.

Instead, I let the patient work out the problems of Oedipal competition in their adult and adolescent derivative forms. He was able to make excellent use of this. He more directly and more elaborately than ever before explored how competition interferes with his ability to form an intimate relationship with a woman: "Going out with a woman always involves competition in my mind—real or imagined. I feel really threatened." The patient always makes every relationship with a woman triangular by bringing in a man whom he fears will punish him. He was then able to connect that insight to other competitive situations, such as golf and his school work.

He recalled a sadistic fantasy scene in a movie, and was thus able to answer a question that I had asked about masturbation fantasies several sessions before. In his masturbation fantasies he is a benevolent despot who uses his complete control over women to give them pleasure. He was able to tell me that now because of an increasing trust in our relationship.

After he was successful sexually, he was able to admit that he had not had sex in about a year. Having confirmed his masculinity with an actual sexual experience that he enjoyed, he no longer had to carry on the pretense that he had been having a great deal of sexual activity.

The patient's comments about therapy helping him to see that all of his problems were related to a common etiology instead of being hundreds of little problems indicated to me that he was making excellent use of therapy. He was able to focus on the central conflict from which all of his other problems stemmed.

At the end of the session I expressed my hope that he would have fun on the camping trip. In the script that he had written for us, he was going to ask my permission to miss the session and I was going to think poorly of him. Instead I wanted to reinforce what I thought was his making good use of the work we had done in therapy thus far.

SESSION 8, APRIL 26   LOVE AND WORK INHIBITION

PATIENT: We went camping but didn't stay overnight. It was bad weather. Things are really moving with Julie. It's the best relationship that I've ever had. We're spending every night together. The first night we spent together she said she wanted to spend the night with me but didn't want intercourse. It turns out that she wanted to but couldn't because of a previous bad experience. We spent one more night together but still didn't have intercourse. She told me how pleased she is that I am considerate of her. I'm not consciously considerate and I have one problem: Whenever I start going with a girl I look at other girls' bodies and they turn me on more than the girl I'm with. It's the old "grass is greener on the other side" thing.

THERAPIST: What happens after you've had intercourse with a woman?

PATIENT: I hate to admit it, but then it becomes even more true.

THERAPIST: What do you make of that?

PATIENT: I think it's a reflection of my insecurity as a man. Like once I wanted to be a great scientist. I thought that would make me a whole man. Now I want a perfectly formed girl. Funny, it has nothing to do with the relationship with the girl. It's more like a possession. I wanted to be an urbane scientist who flys around and has girls up to his hotel room at every convention. I have that fantasy but I don't really think I'd enjoy it. The fantasy just shows the positive side of it. Like the idea of two sophisticated people enjoying each other sexually without becoming too involved. It's like being turned on by other girls. I don't have to be involved with them. I have two hangups: I don't work effectively and I can't have a good relationship with a woman. As soon as things get going with a girl I start thinking about the work problem. Yet Julie excites me as much as any girl I've ever had a relationship with. But it's not enough to get me working. I remind myself of Madame Bovary. She keeps getting involved with other people—rejecting and being rejected.

THERAPIST: Did you have any feelings about spending the night with her and not having intercourse?

PATIENT: The first night I was resentful. I talked to her about it. Partly I felt I wasn't satisfying her. She wants to and feels bad that we don't. I feel frustrated. Not physically, though. The second night I was more ready for it.

THERAPIST: Any feelings of not being a man?

PATIENT: I'd expect that, but I don't feel that way because she really seems to like me. The one time she tried before it hurt. She's not even sure if her hymen is perforated.

(Then he talked some more about his problems functioning well at work and his problems with forming a close relationship with a woman.)

THERAPIST: The problem, then, is to be able to love and to work.

PATIENT: That sounds like Freud, doesn't it?

THERAPIST: Yes, it does.

PATIENT: Now I feel pressed about work because life means more to me. Instead of work this year I've been concentrating on getting along with people. I used to just try to overcome tension. I always felt bad and was trying to get up to neutral. Now I feel relaxed and calm but I'm not quite satisfied with that. Am I going to start accomplishing in work, in my relationships with Julie?

THERAPIST: That sounds like the old problem: that you can't let things develop, you have to push them.

PATIENT: That's what Julie told me. Really, our relationship is moving very quickly. I feel pressure at work. I feel I can never get all the things done. My desk looks like a garbage heap.

THERAPIST: Accomplishing sounds important to you.

PATIENT: Yes. For some reason that reminds me that there was a danger when I was around my father if I didn't accomplish.

THERAPIST: A danger?

PATIENT: Yes. When I was a kid he'd get angry if I didn't accomplish. That would terrorize me. Some unknown danger. I feel it a lot less now. Somehow this thing with Julie allows me to sit down and work a little without thinking I've got so much to do that I can't accomplish anything. Getting a Ph.D. seems less important to me right now.

DISCUSSION

Paul started out by describing his relationship with Julie as the best ever. It turned out that they spent two nights together, but did not have intercourse because she had experienced dyspareunia on her only attempt at intercourse. He then went on to describe how, for him, girls at a distance are safer. From his description of his relationship with Julie so far, it seems that, at least for awhile, she too will be quite distant and safe. He seems happy enough with the relationship as it is, as long as Julie keeps assuring him that their not having intercourse is her problem and not his. One clue to Paul's defensiveness about this is his statement, "We're spending every night together." From just that statement it was easy to draw the conclusion that they were having sexual relations. This was similar to his implying earlier in the therapy that he had a lot of sexual activity when, in fact, he had had none for a year. It should be understood, however, that this was not a conscious lie on his part. It was a bit of camouflage to protect himself from looking at his own feelings of inferiority as a man. It also had transference implications. We saw in previous sessions how his father always belittled him, or at least how Paul felt that his father did. He expected the same kind of belittlement from me if he didn't protect himself. He associated later in the session to a fear of father, but in the work area rather than in the sexual area.

Once again the question of timing of interpretations comes up. During this session I thought about making a two-part intervention. First I would have pointed out the defensiveness involved in his picturing himself one way, when in fact his big fear was that he was just the opposite, that he was ineffectual with women. The second part of the intervention would have been to look at the transference aspects of his doing that with me. My thought during the session was that it was too early for that kind of transference interpretation. The fact, however, that toward the end of the session he was able to make the connection himself between his work inhibition and his father suggests that he might have been able to use the same kind of interpretation about his sexual inhibitions.

In the hour when I did interpret a defensive pattern of his, he at first confirmed it, but then denied it. I said, "That's the old problem. You can't let things develop, you have to push them." Earlier he had described that very style. When he entered a new relationship he would manufacture feelings and try to get it moving very quickly. That always resulted in not moving at all. He responded by saying, "Yes, that's what Julie told me, too." He then went on to say, "I feel a lot of pressure at work; I feel like I'll never get all the things done that I have to do." To me he was just elaborating the same kind of defense, but I think that in effect he was trying to say. "This isn't something I have generated. This is the real thing. The pressure at work is not my doing." That was my clue that he was just defending against the defense interpretation, rather than taking it in as something he could find useful.

His fantasy about being the great urbane scientist with women coming up to his hotel room was a reflection of how he would like to be if he had no castration fear and no work and sex inhibitions. Paul suffers from a special kind of sexual impotence. It is not a physical impotence. He has successfully had intercourse. He had never complained of inability to have or sustain an erection. Instead he suffers from a kind of emotional impotence. He can go to bed with a girl for two nights and not have intercourse. Instead of being upset, he is somewhat relieved. Even when he has sexual intercourse he cannot have complete pleasure from it without anxiety.

SESSION 9, MAY 3   **A RESISTANCE HOUR**

PATIENT: I don't like the way the guy who teaches statistics teaches. I'm doing poorly. I'll probably get a C. We are supposed to have a test today. I'm not ready, so I'll tell him that I'm sick. I don't like doing that, though. It really upsets me. I don't do it habitually.

THERAPIST: Something about using that excuse upsets you.

PATIENT: I don't know if I'm afraid of getting caught or if I feel guilty about it. It's not right to take a responsibility and not do it. It's easy to learn the concepts in statistics, but the details are a pain. They seem silly. But the other part of me feels I'm not scrupulous. I have made the decision not to work hard enough to get a good grade. I act that way but I find it hard to stick with the decision. It's similar with girls. I act without a commitment. But I don't have that conflict with Julie. I'm not giving what is required by the guy who's running the course. Sometimes I feel I'm purposely doing that. I'm not completely committed to sociology and work, but I want to be. The Air Force is a different problem because I just do what I minimally have to do. But I do worry about being caught at it.

THERAPIST: Caught?

PATIENT: Yes, they could catch me at school not really believing in science. A lot of what sociologists do seems worthless. Maybe my resentment of the guy is related to his detailed interest in experimental sociology. My interest is more in attitude sociology, things like changing attitudes toward Blacks, drugs, sex. But I should know analysis of variants.

THERAPIST: You're giving me the reality but you're not telling me what your feelings are about all this.

PATIENT: Something is affecting me I'm not aware of.

THERAPIST: What do you think it is?

(There is a long pause.)

PATIENT: In some ways I feel superior to the teacher and some of the other graduate students because I think I have better values. But I feel inferior to them, too, because they seem to be working steadily. They are very involved in their work. What do you think?

THERAPIST: What about your mentioning of details?

PATIENT: Basically something is wrong with emphasis on details. They make me uncomfortable, but not all details. I enjoy charting grades and making graphs.

THERAPIST: What's the difference with the details in the statistics course?

PATIENT: I have to memorize things that I could easily look up.

THERAPIST: I think it's important for us to understand why some sociology graduate students like it and you don't.

PATIENT: Well, I don't like those people. Maybe they think my abstractions are trite.

THERAPIST: Does a course like statistics display some of your inadequacies?

PATIENT: In some ways. There's no room for disagreement. I do have trouble in statistics raising my hand and saying, "I didn't understand that," but I can ask in sociology because there people are trying to explain their ideas. In statistics I'm afraid they'll say, "Where have you been?" I used to be afraid as a teaching assistant that one of the students would challenge my ideas or formulations, but then I realized that many approaches are okay.

THERAPIST: Sounds like you're having some feelings about compulsive personalities.

PATIENT: Yes. I don't like them. I think they're trivial, worthless.

THERAPIST: Are you compulsive?

PATIENT: I don't know. I wonder about that. Is that what is called counterphobic? Sometimes little things really bug me, but I fight that tendency. There are little things about people that bug me. It depends on my mood. I got upset when we were studying drugs. Pharmacologists use "dosage" instead of "dose" and "usage" instead of "use." I often take a word and run through all the related words in my mind. For example, lovable, lovably, love, loved, lover, loving, lovingly. In other words, all the suffixes in alphabetical order. It's funny. I was so easily able to say that to you. I usually get embarrassed thinking about telling someone about this thing.

THERAPIST: Why embarrassed?

PATIENT: It's silly. I don't know why it seems silly. I only use about four or five words like this. I do it when I'm in a situation that makes me nervous. It's almost a substitute for action. That's the feeling about the people I label as compulsive. What they do is as trivial as what I do with words. It's not fun. It's not a game. It's almost automatic. I don't want to do that with words. Somehow it keeps me out of confrontations.

THERAPIST: All the previous sessions seemed to be connected. This session, at least on the surface, is very different from the last session.

PATIENT: [*laughs*] I laughed because I wondered if you were testing me to see if I remembered the last session. It was about why I'm more attracted physically to women I don't have a relationship with than to a woman I do have a relationship with.

THERAPIST: Perhaps today's session was a reaction to last week's session.

PATIENT: I think so. I think it is related. It keeps me from dealing with what is important. My father emphasized rules a lot. I had to play the game straight. I used to get really angry when people broke rules. I used to get in a lot of fights about it. I'd get beat up. I wonder if I'm trying to satisfy those kids now. People who break rules attract me and they also scare me.

THERAPIST: Rules and details can be used to avoid close relationships.

PATIENT: I never realized that before, but it's true. When I played games as a kid, instead of making friends I got into fights. I wonder if I'm using rules and details now to keep from getting too involved with my work and with Julie.

THERAPIST: And with me and therapy.

PATIENT: Damn. I wasn't aware of that. Of course, by focusing on statistics in such a detailed way I avoided looking at what had been growing clearer and clearer every session, my trouble being really involved in work and my sexual difficulties. Maybe we were going too fast and I wasn't quite ready to look that closely at those things in myself. Especially I didn't want to look at the relationship developing between us.

THERAPIST: Especially with my going away for two weeks.

PATIENT: I had been thinking this past week about your vacation coming up. I was sure it wouldn't bother me any. I just told myself I'd have an extra hour those two weeks to study and work.

THERAPIST: And now?

PATIENT: Part of me is relieved. Part of me really wants to get on with working out my problems. That second part of me is hurt and angry about your going away. It's funny. I didn't have any of those feelings the week I took off to go camping with Julie.

THERAPIST: We have to stop now.

PATIENT: Okay. See you May 28. Have a good vacation.

DISCUSSION

Session 9 raises three main issues for discussion. The first is how to deal with massive resistance when it appears in a session. The second is the developing transference and why it had to be partially interpreted in this session. The third is the severity of this patient's superego, which becomes so clear in this session.

This session illustrates the paradox of resistance in a patient who voluntarily sought psychotherapy. If asked, Paul would reply, "Of course I want to solve my problems with competition, intimacy, and work." For eight sessions he has productively worked on those conflicts. Even when he was away from therapy for fourteen days between the seventh and eighth sessions he was consciously and unconsciously working through his problems. Now, suddenly, in the ninth session, he becomes resistant to a continuation of that work. Why? How should the resistance be handled technically?

The why question is answered in detail in the essay on the working through process. In summary, this patient consciously wants to solve his conflicts but unconsciously defends against the pain and anxiety caused by looking at them. He resists change because it is unfamiliar. Solving conflicts means changing his identity, his self-representation, and his object-representations. These are resistances that all patients share. In addition, there was increased likelihood of resistance in this session because his conflicts have become increasingly clear to him and because it is the last session before my vacation.

Paul was not even aware of his resistance until I brought it to his attention. Many people are consciously resistant to psychotherapy. One of my patients reported that he urged a friend with ulcerative colitis to seek psychotherapy. His friend replied, "I'd rather end up with a colostomy bag than have my head shrunk." My experience with reluctant patients who do come to psychotherapy because of pressure from friends, relatives, employers, or courts is that they have, in addition, the same unconscious resistances as the "highly motivated" patient.

The technical handling of the resistance in this session involved a series of steps. First, I had to become aware of the degree of resistance in the hour. I then had to discover the causes of the resistance by thinking about the overall therapy process up to that point, including the transference, and by listening for specific clues from what the patient was saying in the session. The next step was to help the patient become aware of the resistance. I did this by commenting that this session differed from all the previous ones. This intervention was also an attempt to enlist the patient's aid in finding causes of increased resistance.

With these steps providing a foundation, I then became more interpretative. First I made the general interpretation, "Perhaps this session was a reaction to last week's session." Then I became more specific, relating the resistance to content from the previous session, interpreting transference resistance, and connecting the resistance to my upcoming vacation. The final step was to try to work through as much as possible the insights provided.

In the section on alliance and transference, I listed four reasons for interpreting transference in psychotherapy. One of those, when transference interferes with therapy, was relevant to this session. In individual psychotherapy there are only two people in the office, the patient and the therapist. When Paul talked in this session about his difficulty in becoming involved with his work, with Julie, and in the past with his father, he was also talking about his difficulty in becoming involved with me and therapy. His difficulty in forming a close relationship with me was one of the major causes of increased resistance at this time. This problem was, of course, underscored by my upcoming vacation. One of the most useful ways in which a therapist can help a patient who has difficulties with intimacy is by helping him to form a close, trusting relationship with the therapist. Since the current transference manifestations were interfering with this process, they had to be interpreted. Having looked at some of these manifestations, I then made a connection to my vacation. The patient responded by first telling me how he had denied that my vacation had any importance to him. Later he was able to see his ambivalent feelings about my absence. In spite of this ambivalence he was able to wish me a good vacation at the end. This was another indicator to me that Paul had fairly well developed object constancy.

The severity of Paul's superego became more apparent in this session. He was very upset by his plan to tell his statistics professor that he was too sick to take his test. As the session progressed it became clear that he suffered both from internal guilt and from a fear of being punished by someone else. There are many graduate students who say of certain courses, "I don't think that's important. I'll study just enough to get by and that's it." Like our patient, they consciously make that decision but unlike our patient they don't agonize and feel guilty about it. The same is true about his statement, "They could catch me at school not really believing in science." Most graduate students have some questions and criticisms about their field of study, but not all are upset by their doubts.

His superego problems were long-standing. The patient described a simi-

lar rigidity about rules when he was a child playing games. Piaget[1] ascribes
this kind of attitude toward rules as being normal in a five-year-old. Once a
typical five-year-old learns the rules to the game, he is reluctant to tolerate any
modifications in those rules. The trouble with a severe superego is that it does
not allow for flexibility and it causes a great deal of pain through producing
guilt. The patient's inhibitions around sexuality are also, in part, related to his
severe superego.

SESSION 10, MAY 28   FEELING INFERIOR TO OTHER MEN

PATIENT: I had a final last Friday, so I couldn't have come to see you
anyway.

THERAPIST: It sounds like you are saying that my being away was of
no importance to you.

PATIENT: I'm saying that but I don't completely mean it. While you
were away things started to go bad with Julie. I wanted to talk to you about
that. I'm starting to feel towards Julie the way I did towards Patricia in San
Francisco. I'm turned off sexually and personally. Her everyday conversa-
tions seem silly to me. I don't know how to respond to it. It's an awful
feeling. I feel trapped. I feel more comfortable because she's going out of
town next week. I don't know how I'll feel, though, the day after she leaves. I
think I'll be threatened because I don't have a woman. Before Patricia left I
was glad she was leaving. After she left I wished that she would come back. I
felt she found a group of people more exciting than me. I think this time I'll
maintain some perspective. I'm more sure of Julie's feelings than I was of
Patricia's. I think Julie wants to marry me.

At this point I could have steered the session toward looking at the
parallel between his reaction to his being left by Patricia and his reactions to
my being away. I thought it would be more profitable, however, to follow up
on his statement that he feels threatened if he doesn't have a woman and to
find out more about what is going wrong with his relationship with Julie.

THERAPIST: What is threatening about not having a woman?

PATIENT: I think I should have a woman. Men who don't have a
woman are less of a man.

THERAPIST: It makes you wonder about your masculinity if you don't
have a woman.

PATIENT: Maybe that's too easy an interpretation, but it seems like
that's it.

THERAPIST: If that's too easy an interpretation, maybe you have some
other thoughts.

PATIENT: Well, there are other things important to my feeling masculine. I have a lot of work to do that I can't finish. That makes me feel less than masculine. Last week I had tic fever. I felt really rotten and that made me feel less than masculine. Something about intimacy really turns me off. It makes me vomit. I'm turned on by a woman at a distance, both emotionally and physically, but I'm turned off when she gets closer. It makes me wonder if I'm completely heterosexual. I've had some homosexual dreams. I wonder if it's the dependency aspect we talked about before that turns me off. You know, big breasts, those things. Julie called and said we shouldn't see each other any more. We had seen the movie "Sweet September" the night before. The girl in the movie was dying. She was in love with the guy but wanted a different man every month. Julie liked the movie but I thought it was awful because the moral was love one person. I told her my feelings about intimacy. She took them very personally, which they were. I told her I didn't want to end the relationship because I felt that if I knew what I really wanted, I'd probably really desire her. I hate my feelings. I feel really guilty about them.

THERAPIST: It sounds like you and Julie were getting more intimate and you found that threatening.

PATIENT: That's exactly what was happening, but I don't understand it. We finally started having intercourse and I got a lot of pleasure out of it. I don't have any trouble with impotency. Julie has always had difficulty with sex. It really made me feel like a stud to be able to give her pleasure when another guy couldn't. I used to have fantasies about having a bigger organ. All adolescents have that kind of fantasy, but for me it was a real obsession. It was my predominant concern all through adolescence. That's all I ever thought about.

THERAPIST: And now?

PATIENT: I don't have the same fantasy any more. Maybe it's more unconscious now. The concern is still there but I'm less aware of it. I always felt inferior to my father.

THERAPIST: How so?

PATIENT: For some reason I just can't think of any details about it now. It's just a general feeling of being inferior to him, that he was bigger than I am. My mother and aunts come to mind now. They provided a superficial warmth but that was all. Most people probably make pretty specific statements about how their parents treated them. I remember more about my father than my mother. I have this one image of my mother as a big woman carrying a broom. She's going to swat me. I don't recall anything about her involving real warmth, like her holding me. But she was warm with my brother's children. She would get real excited when they would show her any love.

THERAPIST: You switched from talking about feeling inferior to your father to talking about your mother and the other women in your family.

PATIENT: I think it is all related to my feelings about intimacy and sex but I can't put my finger on it.

THERAPIST: What comes to your mind about the image you had of your mother about to swat you with a broom?

PATIENT: It was like I was doing something wrong. Like I'd left a mess. That could be shit, but what comes to my mind is sex is messy. It's not neat and clean and dry like my mother's house was.

THERAPIST: Women at a distance are neat and clean and dry.

PATIENT: Yes. I'm always surprised that women are never quite what I imagined they were at a distance when they get up close. The quality of sex is different than I expect. People at a distance are more attractive to me. Once you get close to people they are all the same. There is no mystery left. I concentrate on physical things so much. There isn't that much difference in women's bodies. I get turned on by different women's bodies at a distance but that's not true up close. As I get close the softness and warmth turns me off. They're all soft and warm. At a distance they are polished, less flaccid. I don't know what I would expect if they felt like they looked.

THERAPIST: It sounds like you're describing the Playmate of the Month when you talk about a woman at a distance.

PATIENT: Am I a product of that culture? Probably that just helps describe what really bothers me. But, maybe not. Maybe that kind of thing can be influential.

THERAPIST: It sounds to me, from this session, that what really bothers you is feeling inferior to other men and intimacy.

PATIENT: Those things are painful to talk about.

DISCUSSION

After a resistant session and two weeks vacation, the patient returned to the issues of session 8 and the working through process. He again brought up the issue of his attraction to women at a distance, and was able to go much further with it than he did during the eighth session. He gave some specific details about why he is more comfortable with distance. He is upset by both physical and emotional closeness.

The issue here, of course, is intimacy. We know from this session that things are not going all that well with Julie, but we don't know specifically what is wrong. First he reported that she wants to marry him. Then he reported that he told her he has problems having an intimate relationship. She responded by suggesting that they break up. Neither of them took that sugges-tion seriously but their relationship has some problems. They had intercourse, she started talking about marriage and he started finding trivial things about her that annoy him. His problems with intimacy also have to be watched for in the therapy situation. We have already spotted some resistance on his part to becoming involved with the therapist and the therapy. It is possible that if he realizes that he is becoming more involved than is comfortable for him, he will be tempted to quit therapy. For that reason I think it was a good decision on my part early in the hour not to press the issue of his feelings about my being away. As long as the transference feelings were not interfering with the flow of material, there was no reason to elaborate on them.

The other important issue in this session was his feeling inferior to other men. This theme first appeared in this session when he talked about his fantasy that Patricia left him to join a group of more exciting people. Later in the hour he talked more specifically about feeling inferior to his father. When that topic became too painful for him, he defensively switched to talking about his mother and the women in his family. He correctly perceived that his discomfort in talking about feeling inferior to father and his switching to talking about mother are related but he doesn't understand the relationship. I think that the connection is that the feelings of inferiority that he experienced in the Oedipal triangle were revived. The specific anxiety that this aroused in him was castration anxiety.

REFERENCE

1. Piaget J: The Moral Judgement of the Child. Free Press, Glencoe, Illinois.

Chapter 3
Superego Problems

PATIENT: The more I think about castration the more I think it's important to me. It was my biggest concern throughout high school.

THERAPIST: How's that?

PATIENT: I felt my penis was little. I would always get anxious if I thought about trying to attract one of the popular girls. There was a vague feeling that something bad would happen to me if I tried that. But where do I go from there? Periodically I need a woman to demonstrate that I'm sexual. I don't seem to want to have one around all the time.

THERAPIST: Somehow a woman completes you?

PATIENT: I always feel that a woman will complete me when I don't have one. But she never does when I do have a woman. I always think that when I have a woman I'll be able to work hard but it never does turn out that way. But I think I got that attitude from someone else, like my father. Part of it seems to be wrapped up in my insecurity about masculinity. But most of it is just something vague. It seems to be the feeling that it should work that way. But maybe it was related to this thing with my mother.

THERAPIST: What thing with your mother?

PATIENT: I don't know. She seemed so vague to me all the time. I look for outside changes to make me happy.

THERAPIST: It sounds like you don't really believe that will work. You believe it's something inside you.

PATIENT: There is something inside me that tells me I can't enjoy

105

myself. My mother always told me we couldn't enjoy the messy things boys do, like fishing, fixing bikes, things like that. But both my mother and father were kind of subtle. They didn't openly suppress me so I never once stood up to my father. Neither I nor my father are nice to people unless they can do something for us.

THERAPIST: "Messy things?" Like the mess you recalled when talking about your mother last time?

PATIENT: Yes. I have obsessive thoughts. Recently I haven't been able to sleep because I brood about little things I may have done wrong. I worry about what will have to be done the next day. My father is a compulsive, I think.

THERAPIST: He's a compulsive?

PATIENT: I hate him. I'd like to kill him. Mash him up. Really grind him away. I'm capable of that too. I've been in a couple of fights and enjoyed hurting the other guy. The last one was about two years ago. Luckily I was pulled off before I really hurt him. I don't recall feeling that much intensity toward my mother, but my father was really keeping me from doing things I wanted to from about ages twelve through eighteen. I had to be in at nine o'clock.

THERAPIST: You feel you're capable of killing and mashing up your father?

PATIENT: If he were around I'd really be disturbed. I'm twenty-five and I still have never said to him, "Why are you doing that to me?" I have guilt about being angry at him. One reason I never told him was that I was never sure I was right. I didn't know what the hell was going on. When I was ten my mother's mother died but even at that age I still didn't understand what my mother was going through. When I was fifteen my uncle died and it just didn't affect me any. My whole family is pretty messed up. My father has as much trouble as I do expressing emotions and feeling things. I wasn't allowed to express emotions, especially anger. I think I generalize that to all feelings. I push down all strong feelings. Recently I've been better about it. At least with anger. If someone does something I don't like I let him know. I guess I always knew when I felt angry but I didn't express it. I felt sexual desire all along but never loving and closeness.

THERAPIST: Do you want to love someone?

PATIENT: I don't know. In one sense I don't. I put others in the position of loving me but I don't care whether I love them. That makes me feel bad. Like there's something wrong with me for that.

THERAPIST: Something wrong?

PATIENT: Yes. Like I'm missing out on some satisfaction I could get. Most of the girls I get involved with are quite independent. They have strong positive feelings about me but I could never generate the same towards them.

But I still seemed to need the relationship more than they did. But I also felt trapped. I felt that something was wrong. Physically or with the personalities. I don't know. I never tell them but they detect my uneasiness.

THERAPIST: Is Julie still in town?

PATIENT: She left Monday.

THERAPIST: You speculated about how you would feel when she left.

PATIENT: I feel I'm lacking someone to demonstrate my masculinity. I can demonstrate it by screwing. I have to act that out over and over and over. [*Long pause*] I feel like bawling because I really liked Julie. I almost loved her, but when she is around something just digs on me.

THERAPIST: That is a painful conflict.

PATIENT: I feel I have to always demonstrate that I'm a man. I keep noticing little things that turn me off. She is planning to come back the end of the summer and we're going to take a trip. I'm worried because she won't be leaving soon then. I miss her now but I know that unless I change when she gets back I'll feel trapped. I'll feel I can find something better.

THERAPIST: Do you feel that way now?

PATIENT: No, except some girls turn me on more at a distance.

THERAPIST: Where did you get your ideas about what makes a woman attractive?

PATIENT: From the older guys in the neighborhood who had these pictures of big breasted, shiny, smooth, hairless, and sometimes even headless women. The face to me is closer to the personality. Why can't I feel all the time the way Julie does? I'm so abstract. It pisses me off. No, it doesn't. It makes me feel like crying, not like killing.

THERAPIST: Our time is up for today.

PATIENT: Next week is our last meeting until I get back from Reserve Camp.

DISCUSSION

Paul started out the session acknowledging that castration anxiety was one of his biggest concerns. When I asked him for specifics he came forth with several examples: his feeling that his penis was small, his anxious feeling that something bad would happen to him if he tried to attract one of the popular girls, and his periodic need for a woman to demonstrate to him that he still had a penis. Since we had dealt with the first two derivatives of castration anxiety before, I chose to explore further his need for a woman to "demonstrate that I'm sexual."

Paul correctly described how he expects a woman to complete him when he doesn't have one, but how that never works out for him. He even expects a woman to make him more potent in the work area. This is a repeat of the theme of liking women at a distance. Later in the session he demonstrated this vividly by describing how he was becoming bored with Julie and thinking everyone else was more attractive until she left. Then he missed her to the extent that he felt like crying. No woman can satisfy him because no woman is his mother. He wants the idealized woman who represents the image he had of his mother when he was five years old. When the woman comes close, he is disappointed because once again it is not his mother. When she goes away, he starts to idealize her again, misses her, and feels like crying over the loss. He underlined this conflict even more forcibly later when he recognized that he was frightened about the prospect of Julie's return in the fall and their having eight or nine months together. Underlying everything in this hour was his chief dynamic of feeling inadequate as a man.

When he made the statement, "I look for outside changes to make me happy," my intervention was aimed at helping him see that his problem is intrapsychic, not environmental. He responded by saying, "There is something inside me that tells me I can't enjoy myself." That is a very nice description of his severe superego. First he tried to blame his mother for not letting him "enjoy the messy things boys do like fishing, fixing bikes." In effect he was saying that his mother would not let him do what was masculine for an eight-year-old boy. He thought she didn't want him to be masculine. I started to follow up on this but soon we came to the real affect, his feelings about his father. Paul's tremendous anger at his father was not what I anticipated when I asked about his father's compulsiveness. I had expected to learn more about Paul's own compulsive traits by letting him talk about the compulsive traits he was projecting onto his father. I think that the father he wants to kill, mash, and grind away is the internalized father which has become his strict superego. His father would probably be delighted if Paul could have an enjoyable sexual relationship with Julie. His superego, though, is his internalization of the way he perceived his father when Paul was four or five years old. In his unconscious Paul is convinced that his father does not want him to be an adult sexual man. In his unconscious there is still the triangle of him, his father, and his mother, but his mother is now represented by Julie. He externalizes the intrapsychic conflict between his id drives and his superego restrictions. It then becomes a contest between him and his father or his father representatives for his mother or mother representatives. Every relationship with a woman, for him, involves a triangle.

This conflict prevents him from facing his father as one adult man to another. He still has a child–parent relationship going. When he tries to break out of that by doing adult manly things, be becomes very anxious. As a result, Paul remains unproductive at work and unable to have real intimacy with a woman.

The immediate goal now is to keep this theme open for further exploration and elaboration. He needs more help in recognizing that this is an internal conflict rather than an external contest. It is Paul himself, not his father or anyone else, who keeps him from doing the things he wants to do and is capable of doing. One can predict that this conflict will start to be acted out with me in the therapy. He will probably start to attribute to me characteristics of his father and of his demanding superego. This conflict may manifest in competition with me or he may start to identify with me as the transference aggressor.

SESSION 12, JUNE 14   REPETITION: THE HALLMARK OF A NEUROSIS

I started out by informing him that by the time he came back from his Reserve Camp I would have moved to a new office. I gave him my new phone number. He agreed to call me when he returned from camp to set up the next appointment.

PATIENT: There are two main things bothering me. I can't put things in order and I have a problem with feelings. I feel we are getting nowhere.
THERAPIST: So there are three things bothering you.
PATIENT: Yes. [*Laughs*] I know these things take a long time, but it's frustrating. I thought I knew more about myself. Do you think the problem with not being able to order things is related to not being able to finish things? I end up doing a sloppy job at the end.
THERAPIST: Making messes. A sloppy job. Does that bother you?
PATIENT: It bothers the people that I'm around. That does bother me, too. I can lose things and waste money by being sloppy. At least it's screwing up my relations with other people, especially women. They seem to care about neatness. Like the women at my office. I wonder how much of that I ask for. Other people are messier but they get less criticism.
THERAPIST: Criticism from others or from yourself?
PATIENT: Both. Like there are these women at the office. One is about thirty-seven. She's the wife of a professor. Another woman is about my age and a good friend. The third is about thirty and is getting her Ph.D. This woman is a friend of people who own the place where I'm moving out. She keeps offering to help me clean. She was going to meet me at five o'clock to check things over. I thought she had a key so I didn't bother to go up. Maybe I'm sloppy to get attention or something.
THERAPIST: Or something?

PATIENT: Sometimes I see myself as a dashing adolescent who doesn't care about the little things. You know, like keeping my life in order.

THERAPIST: Why does this bother you?

PATIENT: Other people comment on it. But some of these women treat me affectionately, like a little boy. They see me as incompetent in this area.

THERAPIST: They like that?

PATIENT: Yes. These things never bothered Julie. She never mothered me. These women remind me of things I didn't like about the way Mother treated me. I'm consciously trying to disrupt that relationship. I am more independent now. I don't come crying for help from them.

THERAPIST: It sounds like you're struggling with whether you are a little boy or a man.

PATIENT: Yes. Acting like a little boy gets things for me. If I don't do things quite right I still get by.

THERAPIST: And yet you are uncomfortable acting like a little boy.

PATIENT: Part of it is I'm rebelling against their system. But I'm not ready to pay the consequences. I don't even do what I do well. I'm not good at being untraditional. I have new ideas but I never implement them. The real problem is that I don't want to produce anything but I'm uncomfortable when I don't work.

THERAPIST: You are being pulled in two directions.

PATIENT: I do want to produce but I hate actually working. Research at a distance sounds nice but, like with women, when I really get close I don't like it. It's the same with teaching. I've always hated working. I felt trapped there. I wanted to do something important. Now when I'm doing what I choose to do I'm still miserable.

THERAPIST: Who always told you to produce?

PATIENT: My father, I guess.

THERAPIST: Maybe. What about your mother? Like the three women in the office.

PATIENT: Mother really didn't care about actually getting something done. Her emphasis was on getting things to look nice and to be in order. My mother could not tolerate any ambiguity. Like my father wanted to move to California. My mother and her sisters were against her moving. She didn't like to shake things up. I'm trying to satisfy both Mother and Father at the same time. Mother sat around. Father was always out doing things. He was a good achiever.

THERAPIST: You say you're trying to satisfy both your mother and father but you don't do either.

PATIENT: That's how it comes out. Somehow I get the feeling that if I really produce I'll be alone.

THERAPIST: If you produce you'll be deserted?

PATIENT: I'll be out doing things myself with no one to help me. Part of being independent means being alone.

THERAPIST: You seem to be setting up a dichotomy. Dependence is bad and independence is good.

PATIENT: No, there could be a good dependence, a mutual dependence. I often thought I'd like to be a psychotherapist, have contact with people.

THERAPIST: What do you think being a psychotherapist would be like?

PATIENT: I'd be able to get closer to someone. I'd say, "You feel weak. So do I. Everyone does." It would be a way of justifying my own hangups. It would feel good to help someone else. Part of the reason I don't produce is positive. I want to do something really good.

DISCUSSION

Except for my beginning the session with some administrative details, the progression in this session was typical of most therapy hours with neurotic patients. In the time between sessions the patient has a chance to build up his defenses. That is exactly what Paul did. His initial complaint related to his obsessive–compulsive defenses of wanting to put things in order and his problems being aware of and expressing his feelings. Then a third complaint slipped out: "I feel we are getting nowhere." I immediately intervened to try to help him express his anger and frustration about therapy and me. He looked at that briefly but then reverted to anal-level conflicts about messiness and neatness. As I continued looking at the defenses and clarifying the content, he moved back to the central problem, his competition with me. By the end of the hour he was into the transference, talking about issues of identifying and competing with me.

His desire to be a psychotherapist had multiple meanings. His becoming a psychiatric technician in the Air Force Reserves was a form of identification with me. On a more subtle level, it was a way of competing with me. When I asked him, "What do you think being a psychotherapist would be like?" his response seemed to be an expression of the kind of reassurance that he would like to receive from me.

When this session was presented in the psychotherapy conference, one of the students asked an interesting question: "If the patient did become a psychotherapist and had a patient with problems similar to his own, would he be able to see the problems in the patient?" From Paul's fantasy about being a therapist, it appears that he would have difficulty seeing similar problems in other patients until he had worked the problem out for himself. His response was to support the patient's defenses and to identify with the patient. He said that he would like to use being a psychotherapist to be able to get closer to someone and to justify "my own hangups." It was clear from his comment, "You feel weak. So do I. Everyone does," that he would both identify with the patient and support the patient's defenses. That way neither he nor the patient would have to look at the problem. I can imagine Paul's patients saying something like, "I had this mean father who always suppressed me." Paul's response, at least to himself, would be something like, "Boy, I know what he's talking about. I had the same thing." This, of course, is the reason that a training analysis is required for everyone who is becoming a psychoanalyst. Psychoanalysis, or at least psychotherapy, is often extremely useful for all psychotherapists. Some psychotherapists with unresolved conflicts are able to see the conflict in their patients even though they aren't aware of it as clearly in themselves. There is always a danger, however, that a therapist with unresolved conflicts will either act them out with his patients or be unable to help his patients with similar conflicts.

Once again Paul's chief dynamic was feeling inferior as a man and being unable to take the steps that would allow him to really be a man. My pointing out to him that he was struggling between wanting to remain a little boy and wanting to become a man led to our hearing for the first time his fear that if he were productive he would be all alone. This can be seen as both an adolescent and an Oedipal problem. It's the adolescent question, should I be independent of my parents and face the world alone or continue to be a child? From an Oedipal standpoint, it is the question of what would have happened to him if he had indeed won an Oedipal victory. If he had won his mother, he would have been left by his father or his father would have retaliated and castrated him. There are numerous ramifications of this problem. Part of it is his clinging to being a little boy and all of the gratification that comes with that. Part of it is the fear of being left, part of it is a fear of retaliation. Work and adult relationships with women are attractive to him, but they are also frightening.

We have heard this theme in one form or another from the first session on. The hallmark of a neurosis is repetition. There are innumerable variations on one theme but the variations become more and more elaborate and lead to better and better understanding of the ramifications.

With only slight exaggeration, one can say that nothing new ever happens to a neurotic. Through transference, the present is distorted by the past. Every new person in a neurotic's life is expected to play an old role; every new situation is expected to fit into an old plot.

Paul is not yet consciously aware of the competition theme. When one of the ramifications of his problem with competition with other men appears, he is not yet able to say to himself, "This is another facet of the competition theme." When he is able to see and work with this theme without help from the therapist, he will be in a position to give himself therapy. When the patient is able to do that fairly well on his own, it is time to start thinking about termination. Learning to do self-therapy is usually extremely exciting and rewarding.

During the last several hours, Paul has talked a great deal about obsessive–compulsive issues. Even though he does have some obsessive–compulsive traits, I do not think that is an important problem for him. Instead, it serves as a regressive defense. If he can regress to the earlier level where those were the issues, he does not have to deal with Oedipal issues which are really central in his life.

SESSION 13, JULY 2   **THE STRUGGLE WITH FEELINGS**

PATIENT: Hey! This is a nicer office.

THERAPIST: Uh-huh.

PATIENT: At Reserve Camp we had one-and-a-half-hour group sessions. I learned a lot. Many of my ideas about what bothers me changed. I don't think it's castration. With my father I just feel it is dangerous to be close to him. The last group session, I told the group how I really got messed up in the Air Force. I told them I got threatened by men, especially in showers. The nurse said that I sounded like I wanted to be a homosexual. I don't think so. I think I'm just threatened by other men's masculinity. I started talking about my father. I mentioned wanting to hurt him. The psychiatrist said, "You really don't want to hit your father. You want to hold on to him and be nice to him." That's sort of right. I want some affection from him. He has tried but he can't. He gets nervous when he tries to be affectionate to me. That's how I feel when I'm in a situation which implies affection with men.

THERAPIST: Earlier you said you feel it is dangerous to be close to your father.

PATIENT: That's just a feeling. I can't give incidents. Even when he tries to be nice to me, he's very business-like. We both feel it's dangerous to express feelings. I did a little in that group. I really felt good those two weeks. My mind wasn't racing around.

THERAPIST: It sounds like the group experience was a good one for you.

PATIENT: It was. I started out very intellectual. I'd talk about feelings but I wouldn't express them. The psychiatrist pointed that out. I started expressing feelings. I've felt more serene since. I can get into what I'm doing. I used to think about the future and the past. Now I'm more into the present. I've been telling some of my friends about my experience and they say it is childish to express feelings directly. How do you feel about that?

THERAPIST: I think you are wondering if it's dangerous to feel close to me.

PATIENT [*his eyes filled with tears*]:   I know that you have always encouraged me to express feelings, but I keep fearing that you will be like Dad. Suppressing emotions can get to the extent that one is no longer aware of them. Mother was like a delicate china closet. Feelings were dangerous. I think it's part of my mother's Norwegian culture. Especially when they came to the United States they were afraid of upsetting the system. I think I understand what my father did. He tried to like me but it scared him so it scared me to be close. But, I don't know about Mother. She was never warm with me. She could express warmth toward the grandchildren. She scolded me and expressed disgust, but in subtle ways.

THERAPIST: You once told me that she controlled you and your father through guilt.

PATIENT: Now I don't know if it was really her or my father.

THERAPIST: How's that?

PATIENT: He would say, "Mother's had a hard time. Be considerate." He communicated that she was different from other mothers.

THERAPIST: How did that make you feel?

PATIENT: Ashamed of her. Not the polio, but the eyes. People noticed her eyes. Her puffy face made her eyes look very small. They almost disappeared. When I was thirteen, fourteen, fifteen, I was afraid to bring girls home. I was afraid they wouldn't like me because of my mother's eyes. But, then I'd feel ashamed of my feeling ashamed of my mother. I'd forgotten about it. Is it guilt or shame?

THERAPIST: Why do you want to make the distinction?

PATIENT: I want to understand.

THERAPIST: I think it's your way of getting distance from the feelings.

PATIENT: I do that a lot, don't I? I intellectualize to get away from emotions. [*Pause*] I had some of the same feelings about the girl in San Francisco. She had a bad reputation. I've never told you because I have a hard time admitting it. I found out that she had false teeth. That really bothered me. I felt I should feel responsible for her reputation and bad teeth. I felt I had to make up for it. I felt that I wanted to cry and say, "I'm sorry."

THERAPIST: Did you feel responsible?

PATIENT: I felt that I, too, was a man, so I was just as guilty as the guy who slept with her and told everyone.

THERAPIST: You thought you were responsible for your mother's diseases and for Patricia's problems.

PATIENT: Contact with me was destructive. But maybe I can't be involved with someone who doesn't have something seriously wrong. I feel that girls who are perfect physically won't like me. If they have something wrong, I can help them. But, I don't help them, I just feel sorry. That's one reason it didn't bother me when Julie couldn't have intercourse at first. I did help her. I had that feeling very little with Julie and surprisingly I was less nervous in my relationship with her. Physically, masturbation satisfies me more than intercourse. Something is wrong with that. It's important to me that the woman has an intense gratification and not important that I do. But then I get pissed off and blame her.

THERAPIST: What would happen if you got gratification yourself?

PATIENT: Some fear of being alone.

THERAPIST: That's similar to the last session, when you said that obtaining your Ph.D. would result in your being alone.

PATIENT: Funny. I don't feel it much right now. I feel more at ease.

THERAPIST: You were enough at ease at the beginning of this session to say, "Nicer office." One thought that communicated to me was that you were also saying, "I feel good that you got a nicer office."

PATIENT: It really makes me feel good that you understand that, because that's what I was feeling.

THERAPIST: You may also have experienced some angry and competitive feeling..

PATIENT: [*Laughs*] I did, but I immediately repressed them. Now I recall that my first thought when I walked in to this office was, "The S.O.B. got a promotion," but I did also feel very good about it. It's really important to have feelings and to be aware of them.

THERAPIST: When you first came to Dr. Krueger you asked for Dilantin. Then you said that your problems were psychological and that you wanted to understand them. Now you seem to have gone another step. You are saying that you are going to have to feel and experience, too, in order to make progress.

PATIENT: Since I've taken this third step, I'm feeling more optimistic about my chances of improving.

DISCUSSION

The patient's opening comment about my having a "nicer office" could have been dealt with immediately. But since we had not met for over two weeks, I decided to wait until I could determine where he was in the transference. During the course of the session it became clear that his struggles with his wishes and fears about having a close relationship with his father had come to the forefront. It also became clear that he was defensively de-emphasizing his anger and competition with father and his fear of his father's retaliation.

When I returned to his "nicer office" comment near the end of the session, I was able to make some specific interventions about the ambivalence he was expressing. First I acknowledged that he did feel pleased that I had obtained a nicer office. Then I was able to help him look at the angry and competitive feelings that he was expressing as well. He responded with laughter which we have learned is his unconscious saying "yes" to an intervention. My intervention helped him to recall his thought, "The S.O.B. got a promotion," that he had repressed before. One of my goals was to help him differentiate me from his perception of his parents. I wanted him to understand that he could experience both positive and negative feelings toward me without my retaliating by either rejecting him or physically hurting him.

In some respects my handling of his comment about my office involved transference interpretation. Earlier in the session I made a direct transference interpretation, which I rarely do in psychotherapy. I said, "I think you are wondering if it is dangerous to feel closer to me," (as he had earlier expressed about his father). The patient's emotional response with tears welling up in his eyes and his connecting that to his father made it clear that it was a correct interpretation. I decided to deal with that aspect of the transference because I was convinced that to do so would facilitate the alliance.

Later in the session I again commented on his need to keep distance from his feelings, but that time it was an interpretation of a defense. He had been talking about his mother's polio and her endocrine disease. Although eye changes are not an obvious feature of Cushing's disease, they were the center of attention for the patient. In an earlier session we had seen that his mother's shrunken leg and her eyes represented deformed, castrated genitals to this patient. When talking about his mother became too anxiety-provoking, Paul started to intellectualize by asking me whether he was dealing with guilt or shame. Rather than answer the question I helped him see how he was using it in a defensive way. He was then able to associate his mother and the woman in San Francisco, Patricia. He was able to tell me for the first time about what he saw as defects in Patricia. He also saw why he repeatedly picked women who were in some way defective, at least in his mind.

I ended the session by summing up the changes in his conceptualization of his problem. He agreed with my description of the progression in him. He then went even further and stated that, unlike his pessimistic feelings in the previous session, he now felt optimistic about his chances for change.

SESSION 14, JULY 9   "WOMEN TREAT ME LIKE A LITTLE BOY"

PATIENT: There are a couple of things I want to tell you. The first is my reaction to women. Most women treat me like a little boy. That really makes me angry. But Julie doesn't do that.

THERAPIST: Women don't treat all men like little boys.

PATIENT: I do something to put myself in that position. I have a conflict between wanting to be an adult and wanting to be a little kid. Like the affection a little kid gets, but not the other stuff. Mother must have done that to me, too.

THERAPIST: You make it sound like mother said, "The price of affection from me is to remain a little kid."

PATIENT: Well, my aunts rewarded me for that. Mother just never gave me the affection no matter what I did. I really got more affection from father than mother, although he wasn't comfortable giving it either. I can't recall a single instance of affection from my mother. The closest she came to giving me affection was to say, "How could you do this to me?" Like when that girl left Nebraska. I felt rotten. Dad tried to understand. Mother just said, "Shape up." That was the point at which I came closest to killing myself. I decided to leave school. I went to Aspen. I told Mother I was leaving. She gave me fifty dollars. She was really disgusted with me. I tried to kiss her and she just turned away.

THERAPIST: You must have had a strong reaction to that.

PATIENT: I felt the same way as when the girl the other day bawled me out for looking at her mail. Guilty and ticked off.

THERAPIST: Guilty?

PATIENT: She made me feel that it wasn't just the act that was so bad, but that I was a kind of bad person who'd do such a thing. One thing that ticks me off is that people paid attention to Mother's problem. Father did. But I wasn't supposed to have any problems. I wasn't supposed to have feelings either. She felt people just shouldn't talk about emotions or emotional problems. The only feelings she expressed about me were irritation and disgust. When I felt so bad at that time I didn't even think of going to my parents for help. I went to a school counselor. I felt really weak. That's one reason I became immediately attached to the University. There was an awareness that people get messed up and need help from others.

THERAPIST: You're describing an emotionally barren childhood.

PATIENT: I think so. Especially because I can't recall anything more than ten or fifteen years back. I'm hesitant to say it was barren because sometimes my father would try to be warm, but his way was to try to teach me all the skills to prepare me for the world.

THERAPIST: You said that your mother only expressed irritation and disgust.

PATIENT: I like to think there were other feelings but I don't see them. I had a recurrent dream as a kid, before I was thirteen years old. A huge icebox-type thing would be falling on me. I felt I was growing smaller and smaller down to nothing.

THERAPIST: What pops into your head about that dream?

PATIENT: Coldness, I guess. Almost all my dreams are bad ones. One reason I restrict myself is that when my feelings get out they're scary. Like when I'm on grass I keep getting the feeling that cops will come. The only good dream I've had, and this was the only one I've had in color, I'd run down the street jumping higher and higher until I was almost flying. It just made me feel free. No people in that dream. Just trees and cattle and fields. I keep wanting to go back to the icebox. The two dreams are really different. The first one is cold and restricting. The second one seems free and adult. Iceboxes make me think of a cold mother. Mother was around the icebox a lot when I was a kid. The box would never really engulf me but rather would come toward me and I'd retreat and get smaller. I've always been afraid to stand up for myself. There was a strong feeling among my mother's family that one doesn't go beyond the family except to get a mate. Then you bring the mate back into the fold. Hey, I'm ashamed of the fold. I don't want to bring my mate back. I'm ashamed of my father, too. A guy just came back from Boston. He reminds me of my father. He's aggressive. He said to me, "Let's play golf." When I didn't want to he ridiculed me. He brags about himself. He pushes me around, dominates me, and I can't stop it. I can't let him do that to me.

THERAPIST: Sounds like something makes it hard for you to stand up for yourself.

PATIENT: I feel sorry for him. He really needs me. He hangs around me. But he pretends that I need him. It's the same with my father. He used to make me drive three hundred miles with him on sales calls and he'd make it seem that he was doing it for me. Doing me a favor. Really he just wanted the company.

THERAPIST: But something keeps you from saying to this fellow, "I don't feel like it."

PATIENT: Yes. If I say that he won't be my friend any more.

THERAPIST: So?

PATIENT: Right. I don't need another friend. I just get angry at him anyway. But I still can't do it. Last night I wanted to go to dinner with a woman in the office. He hung around until I agreed to eat with him. If he were more mature I could have just told him. It's the same with my father but usually he tries to take my feelings into account. There are some exceptions. Like when I'm with my father I have to drive exactly the way he wants.

THERAPIST: Did you want to eat with him?

PATIENT: No.

THERAPIST: But that was the result of your actions.

PATIENT: That's right. This is my secret life. I even gave him some marijuana. I thought then he'd feel I still liked him even if I didn't want to eat with him.

THERAPIST: What do you mean by your secret life? Did you think I'd make some judgments about your using marijuana?

PATIENT: No. I really don't like it but I feel pressure to take it and I can't just say, "I don't feel like it." My wanting or not wanting to do something never seems like enough justification. Like if I take a girl to bed I have to tell myself I'm doing it so that we will feel emotionally closer.

DISCUSSION

This session had four closely interrelated themes. Paul started out by saying, "Women treat me like a little boy." He then went on to the next theme, "I can't stand up to another man and demand what I want." Originally he was talking about his father, but then he went on to the third theme: that he can't even stand up to one of his peers. He not only ate with this fellow when he didn't want to, but then felt guilty about having had the thought that he didn't want to eat with him. He tried to placate his friend by giving him some marijuana. The fourth theme was his repressing his sexual feelings toward his mother by convincing himself that she was very cold, had no compassion, and was disgusted with him. Repetition of the type I described in the discussion of session 12 ties these four themes together. As I mentioned then, every person he meets, including me, immediately becomes a transference object, a character playing a distorted role in a rerun of his childhood drama. Paul's self image is still that of an inadequate, poorly equipped little boy. Last session we saw how he made Patricia into a younger version of his mother. This session he turns the fellow from Boston into a younger version of his father. He is unaware of his options. All he can do is repeat his past relationships with his parents in a new edition. Every action continues to be determined by his fear of belittlement, castration, and rejection.

My first intervention, "Women don't treat all men like little boys," was aimed at helping him see his role in eliciting responses from others. To the extent that he is able to see how he contributes to and generates these problems it is a real advance. In the past Paul had largely blamed the situation on other people. For a patient to realize that his problem is intrapsychic is a very important early step in therapy. Taking away the patient's defense of blaming others will often depress him at first. He cannot yet realize how that enables him to deal with the problem and change it. As long as Paul clings to the idea that there are all those bad women in the world who are always going to treat him like a little boy, no change can take place. Until he sees his part in creating the problem, he will continue to make every woman treat him like a little boy no matter whether she wants to or not. If she is not willing to go along with the script he has written for her, he just won't have a relationship with her. Once he understands his role in the problem he can start working on understanding why it is so hard for him to tolerate an adult-to-adult relationship.

I emphasized that helping him see the problem as intrapsychic is only a first step. He is not going to easily relinquish his neurotic solution. Carrying around the representation of himself as a little boy made him feel safe with his sexual impulses toward his mother and his aggressive impulses toward his father. A little boy could not possibly carry out those sexual or aggressive wishes. Even though that once served as a solution, it is now greatly interfering with his adult relationships with both men and women. Nevertheless, he does not yet see that there is a very different and better solution for him as an adult. At this point for him to give up that symptom would be experienced as a loss. When he finally does give up the symptom he will probably temporarily feel some sadness and depression until the better adult solution starts to become effective and starts to be integrated into a new self-image. All of this is part of the working through process. It is one of the reasons the therapist can't say to the patient during the first session, "I see your problem, this is what it is, and this is what you should change."

The two dreams were interesting. Childhood dreams recalled during therapy are always significant. His associations were revealing. It is not surprising that he recalled the icebox dream, because it fits in with the same defense against his Oedipal strivings that he has been describing in this session. As long as mother is a cold icebox and he is very small, he can avoid his sexual impulses toward her. The dream points out how fixated Paul is. In reality Paul is physically well developed, good-looking, and obviously bright, yet he feels very inadequate and inferior to other men. As a little boy he cannot stand up to anyone and cannot go after the things he wants. Part of him wants to remain that little boy who gets affection and mothering. The part of him that wants to be "free and adult" is represented in the second dream. The second dream describes how he would feel and act if he did not have any castration anxiety. Then he could jump "higher and higher until I was almost flying." In this dream I think the jumping higher and higher and almost flying represents having a penile erection.

Paul was obviously very bright, very talented, and could have had tremendous social skills if he were not so frightened of standing up to people. It is important to ascertain the patient's potential in order to set realistic therapy goals.

SESSION 15, JULY 17   FURTHER CLARIFICATION OF THE
                                        INTRAPSYCHIC CONFLICT

(The patient walked in carrying Philip Roth's book, *When She Was Good*. On the cover was a picture of lips.)

PATIENT: There are two things I want to talk about. I can't decide which is more important. The first is that I'm having increasing difficulty working. Maybe that's what I should talk about. The insight about what I want to do, that I got from that group, seems counter to working. I get really tense when I try to write a paper. Why be miserable when I could get a job I like? For example, working directly with people. Maybe I could work with Mexicans. But I don't want to give up graduate school. The other time I felt really calm I had the same damn feeling about graduate school; that it involved a lot of foolish stuff, and I quit. I feel like quitting again. Things seem too hard for me. They require too much care for details. I may do some little thing wrong. That really bothers me.

THERAPIST: What if you do some little thing wrong?

PATIENT: I don't know. It scares me. I haven't written a paper yet in graduate school. I used to always get A's on papers as an undergraduate. I've got all the information and ideas but I just can't put it down on paper. I get tense, start smoking.

THERAPIST: What do you mean by tense?

PATIENT: About the fear of making a little mistake. Maybe grammatical, or I think, "Is this exactly what I want to say?" I'll be sitting there. I'll almost have a paragraph written out in my mind, but I'll forget it when I try to write it down.

THERAPIST [Trying to enlist the patient's observing ego]: What do you make of being able to think what you want to write but being unable to put it on paper?

PATIENT: Well, I'd say I'm afraid to have anyone look at my work, and I shouldn't be that afraid. I expect the worst. Instead of looking at graduate school as a place where I'm learning, I feel I'm being continually evaluated, and have to come up with a beautiful paper. Something perfect. Goddamit, the place has a compulsive, competitive quality [*said with great anger*]. Like one guy is always asking questions. He makes me feel that I should. All these feelings—it has to be perfect; it has to be better than someone else's. It's just messing things up.

THERAPIST: What if the professor isn't pleased with your work?

PATIENT: That would really bother me. Like when I got so ticked off with that guy who was asking questions in class. What bothered me was that I thought the professor was getting irritated.

THERAPIST: Even when the professor was irritated with someone else?

PATIENT: Yes. That's happened a lot. Like whenever someone is doing something in class, or in the Air Force to irritate an officer, I get anxious and nervous.

THERAPIST: You look anxious now just talking about it.

PATIENT: Yes. I don't know what shakes me up so much about it. Somehow it's related to my father. I always feel on guard with him, careful, alert. He says things that sound friendly, but there are a lot of things he doesn't let me talk about. I called him two nights ago. I'd bring something up and he'd say, "Yes, I know all about that," and he'd want to talk about something else. In class I really fear something awful is going to happen to me. That the guy will really get ticked off. It bothers me tremendously, even if it is someone else. If I were talking I'd be less anxious because I could just stop talking.

THERAPIST: You are experiencing a great deal of emotion now.

PATIENT: It just snuck up on me. The feeling of wanting to cry, but anger, too. In the classroom it's anger and fear and feeling jumpy and I start sweating. I get enraged at the people who are causing me to feel that way. My boss told me I'll have to live with this tension, but I can't. It's just too much. Either I have to solve this or quit school. When I start to feel this tension the papers become very important. Sort of life-or-death matters. I'm afraid to be evaluated. It's all or nothing. I feel my paper will either be really great or just a pile of shit. All this is really stupid, but I can't stop it. There's something dangerous that I feel here. It makes me angry that people are demanding papers of me.

THERAPIST: Would it make any difference if you had women instructors?

PATIENT: I don't know. I fear all men in the same way. It depends how women act. If they scold me I get furious. If they don't I can like them. There was a nurse captain at camp whom I was able to contradict. She said something that I knew was wrong and I told her.

THERAPIST: What if she had been a man?

PATIENT: There was a psychiatrist in the group. I really started to hate him because he would make comments about me and then end it. Like he'd say I'm trying to be a scapegoat. I felt I wanted to fight what he was saying but he didn't give me a chance. My father does that. He'll say, "I don't want to argue about it." He used to say, "Do what your father tells you."

THERAPIST: Last week you were talking a little differently about your father.

PATIENT: It sounds contradictory, but that's true, too. This "do what your father tells you," I guess, is an earlier picture. I've got feelings about him that he would never let me do anything. Everyone else in the neighborhood could stay out a little late once in a while, but we had to be home on time for supper. In the ninth grade I came home at 1 AM instead of 10 PM. He said, "We'll talk about it in the morning." I was really scared, couldn't sleep all night. He didn't do much, though.

He did have some sadistic characteristics. Like when he'd want to get me out of bed he'd grab my toes and pull. That hurt. I wanted to hit him. I wish I'd really busted him up. He would humiliate me. When I was an adolescent he made me pull my pants and shorts down, put me over his lap and pretended he was going to hit me with a strap. I felt humiliated, mortified, angry. I wish he'd try something now. I'd kill him. Well, I don't think I really would. Geeze, I remember those days when I was a kid! I was so afraid of him.

THERAPIST: Is someone going to pull your pants down if you hand in a bad paper?

PATIENT: There is some of that feeling that I'll be ridiculed, but mostly that just something really bad will happen, something I can't define. Like my whole graduate career will be destroyed. Something vague and unknown. Like I never really knew what my father would do. There was no "If you do this wrong, this will happen." Anything could happen.

(His high emotional level was continued throughout this hour from the time that I first pointed it out. He no longer had tears in his eyes but there was still the anger, frustration, anxiety, and feeling of disaster. It was nearing the end of the hour. I had recalled his saying at the beginning that he had two things to talk about, and so far had only talked about one. I wanted to at least find out what the other was, so I asked him directly.)

THERAPIST: What was the other thing you were going to talk about?

PATIENT: I was reading *When She Was Good*. It reminded me of high school. There was nothing I liked about high school. It was just a lot of competition. I have a real hatred of competition. I was a really good golfer, but I never won. I was afraid to win. I really wanted to but I couldn't let myself do it.

THERAPIST: So the two things you wanted to talk about today were closely related.

PATIENT: Yes. I realized that as I was talking just now. For the first time I'm starting to feel some worth. I used to tell myself I was King Shit but I never believed it.

DISCUSSION

My initial interventions in this session were aimed at helping the patient to elaborate the material, to be more specific, and to be less intellectual. For example, while he was talking about the whole graduate school, he was able to keep a great deal of distance. When I reduced the institution to a professor, he became much more specific about the feelings he was experiencing. I then made a different kind of intervention: "You look anxious now just talking about it." That intervention was different because it was speaking to his interaction with me. It was not quite a transference interpretation; I did not say to him, "I think your dealing with me makes you just as anxious as dealing with the professor or your father." I did something less, something that I have called a pre-transference interpretation. I commented on his mood but did not make the connection for him that it was related to his dealing with me. If he was able to make that connection, fine. If not, I let it go because I assumed he was not ready to examine his interaction with me.

What is the etiology of the anxiety he was describing? Implied in my statement, "You look anxious now just talking about it," and my calling that a pre-transference interpretation, is the idea that Paul was transferring early feelings toward his father onto me right at that moment. The etiology is his early interaction with his father. This is a direct continuation of the last session, when he talked about his inability to confront men, and gave the example with his friend. Now he is working that through further with examples from school. He is afraid of putting forth his ideas on paper to give to a professor because the professor might not approve. He sees writing papers as competitive. He became anxious telling me about it. He wondered how I would respond. We have heard prototypes for this in his description of his early interaction with his father. I did not think he saw the connection, but he clearly did, since he responded by relating the anxiety back to his dealings with his father.

This session represented an advance in the therapy. Paul was talking about the central intrapsychic problem now, his fear of castration and its derivative, fear of competition. There was also more transference in this hour than in most previous sessions. There was no need to interpret the transference any further than I did with the pre-transference interpretation. There were other times when I could have pointed out the transference quite directly. When he related being able to stand up to the woman captain at camp and I said, "What if she had been a man?" the first person he thought of was a psychiatrist. There was only one psychiatrist in the office at that time. At least, some of his comments about the psychiatrist were about me, whether he was aware of it or not. Then he associated the psychiatrist with his father, who would never listen to him or let him develop.

Paul's description of his father's behavior in pulling him by the toes to get him out of bed raised two questions in my mind. The first was: What was Paul's role in provoking that kind of behavior? The second was: Is Paul distorting his description of his father? I did not pursue those questions because the material that he was presenting about competition was more central. If I had wanted to find out the answers to those questions, I would have asked for more details: "Your father used to pull you up out of bed by the toes. When would he do that? Do you remember some specific times?" We might have found out that Paul was so passive–aggressive that he provoked his father into that kind of behavior. We may have found out that Paul was extremely dependent and needed a push. I do think that some of Paul's memories about his father are distorted in the service of defense. We have obtained enough evidence that his father cared about him, wanted the best for him, and was more playful than sadistic. As long as Paul can maintain his distorted view of his father as a mean, sadistic man, he can justify his fear of competition and his anxiety.

We can now be more specific about why he is having trouble in school at this time. Paul stated that he did extremely well in college, receiving an A on almost every paper he wrote. When he reached graduate school a number of things happenend. First, it struck him that things really counted now. His goal, obtaining a Ph.D., now means working in a particular field and eventually competing with his professors. In college there were large classes. The competition was anonymous and vague. In his highly specialized field in graduate school, there are only about a half dozen other graduate students, all of whom he knows very well, all of whom are working for their Ph.D.s, and all of whom are in direct competition with him. In college he used the defense of denial to pretend there wasn't any competition and he was able to function very well. He is extremely intelligent, and was able to go through college obtaining A's without much effort. Now he is competing with graduate students who are as bright and as well-prepared as he is.

There is real competition with his fellow students. There is also his fantasized competition with his professors. Both are involved in Paul's anxiety, but the fantasized competition with his teachers comes closer to the old competition with his father. This would probably be surprising to most of his professors, who think they are teaching and working with Paul. Unfortunately, that is not always true. There are some teachers who fear the competition from their students. Those teachers do not like taking part in the relay race of life, passing on to their students what they have learned from their teachers. We have talked about the patient's Oedipus complex. The teacher, or parent, who fears competition from his student or child can be seen as suffering from a Laius complex. King Laius, fearing the oracle's prophecy that his son Oedipus would grow up and slay him, sought to kill Oedipus by abandoning him in a field with his ankles tied. However, none of the professors described by Paul so far sound like King Laius.

Paul started the hour by saying that he had *two* points to discuss because he didn't realize that they were both about competition. His first point was, "I have increasing difficulty working." The second thing on his mind was the book he was reading, which reminded him of high school. At the beginning of the session he didn't realize that the increasing difficulty working was caused by his trouble with competition, and that what bothered him most about high school was the competition. In high school, the competition was sexual rather than academic. One of the goals of therapy is to help him see what is central to both. With Paul, no matter what material he brings in, it generally relates to

his fear of competition. We have realized that for a long time. Paul doesn't
quite realize it yet, but it is so close to consciousness that it keeps surfacing.
When he does realize it, he will react with increased anxiety and defensiveness.

SESSION 16, JULY 24   **SUCCESS IS FRIGHTENING**

PATIENT: I'm really in a panic. First of all, I've got a new job with
some sociologists. That means we're going to have to change my appointment
time here. Another thing is that Julie wants me to come out there. I want her
to come here but it scares me because I know she'd come back because of me.
That puts me on the spot. Before she met me she was thinking of not coming
back. I just can't say yes or no. The third thing is, I'm having trouble
sleeping. I can't fall asleep and I'm waking up early. I just can't sleep from
about 6 AM on. I used to feel like that all the time. I have the chance to make
a lot of money on this new job. If I do well I can generate enough data for a
dissertation, too. I still have these other projects that I really should finish. I
told the professor about my fear of handing in an imperfect paper and he said,
"Why don't you just hand in a rough draft that won't count?" I want to
continue therapy, but I also want that job. I will call you as soon as my job
plans are final and I know the exact times, so that we can work out a time to
meet. I'll be out of town a lot.
THERAPIST: I will be consulting at the mental health clinic at your
school one day a week starting next week. Perhaps we can meet there.
PATIENT: I can put off my dissertation, but I have to act with Julie.
The work thing will probably work out okay, too. But Julie is threatening.
She's in New York now and not enjoying it. I want her back, but maybe she
should wait until the end of the summer. I'm afraid of becoming obligated,
but maybe that would be good for me. I want to be able to step out of
emotional situations.
THERAPIST: Emotional commitments still frighten you.
PATIENT: I feel there will be something wrong with Julie that I don't
know about. For example, I picture her as an adult but maybe that's an
illusion. Maybe I'm projecting my own uncertainty. Knowing that doesn't
help me, though. One day I feel I'd like to spend years with her. Another day
I think I could find a girl with a nicer body or something. When a girl gets
turned on in bed I get turned off. I used to think it was because I envied their
better sexual response. But really it is that I think they are responding to some
kind of power in me and what if some guy comes along with more power?
[This is a central fantasy of his.] I had a dream once where a lot of other guys
were screwing Julie and I felt miserable. I felt I could be one of those guys but

nothing special, not the exclusive object. I felt she wouldn't let me have that exclusive power.

THERAPIST: Were these guys that you knew?

PATIENT: I felt they were high school kids from a lower-middle-class, very athletic high school. I felt these were perfect men with more power than I had. I saw them as cold and powerful. I wanted that power but I felt I didn't have it.

THERAPIST: That must have been a miserable feeling.

PATIENT: Yes. I've had that feeling as long as I can remember, from grade school on. I always felt there was a group of guys my age with more power who knew how things worked. I'd wonder, "How do I become one of them?"

THERAPIST: You also said last week that you were miserable when your father told you you did something wrong.

PATIENT: Yes. I think he was trying to help me, but he always felt I was wrong, my work was no good. This is a little different feeling. It's guilt and shame. The other feeling is anger and impotence. Somehow there is a difference between being competent and being powerful. Being competent has to do with work, other men. Power is related to my ability to get women. [He then related this to the guilt he felt when he beat out a friend for this new job.] It sounds Oedipal, but I can't think of any specific things that have happened to me.

THERAPIST: You can't?

PATIENT: I get so nervous talking about it, there must be something there, but it seems silly. [Pauses, strokes his moustache, obviously very anxious.] If I think about the possibility of . . . [Pause] I can't say it. [Pause. There's a real struggle going on inside him. Finally he blurts out:] of competing with my father for my mother. [He gets very upset. Long pause.] I'm really shook up now. I'm trying to laugh but I just feel scared. [There are a lot of anxious gestures throughout all this.] Father always made me feel guilty about mother. What's that about? Was it the same problem I have—have to justify loving someone, make it up to her? [He goes on with this in a repetitive way, trying to work through this feeling of competing with father for mother. At the end of the session he says] I'll give you a call as soon as I know my plans more definitely. Actually, I wish I could come here more often. I'm letting myself feel things. That makes me anxious, too.

DISCUSSION

This session is both a continuation of the previous hour and another step forward. We continued to hear derivatives of the Oedipal struggle, but we also hear the clear statement from the patient that he suffers from an Oedipal success neurosis. The precipitants for his anxiety were two successes: He triumphed over his friend for a desirable job, and Julie expressed the desire to come back to him. I suspect that his having gained some insight about his problems with competition allowed him to compete more effectively. The anxiety arises out of his unconscious transference fear that I am going to castrate him for being so successful.

Paul was expressing some ambivalence about therapy in this session. When he talked about wanting to step out of emotional situations such as his relationship with Julie, he was also talking about therapy. Part of him would like to use his new job as a way of ending therapy. Another part of him, as demonstrated at the end of the session, would like to see me more frequently. As we deal more and more directly with the central conflict, therapy is growing frightening to him, but he also realizes that it is helping him. Unless the ambivalence starts to move toward the side of his wanting to terminate therapy, I have no need to interpret it.

This session is a nice example of the working through process. Paul was elaborating old themes. This expanded awareness on his part of his central problem is extremely important in bringing about change. This is the real work of therapy. For many sessions we are going to hear a working through of all the various aspects of his problems with competition. It will be interesting to observe the complexitity of working through. The patient will go through a repetitive process. He will gain some insight, look at it, become anxious, defend against it, and then gain more insight. The resistance and the push to get well will compete against each other. When the resistance dominates, the patient will repeat the same things over and over again. He will be quite comfortable because he is defending so well and there will be very little emotion. During those times I will confront his defenses. As long as there is good progression I will help facilitate further elaboration and try to help him gain additional insights. Working through will continue to dominate until we start the termination phase of therapy.

Paul has one core problem: his Oedipal success neurosis. The competition problem is its main manifestation. It also has dozens of derivatives. The working through process is looking at each of these derivatives and relating it to the central problem.

SESSION 17, AUGUST 5   **A PROBLEM WITH ASSERTION**

PATIENT: I like it more up here. I don't like those big buildings in Denver. I've been on my new job for a week. I don't like it because I don't like most of the guys and having to go out of town. It's hectic work. I wanted to get work over as quick as possible so we could go out and have a good time. I started smoking. That made me even more nervous. Sometimes we'd work until ten at night. Another problem was that I have a hard time imposing myself on these people. Like farmers—to tell them that I'm from the university, or doing research, and so on. I'm afraid they'll ask, "Well, why are you prying into my life?" Also, I have some guilt. Like I shouldn't be using these people. The only value this research would have is to get information from them which would enable the government to talk them into government programs. It makes me mad when parents are that way. They think they know what is better for their children than the children do. It's the same with the government. The government is setting up weather control stations to seed clouds, control the rain.

We study three areas. One in a target area, one out of the target area, and one in the periphery. We ask the farmers how they feel about modifying weather and they say things like, "Oh, that's good," or, "It's against God's plan," or whatever they think. We will interview them again after modification has been going on for a while. It's interesting, but it's still bothering people to question them. It's like when the sociology department makes us be subjects for experiments. If I were a beginning student in sociology now I would refuse, even if it meant a lower grade. The whole sociology department accepts this imposition on others. I'm afraid a farmer will ask me, "Why are you doing this?" Some of them have and I tried to explain it. But we don't tell them exactly why we are doing it.

THERAPIST: Do you understand what's bothering you?

PATIENT: Maybe I don't like asserting myself. Other people I work with see people's objections as an impediment which has to be overcome. I got nervous doing some of the interviews. I even started stuttering a little.

THERAPIST: It sounds like there's something about asserting yourself that you don't like.

PATIENT: I'm afraid they won't accept me. That's a problem in all situations. I'll do a lot of things to be accepted. Maybe that's less important for the other guys.

THERAPIST: What if Rancher Brown says, "This is nonsense. Get out of here."?

PATIENT: That wouldn't bother me. I'd be rejected and that would be it.

THERAPIST: It sounds like there's some fear here that is still unknown to you.

PATIENT: Yes. It's like I'm projecting something onto them.

THERAPIST: Something?

PATIENT: I get some apprehension. Afraid they'll do some bad thing that will mess me up. If I could get over that I could enjoy that work. There are some real moral considerations, but there is something wrong with the way I'm handling it. I can't write a paper feeling the way I do.

THERAPIST: Last session you thought that you would be able to obtain enough data from this work to write a thesis.

PATIENT: Someone could do that, but I don't know if I can. I'm on academic probation because of a C in statistics, but I think I have two A's coming up for my research courses, so that will bring me up to a B average easily. It's not really a problem. Why am I having this trouble? This problem with this work? [At that point I made a clarification, showing him that this was part of a larger pattern—his inability to complete things for his Ph.D., his inability to write papers, his inability to work. I related those difficulties to his fear of asserting himself.] Yes. They do all seem related. If I continue to be too uncomfortable I'll just get a job in a small school with my Master's degree. Maybe I could teach sociology courses and throw some other things in, like Eastern philosophy and far-out thinkers. I don't want to be doing a lot of research. I don't have a Master's yet but I could very quickly. I just need a thesis and two papers beyond my M.A. to get a Ph.D. I'm about a year away now from a Master's. I need about two more courses and to complete two papers. When I was working on a paper the last few weeks my stomach got upset. I had trouble sleeping, like when I was studying for my preliminaries. I just thought my paper wasn't worthwhile.

THERAPIST: Not even for a rough draft?

PATIENT: No. I seemed way off track. I would have had to stay up all night to finish it on time. I used to punish myself as an undergraduate to do that. Now I feel deficient. I'd like to get the papers over, but I get so nervous and angry that I can't. I don't want to go through that misery. I get frantic. [He jumped up in the chair and told me that as he was talking about it his palms started sweating and his stomach was getting very upset. At that point I ran out of paper in my notebook, so I put it down.] I've never liked you taking notes. The information I give you doesn't seem worth it and it seems like a lot of work for you.

THERAPIST: Like your paper.

PATIENT: Maybe you think it's worthwhile. Anyway, I couldn't do that paper for Friday. I was afraid that he would criticize me. My friends say, "Just do it," but I can't.

THERAPIST: What if it could be guaranteed that your work would not be criticized—that he would say "good paper" or at least "good start"?

PATIENT: I'd sit down and write it with no trouble.

THERAPIST: He seems to be quite understanding. [This is the professor who told him to just do a rough draft if he could not do the paper. The patient started to cry. I commented on his tears.]

PATIENT: He is understanding. Realizing that made me feel there is some hope, but I'm still afraid he will criticize me.

THERAPIST: What would you like for him to do?

PATIENT: I want him to put his arm on my shoulder and say, "It will be all right" and encourage me and be comforting. I guess I want from him what I want from my dad. It isn't that I can't take criticism. Like you could criticize me—well, I guess you'd have to be pretty gentle or I'd get upset. Not like that woman who gave me hell for leaving the typewriter on the other day.

DISCUSSION

This is the first session in which I saw Paul in a small university town instead of in Denver. His opening comments were, "I like it more up here. I don't like those big buildings in Denver." As the session progressed, we saw that the big buildings symbolized all the big men with their big penises who frighten him so much. Throughout the session he described all the men he encounters as being like he imagines his father to be. I emphasize the word *imagines* because I do not think his father is really the tyrant Paul often describes. In Paul's mind all these farmers and ranchers are going to castrate him if he interviews them too assertively. He also says that he can't write papers because all of his professors are so harsh and frightening. I finally confronted his defense against being productive by commenting that at least this one professor "seems to be quite understanding." The patient responded by starting to cry. That is not an unusual response, because when a defense is confronted, the patient suffers the loss of the defense if he accepts the confrontation. When I commented about his professor, Paul realized that he had been distorting his perception of that man. My speculation is that all the anger that Paul thinks these men feel toward him is really a projection of the anger he once felt toward his father.

There were also many transference issues in this hour. A prominent example is when he talked about wanting his professor to put his arm on his shoulder and say, "It will be all right." He was also saying that he would like that from me and in the past would have liked it from his father. I think that after his defensive distortion of his father was interpreted, he was able to get a glimmering that not all men are like he imagines his father to be. He was then able to express his wish for warmth and kindness from a man.

Another aspect of his job difficulty is that he sees the farmers and ranchers as being like children who are being used by the government, which he sees as a parent. Suddenly, as part of this job, he finds himself as part of the government. This clashes with his self-identity because he still sees himself as an adolescent. He equates the government and the sociology department with a parent, but he identifies with the farmers and the sociology students who are used as subjects for experiments.

SESSION 18, AUGUST 17   SUPEREGO STRUGGLE REVISITED

PATIENT: I want to talk about women and guilt. I'm reading Philip Roth's book, *When She Was Young*. The woman in the book is a real bitch. She wants her husband to be duty bound. If women want people to be responsible, just telling them to be responsible isn't going to do it. Like with that woman who got so angry at me for leaving on the typewriter. That really gets me mad. I feel all those women want to keep me tied down.

THERAPIST: Which women are you talking about?

PATIENT: Those women around my office. I used to think they were nice people, concerned with civil rights. Actually, I'm not that involved with some blacks in a ghetto myself and I don't believe they are. I feel now that the most important thing for me is to be happy. If I can make them happy without taking away my happiness, fine, but I'm miserable enough as it is. I spent a lot of time putting down people with conservative views. But, that's wrong. Like those farmers and ranchers I'm working with now. They've been real nice to me even though they have very conservative views. I feel these women got me further into it than I wanted. I thought that by joining liberal groups in college I was asserting my individuality, but really I was using these groups to rebel against my parents with their conservative views. I couldn't do it by myself. I was afraid of being alone if I asserted myself.

THERAPIST: You seem to think that asserting yourself will somehow lead to your being alone.

PATIENT: That's right. That very thing happened since I last saw you. The example was further complicated because I wanted some time alone. I wanted to do some fishing while we were working in Montana, but I was afraid to. Finally, I mentioned it to my boss and he said, just like you do, "Do whatever you want to do. You're doing a good job here." That really made me feel good. I was able to do what I wanted and he didn't reject me. Now I want to do the work, too. After that response from the boss, I felt I could both do the work and enjoy myself. I'm less wrapped up in morbid feelings about responsibilities. That's why I'm so damned mad at those women. They try to make me feel guilty. Those women have the capacity to scold me, but I'm attracted to them, too. I'm trying to work it out with them. My mother used to do that a lot. They generate feelings in me that I think I'm supposed to have, but I realize they don't do any damn good.

THERAPIST: Feelings like guilt.

PATIENT: Yeah. And, like I thought I was supposed to miss Julie. Julie is different. She got angry at me because I didn't write, so she told me that but she didn't make me feel guilty.

THERAPIST: She said, "I'm angry because I'd like to get a letter from you," not "You are a bad boy because you didn't write."

PATIENT: That's right, and that's a big difference. It didn't bother me at all. In fact, I felt like writing her after that; but these other women are really castrating.

THERAPIST: How so?

PATIENT: They say, "Satisfy me. Don't go out and be a man and do what you want." When it is going on I just feel confused and angry and guilty and feel I have to do for them. I guess one reason I call this castrating is that in the novel her uncle calls her a ball-breaking bitch. She's like these women —always talking about castration. A friend of mine said these women attack me because I appear to have a good time with my work and they can't stand that. My mother was that way—duty, responsibility. She didn't like people being happy but dammit, they're so subtle. They reward me and praise me when I carry out my duties. I've been reading some of the forerunners of Zen. Mystics who talk about salvation through enlightenment. Like if you feel good you'll do good things, not the other way around. I struggle too damn much doing it the other way. Tao philosophers talk about action and non-action. They encourage acting without exerting effort. I used to run around frantically. Now I take my time and get a lot more done and I enjoy it.

THERAPIST: Great!

PATIENT: I get in a circle, like with my graduate work. I think it's very important and I'm going to screw up. Then I try to deny that it is important and I do screw up. Somehow, whenever I feel afraid, like when I try to do something I want to do, I feel guilty. I'm afraid someone will destroy me. I just had a weird thought. Someone will destroy me or someone else will be destroyed.

THERAPIST: Both of those ideas do affect you. You think that to be successful you have to destroy someone else and you also fear that if you are successful, someone will try to destroy you.

PATIENT: That really makes sense to me. I feel like I always do that but somehow I didn't really know it until you said it now. It isn't exactly the same, but masturbation comes to my mind now. Masturbation is frightening because it involves satisfying oneself without anyone else, and parents don't like that. I always felt uneasy about masturbation, even though I didn't think it was wrong. When the older guys first told me about it, I was about ten or eleven. I never felt that there was anything wrong with playing with one's genitals, but I still feel uneasy about it. In fact, I get the same anxiety going to bed with a girl. I don't feel guilt about feeling dirty or anything. I just feel anxiety about doing something I want to do. I can't accept doing that. Well, I'm starting to be able to accept it a little now. I think about castration but at the same time I think about separation. I feel I'll be deserted if I do what I want to do. I feel that the only way I can be on my own is to go and be a man, but that the only way I can relate to women is like a guilty little boy. Remember I told you that I never remembered trying to go after my mother and being threatened by my father? It's funny. I can talk to my friends about that without getting anxious but as soon as I bring it up with you, I become very anxious.

THERAPIST: Why do you think that is?

PATIENT: Somehow you have more power. Like to help me change, and that scares me. Do you think that somehow going after what I want is a main conflict?

THERAPIST: You did get anxious talking about it.

PATIENT: Going off and being on my own seems related, too.

THERAPIST: Before we stop today I want to tell you that the Student Health Service will be closed for the next two weeks because of quarter break. We will have to meet in Denver for the next two times.

PATIENT: Oh, I forgot to tell you. I will be away for two and a half weeks. As soon as we finish our work in this area we're going to the northeast.

THERAPIST: How do you feel about our not meeting for three weeks?

PATIENT: I feel that I can get along without it. I also feel that we are really moving. How long will you be available to see me?

THERAPIST: Until June.

PATIENT: That makes me feel good. I was afraid you were leaving sooner. I would be upset about our not meeting for three weeks if you were going to be leaving in a few months. I'll call you as soon as I get back.

DISCUSSION

The patient began the session saying, "I want to talk about women and guilt. I'm reading Philip Roth's book, *When She Was Young.*" Those two sentences allowed the therapist to predict the content of the hour, the prevailing defense that the patient was going to use, and the patient's regressed ego state. For Paul, women lead to guilt and men lead to anxiety. For the previous two sessions he has been talking about how being successful and assertive leads to anxiety. Now he is going to talk defensively about women and guilt instead of men and anxiety.

In the second sentence he made an important slip. The real title of the book is *When She Was Good*, not *When She Was Young*. For Paul, being good means being assertive and successful, which is very anxiety-provoking. Regressing to a time when he was young is much more comfortable. During much of the hour he vacillated between sounding like a latency-age boy and a fifteen-year-old. As a latency-age boy all he had to worry about was doing what his mother wanted so that he wouldn't feel guilty. As a fifteen-year-old he had some revival of the Oedipal struggles, but those struggles are easier for him to talk about than current-day problems with competition and winning. The Oedipal struggle is safe because he lost it to his father. The only time talking about Oedipal material makes him anxious is when he discusses it with me, because then he is reliving it in the father transference. The feelings of being little are in the service of avoiding looking at adult competition.

Later in the session he said, "I used to run around frantically. Now I take my time and get a lot more done and enjoy it." My response was, "Great!" Conventional psychotherapeutic wisdom dictates that my response be, "How does that make you feel?" or, at most, "That must be a good feeling." The argument for the conventional therapist's response is that it allows the therapist to retain his neutrality and to act as a mirror that reflects back the patient's feelings and thoughts. This does make some sense in psychoanalysis when one is trying to foster a deep regressive transference neurosis. In this case, Paul was already in a usable father transference and he was having a superego struggle. I think it was much more productive for me to directly reinforce his being able to work and enjoy his accomplishment. My goal is to modify his harsh superego, which does not allow him to enjoy sex, work, or success. In psychoanalysis this is done in the resolution of the transference neurosis. In a briefer form of psychotherapy such as this, the modification in the superego is brought about by the therapist providing an adult, reasonable superego as a model and through interpretation.

We gain more understanding of his fear of success in this session when he explains that he sees being successful as being destructive; either he or another person will be destroyed. He still has the primitive notion, at least in his unconscious, that to be successful involves depriving others of success, and thus destroying them. The only alternative is that others will retaliate and destroy him. This leaves the patient only two choices: He can either be a guilty little boy or a lonely man. For Paul, being a man means doing things not approved of by his superego. In this session Paul described a fear of castration and a fear of separation, two basic forms of anxiety.

When I told him near the end of the session that we would have to meet in Denver for the next two weeks, he remembered that he was going to be away for the next two and a half weeks. Once again he could not announce a change in the therapy plans until I had announced that I had to make the change. I was tempted to bring this to his attention but decided that in the context of this session, it would have only been guilt-provoking. Instead, I asked him how he felt about our having a break in the therapy. That question reminded him of a concern that he had never before mentioned: how long would I be at the medical center and available to treat him. Since it was near the end of the session and we were about to have a three-week break, I answered him directly. If that had come up earlier in the session I would have explored his thoughts and feelings about it before answering. To do anything other than directly answer it at that point would have caused him to experience anxiety for the next three weeks until our next session.

SESSION 19, SEPTEMBER 7   A SUPEREGO INTERPRETATION

PATIENT: A couple of times when I've been desperately anxious since I last saw you I tried to think of incidents from my youth to explain my feelings. I thought of a couple times when kids in the neighborhood encouraged me to do things that I thought were bad. For example, they wanted me to light a firecracker on someone's porch. They went up on the porch and I stayed on the sidewalk. He saw them. They ran past me and he caught me. I told on them. I didn't want to go along with what they were doing, but I didn't want to be rejected by them, either. That's very similar to what I do now. When I'm with people who smoke grass I might take a puff or two or just sit there. If I start to get at all high I get afraid that the police will come. About a week ago I had a dream. In real life there were two boys down the street who I thought were more popular and stronger and developed earlier than I did. One was a year younger than me, the other about a year older. Even the younger got pubic hair before I did and he teased me about it. In the dream he told me not to come around any more because I never said anything interesting or worthwhile. I got angry and left. It was on the front porch of his house. I think I might have started crying, too. That's related to a lot of things. If I'm in a group I feel a desperate need to say something and I want feedback to make me feel what I said was interesting. It reminds me that my father would also respond to what I said by telling me, "Tell me something I don't know." In high school I would go along with shooting spitballs and things like that even though I didn't want to.

THERAPIST: I'm trying to understand why you are talking mostly about the past this session.

PATIENT: The present is in limbo. Julie isn't here and I don't know what I'm going to do this fall. I want at least a Master's degree but I can't do those damn papers because I get so nervous. I thought I'd take a semester off and try to get those papers done. The job is going well, though. There's nothing else to do but work, so I'm doing that well. I've done half the interviews even though there are three of us working. I don't particularly like the job, but I feel good about doing it well. I would like that feeling in graduate school, too. I decided they would look badly at a leave of absence, so maybe I'll take one course.

THERAPIST: The central issue seems to be why you can't do those papers.

PATIENT: Yes. I try to avoid talking about them. They scare me more than anything. Julie and I are planning to live together this fall. That should scare me more, but I'm really looking forward to it.

THERAPIST: Any idea of what keeps you from getting on with the papers?

PATIENT: It's scary to present something to someone. They'll say it's awful. But I'm afraid of succeeding in general.

THERAPIST: Just a minute—that's contradictory. You say you're afraid they'll say it's awful and then you say you're afraid of succeeding. Maybe you're afraid they'll say it's good.

PATIENT: I used to play in golf tournaments. I felt, "If I win I'll be like my old man and I really don't like him that much." I'd get angry if I lost but I really can't handle winning. I'm ashamed of it, somehow. If I win my father won't be the only one to have the limelight. He'd have to share it with me and he wouldn't want to.

THERAPIST: If you win something you'll have to take something away from someone else?

PATIENT: It seems that way to me but, really, if I do well in graduate school it doesn't hurt anyone else. It's funny; now I can succeed with a girl and I no longer feel I'm depriving someone else of her. Things don't seem so conflicted in that area.

THERAPIST: Dad won in the battles you and he had for Mother.

PATIENT: That's true. But the golf and work and things like that are still a struggle.

THERAPIST: Again this hour you've been talking about how little you are, how slowly you developed.

PATIENT: That represents how incompetent I am.

THERAPIST: All in the service of not winning.

PATIENT: [Pauses] Yes. [Pauses] If I have that view of myself, then I can't win and I don't have to worry about it. Winning and losing shouldn't be the focus, though.

THERAPIST: How's that?

PATIENT: Whether or not I enjoy what I'm involved in instead of trying to get the prize or satisfy a superior should be important. If I don't worry about doing a good job I always do.

THERAPIST: You mean if it doesn't count.

PATIENT: Yes. If it's not to be evaluated. Tao agrees with that. They have a thing. The man who places himself behind everyone else comes out first. I always get tense when I compete with someone for something.

THERAPIST: Like you did for this job.

PATIENT: Yes. I found out that my friend really didn't want the job much. I was tense on the job at first because I felt I had to act a certain way, but then I decided I could just be neutral.

THERAPIST: Be neutral or be yourself?

PATIENT: Really more like be myself. But I used to think I had to force feelings. I'm getting angry as I talk about this. Angry at my mother and father. They made me feel I had to have good feelings about them all the time.

THERAPIST: It's hard to force feelings.

PATIENT: That's right. They happen. I almost went into psychology instead of sociology because I wanted to understand and be able to control feelings, and also it was a competitive thing. I wanted to show all the people in Omaha that I understood people and they didn't. The same thing as a guy coming back after winning a battle in the war. It shows that he's competent. But I don't know what I can do about those papers. Guess I'll sign up for one course and try to do those papers, too. But I'm a little afraid they may throw me out if I don't start producing more. If worse comes to worse I'll tell them I'm trying to work out my problems. Seeing you is the evidence for that. Anyway, now I've been just letting myself be. If I don't feel like saying anything in a group, I don't. But then that seems schizophrenic to me, like I'm withdrawing.

THERAPIST: You assign values to what you do. [This was one more attempt on my part to get him to look at his superego and how it was controlling him.]

PATIENT: Yes. I shouldn't have to do that. I should just let myself feel and do as it happens. Not try to act or feel a certain way.

DISCUSSION

Paul began the session by relating that he had been desperately anxious a couple of times since our last meeting. He tried to deal with the anxiety by looking for an etiology in his childhood. Paul was identifying with how he thought I would handle the problem. Even though his understanding of how I would deal with his anxiety was not completely correct, it was a sign that we had a working alliance that functioned even between sessions. The dream that he had during the period away from therapy was related to his childhood memories. The most important aspect of the dream was that Paul was able to see that the strong, sexually mature boys from his youth represented his father.

My first intervention in this session had two aims. Most patients after a three-week absence from therapy begin the first session upon returning by describing what happened during those three weeks, rather than going back to childhood. I did want to know more details about how he functioned during those weeks, and whether any important changes had taken place in his life. The other reason I made that intervention was that in the previous session he had remained defensively regressed. I thought that at this point it would be useful to interpret forward. It might have been smoother and more tactful to simply have asked him, "What has happened since we last met?"

In this session the patient made the clearest statement thus far about his fear of succeeding. Many previous sessions built up to his understanding his anxiety about competition and his fear of success. Everything is a conflict for Paul. If he succeeds, he is anxious, and if he fails, he is guilty. He treads a narrow line, unable to really enjoy anything he does. His superego is continually evaluating his behavior. He always seems inadequate by the standards of his superego. Part of his fear of producing is that he projects onto others that they will evaluate him as harshly as he does himself. It is not surprising that Paul is attracted to the Taoist philosophy that states, "The man who places himself behind everyone else comes up first." If that were true, Paul would reach his goals without having to compete.

Many of my interventions throughout the session were aimed at helping him see how his superego was affecting his behavior. Even my last intervention of the hour was an attempt to help him see how he is continually judging himself. Earlier in the session Paul had said, "Things are going well with Julie but I'm still having trouble with work." I responded that Dad won the battle for Mother. I was trying to help him see that he was able to have a woman for himself because he was becoming aware that he had lost the real Oedipal struggle with his father. Paul then pointed out that he was still having difficulties with other derivatives of the Oedipal struggle, such as succeeding in sports and work. Eventually I expect him to realize with conviction that he can succeed in many areas without destroying anyone or being destroyed in retaliation.

Chapter 4

The Effects of a Current Life Stress on Therapy

SESSION 20, SEPTEMBER 10

"SOMETHING TERRIBLE HAPPENED TO ME"

(The patient had called the previous day requesting an earlier appointment. That was the first time he had called me between sessions.)

PATIENT: Something terrible happened to me. Saturday Julie came back. She has been having an affair for two weeks. I've been throwing up since I heard about it. She did come back to Colorado, but is thinking of going back to New York. I think she likes him more than she does me. Since this happened she has been the most important thing for me. On top of this, I found out this morning that we have to go to upstate New York for two weeks to interview farmers there. I wouldn't want to have a relationship in which I am always worrying. For a while I felt that she was like a cold witch. I don't feel that so much now. I looked at her body and I wanted to throw up. Just a week ago all sorts of women could turn me on. Now they all turn me off.

THERAPIST: You were hurt by a woman. [He is having two reactions to Julie's affair: hurt and anger. During the hour I will help him look at both. I responded to the hurt first because it seemed closer to the surface.]

PATIENT: Yes. A week ago I just thought I'd enjoy being with her and I had a lot of plans. Now I want to possess her and not do anything else.

THERAPIST: How do you feel about the other man?

PATIENT: I found out she went to bed with him. It really bothered me when she said he was an unusual person. It reminded me of Patricia [the girl

141

he followed to San Francisco] going off with a bunch of interesting guys. But I also felt that he could screw better, that he was stronger, more attractive than me.

THERAPIST: That sounds like your old idea that some men have more power than you do.

PATIENT: Yes. I was pretty charming with her before Saturday. Now I can't make her laugh or anything. I just feel sorry for myself and she wants to be left alone. One reason it was so hard is that Sunday morning I had to go to Reserves and they were teaching us psychodrama. I finally broke in and said I had to tell them what happened. What really bothers me is that her being attracted to someone else makes me feel worthless. Before that I wasn't even sure I loved her. I just felt like throwing up.

THERAPIST: Throwing up?

PATIENT: Yes. First I feel like I'm choking and then I feel like throwing up. The same thing happened twice with Patricia. I feel pretty good right now but it comes back as soon as I'm alone. Isn't that a part of depression?

THERAPIST: Is depression what you're feeling now?

PATIENT: Most of the time, but also confused and helpless. This seems related to my self image.

THERAPIST: Yes. It is a blow to your self esteem. It makes you wonder how lovable you are.

PATIENT: Oh yes. I feel I want someone to hold me and comfort me and tell me everything will be okay. Especially I want Julie to. I'm angry and ashamed.

THERAPIST: It sounds like the main thing you can't handle is your anger, your rage. As soon as that starts to come up you start vomiting.

PATIENT: Well, I understand that things like this happen, but I was really so strong this past month or so. I felt there were still some dangerous things in the world but that I could handle them. Now I just don't want anything. I just feel miserable. I feel a little like crying, but I'm not. I'm angry with her. Saturday I wanted to grab her by the throat. But I'm angry with myself, too. I feel I did something wrong. At the Reserves they told me that. They said I should have told her that I loved her more. But that was bad advice. I ran back to tell her that and it didn't do any good. It just increased my own feeling that I did something wrong. She seemed so cold and unresponsive. Her parents always make her feel guilty and she's afraid that I will too. I don't want to get her back through guilt. She has to want to be with me. But I still tend to make her feel guilty just by being so miserable. So I'm going to stay away from her for awhile until I can be a pleasure to be with. I feel I'm fighting off a panic. Like I got here early so I had to walk around the block. I couldn't just sit here. Thursday I have to start interviewing in New York. I'm afraid I won't be able to. In the middle of the interview I'll think of Julie. Like yesterday, I asked one of my advisors about requesting a leave of absence. We discussed all the reasons and I wrote up the request, but I left out three quarters of the reasons. I'm afraid I'll go to Julie's house and she won't be there. Like the dream I had about Patricia. I was in a huge house with a lot of doors on a cliff. I kept knocking but no one answered. I looked over the cliff and saw her. I ran down but she kept getting lost in the sand and I could never find her. During that time I was really afraid of losing my mind. I saw my mother in San Francisco. I wanted her to hold me and empathize with me. No one's ever done that for me. I never felt I could get strength from anyone else. I'm still trying to. Julie said she always felt I needed her but didn't care for her. She was doing more of that than I was. Partly I was so sure of her feelings that I didn't have to act like a wimp. But now it's the opposite.

THERAPIST: Of course you're furious with her, but you're afraid of your anger.

PATIENT: I'm angry because I did some things for her and then she hurt me. She had difficulty with intercourse before sleeping with me and I helped her with that. But now I feel she doesn't appreciate it. Maybe she will. She's under a lot of strain now, too. I really feel wronged. I also fear I'll do something like I did with Patricia. I dropped out of graduate school then and joined the Air Force. Even the next spring when I saw her and was involved with another girl I still felt wronged. I'm afraid now that even if Julie comes back to me I won't get over feeling she didn't treat me right. I would always be afraid that she would leave me again. I wouldn't trust her. I could be married to her and have to leave for a while. She made it almost sound like she had no control over it. He pestered her until she gave in.

THERAPIST: How concerned are you about leaving for two weeks?

PATIENT: I feel it might be good, but what if she's gone back to New York when I return. I have no control over what happens. I'll ask her to leave a note in my office if she moves. Should I stay in Colorado?

THERAPIST: I don't know.

PATIENT: I knew you'd say that. If I don't know, how could you? Could you give me some kind of medicine?

THERAPIST: I can't think of a medicine that would help. I wonder, though, if you are asking for medicine as some kind of symbol, like a gift from me. Or something from me that you can take with you.

PATIENT: I think that's true. I'll call you when I get back, but you will probably be very busy then with school starting.

THERAPIST: What brought that to mind?

PATIENT: I guess I'm afraid you won't have time for me, either. You don't think this is as serious as I do, do you?

THERAPIST: I think you have good reason to be depressed and angry and that you are hurting a lot.

PATIENT: [*Starts crying*] It's odd that I don't cry when I'm hurt, but I do if I feel someone is understanding me. Your saying that felt like you had put your arms around me and comforted me. I don't think I need any medicine after all.

DISCUSSION

Paul requested an earlier session because he had been deeply hurt by Julie's having an affair with another man. I tried to empathize with Paul by thinking about how I would feel in a similar situation if I had Paul's personality. I thought of a multitude of responses, the two main ones being hurt and anger. Paul was hurt and angry, but his anger frightened him. As soon as his anger would start to surface, he became symptomatic with nausea and vomiting. I then made a number of attempts to help him accept his anger and to help him understand how it led to his vomiting. For example, I said, "Of course you are angry and furious. That anger frightened you and you started vomiting." In spite of my attempts I do not think that I was really with the patient until the very end of the hour. My clue that I wasn't responding appropriately to him was when he asked for medication. My first response when he made that request was to make the most common interpretation, "You want a gift from me." I then made it slightly more specific by suggesting he wanted to take the medicine with him to New York to have something symbolic of me. Even though he agreed with these interpretations, it was clear to me that he felt I really wasn't understanding him. When I finally made an empathic comment that showed him that I did understand, he began to cry. Then, he no longer needed any medication.

We never did learn why anger is so frightening to him. My speculation is that in his unconscious, acting on his anger would mean killing either Julie or her lover. For Julie to have an affair with someone else is a terrible narcissistic blow to Paul. It confirms all his fears that he really is little and inadequate and no one could want him or love him. This same fear was expressed in the transference when he said that he was afraid that I wouldn't have time for him, either.

His problems with anger also contribute to the inhibition of his ability to get on with his graduate work. In the last session he told us that one time he had wanted to become a psychologist. His motivation to become a psychologist, though, was of a very angry nature–he wanted to be able to go back and show all those people in Omaha that he really is better than they are in some way. That adds a hostility to the competition, that even further increases his inhibition. He probably has similar motivation in his decision to become a sociologist.

When he asked me point-blank, "Should I go to New York or stay here?'' I said, "I don't know." If I had told him, "You should go to New York," he would have heard that as his father or his superego saying, "Look, you've made a contract and you should carry it out." He would not have heard it as, "I think it would be healthy for you to be able to do that." He himself was able to make the decision to go ahead with his work assignment. It would not have surprised me, however, if he had said, "I'm going to cancel this trip. I feel I have to continue seeing you right now and work this out with Julie. I can't take the chance of her leaving while I'm away."

Paul's many trips raise a side issue. Usually the patient and therapist agree to regularly scheduled appointments with a minimum of interruptions. All of Paul's interruptions have been in the service of healthier functioning. First he took the trip with Julie, which was a move toward having a close relationship with a woman. His other trips were involved with carrying out his work assignments. When he is away he appears to remain highly motivated and to do self-therapy. Although it is usually preferable to have sessions at a regular frequency and without interruption, the therapist has to remain flexible and to allow separation when it is in the service of growth.

This was one of those psychotherapy hours where the patient is hurting at the beginning of the session and is still hurting at the end. The difference between the beginning and the end of the session, though, is that the patient understood better why he was hurting and was able to go on functioning. I had no doubts that Paul would be working on the pain on his own during the weeks he was away from therapy. Many beginning psychiatrists are uncomfortable with this kind of session because they became physicians with the idea of ridding people of pain. It is only with experience that one learns that the best medicine in psychotherapy is understanding.

SESSION 21, SEPTEMBER 30   **"ACTUALLY DAD ISN'T THE TYRANT I PAINT HIM TO BE"**

Three weeks later.

PATIENT: I feel a lot better now.

THERAPIST: Good. How come?

PATIENT: I know that Julie really cares for me. I felt lost three weeks ago.

THERAPIST: The one thing that was missing the last time we met was how much anger you were feeling. Even though I brought it up a couple of times you never really responded.

PATIENT: Yes. I noticed that, too. Especially in the past I was afraid to express anger to anyone. It was frightening.

THERAPIST: How so?

PATIENT: I never saw my mother and father fight. Lutherans never get
angry, especially my mother's family. Last week I saw my Dad. I finally told
him I felt miserable and that I have for years. We talked for about three hours.
I told him how I was afraid to do things. It turned out that Mother developed
her endocrine problem right after I was born and continued to be bothered by
it for years. I told Dad I could never recall being held by him, but he denied
that. He also told me that I was breast fed for eight weeks. He said that
Mother loved me very much and was proud of me. For some reason I still feel
that she was very cold. Maybe it's related to those first two or three years.
Maybe my trouble with sex is that it's like being held by my mother.

THERAPIST: Do you feel that?

PATIENT: Not really, but it seems like an explanation. I don't really
enjoy sex when I get it and sometimes I hold back from getting it. The other
night I was making out with Julie and I really felt as turned on as I ever have
in my life. Partly it was because she was turned on and partly because I just
felt good. When Julie gets turned on about something that has nothing to do
with me I don't feel warm toward her.

THERAPIST: It sounds like how you feel about yourself is related to
how she responds to you.

PATIENT: Yes. That's true. I think one of my main problems is that
I'm too self-conscious. If she says something I like and I'm self-conscious I
don't enjoy it. But if she says the same thing when I'm just a little drunk I
enjoy it and it's not a threat.

THERAPIST: For example?

PATIENT: It's hard for me to think of one because it makes me uncomfortable. When she was in New York she went to an old fishing village in
Maine. She really liked it and that was threatening to me.

THERAPIST: Threatening to you?

PATIENT: Yes. I wouldn't get as excited about it as she would. I feel
she is more mature than I am. I'm afraid she likes other things and other people
more than she does me when she gets excited about them. I really feel
uncomfortable talking about this. I feel it will always be true. Julie doesn't
like my seeing you. Like last spring when she felt strongly for me she'd say,
"We don't seem to have problems. If we do, why can't we work them out
together, you and me?" The night she told me about that other guy she told
me that my coming to see you is a sign of weakness. She has problems with
her parents. They want to hold on to her but she feels she's broken away. To
her my seeing you is like if she went back to her parents. Last night Julie and I
talked in the park. I told her I didn't want to settle down to one job until I was
about thirty-five and she said she didn't want kids until she's about thirty-five.
She said maybe we could get together in about ten years and have some kids.
That really got me mad. It made me feel she wants to live alone for ten years.

THERAPIST: Julie says your seeing me is as if she went back to her parents. How do you feel about that?

PATIENT: I don't feel that way. I feel if I didn't come here I would go looking for a parent, like someone in a job or something. My idea is that I come here so that eventually I won't have to. I don't like the fact that I need help from someone. Julie is afraid it will change me or make me attached. I used to feel that way, but I don't anymore. Stubbornness just doesn't work. I told my old man off for the first time when I was home. He told me to visit Mother's grave. I said, "Don't tell me what to do. You remarried right after Mother's death." I was about to ask Ruth, his wife, to dance when he leaned over and told me to. So I didn't. I didn't visit Mother's grave, either. It's confusing. He's really trying to help me out but then I won't do it. It makes me mad. That makes me more angry than when he criticizes me. It's worse to be told the right thing.

THERAPIST: You seemed to be happy when you said that you told your dad off.

PATIENT: Yes. I was happy. I was hoping we'd get into a real argument. But actually Dad isn't the tyrant I paint him to be. In fact, he's uneasy around me. He just accepted what I said. I was looking for a fight. In fact, the reason I still felt good was that I was able to recognize how I felt and express it. That whole time with Dad was a real success, both the warm talks we had and my telling him off, but I can't quite believe it happened.

DISCUSSION

In spite of the three-week break, there is good continuity between this session and the previous one. Paul's returning to the problem with Julie provided another chance to help him look at the anger that was missing in the previous session. Now he is able to recognize the missing anger and to relate his own problems with expressing anger to his family's attitudes.

Paul found out from his father during a three-hour talk that his mother loved him very much and was very proud of him. Nevertheless, Paul still feels that she was very cold. From this session we see that Paul carried around a misconception about his father. Father is willing to talk to him, is not a tyrant, and is just confused when Paul tries to start a fight with him. Was Mother really cold as Paul thinks? Was she as unable to express warm, loving feelings as she was to express anger? That is a possibility, but it is just as likely that Paul could not recognize and accept expressions of warmth from his mother.

During the session, Paul made an intellectualized statement that sounded as if it came straight from a textbook of psychiatry: "Maybe my trouble with sex is that it is like being held by my mother." I confronted that intellectual defense by saying, "Do you feel that?" Paul admitted that affectually the statement had no meaning to him. He then described some very meaningful feelings he does have about sex.

My next intervention, "It sounds like how you feel about yourself is related to how she responds to you," was aimed at his narcissistic line of development. Paul is not completely devoid of an internal structure which can tell him such things as, "Good job, well done," or, "You are a good person." However, that structure is fragile enough so that it seemed worthwhile to point out to him his need for external narcissistic supplies.

Paul was uncomfortable telling me Julie's feelings about his seeing a psychotherapist. Julie's disapproval of his therapy demonstrates the kind of opposition patients often run into from their friends and relatives. I can only speculate about what is behind Julie's opposition to Paul's therapy. It may be that she is threatened because it is the kind of help she would like herself, but which she associates with being weak. She may be jealous of his relationship with me. In her fantasy she may imagine him talking to me about much more intimate things than he discusses with her.

It is clear that Paul understands the therapeutic process and what he can gain from it. During this session he said, "My idea is that I come here so that eventually I won't have to." He sees that psychotherapy is helping him individuate and separate from his parents. As the therapy continues he is seeing his parents, especially his father, more realistically.

There are still, however, many areas of conflict with his father. For example, why should Paul object to his father remarrying? Paul is still conflicted about his sexual feelings toward his mother and his competitive feelings toward his father. When his father remarried, Paul saw his father as sexually successful and free and winning again. Father had Mother, the woman Paul wanted, and when she died, Father quickly found another woman. Paul sees himself as still being bettered by his father in the competition for women.

SESSION 22, OCTOBER 7   **ANGER–JEALOUSY**

PATIENT: I'm so pissed off, I want to kill Julie. I felt good last Monday when I saw you. I went out with her that night. We made love. It was the best sex I ever had. But afterward [*pause*] well, for a while it was nice, but then I was gone until Saturday. I saw her Saturday night and last night. I think I really love her and she won't open up to me. She's afraid. She said yesterday that she wouldn't plan to get married for ten years. I was so pissed off I started throwing up again. I was angry but I couldn't do anything. I had fantasies of grinding up her body, of destroying her. I know she has feelings for me but she won't let them happen. It's so infuriating, I'll have to stay away from her.

THERAPIST: Of course you're angry about all this, but why is expressing anger so frightening that you end up vomiting?

PATIENT: [*pause*] Maybe it's the fantasies that I have. Maybe I'm afraid I'll really act on those. I really want to just destroy her. I've got to express the anger some way. I can't go on like this. I have a hard time with anger. I feel hate and rage toward Julie now. Our roles are reversed now. I used to be the one who wouldn't commit himself. I just don't want to be around her like this.

THERAPIST: You say you have to express this anger some way.

PATIENT: Yes. I rehearsed last night. I thought of terrible things to tell her, but I'm not sure I'm right. For me to say, "Pig, I hate you" really isn't right, because she's not a pig and actually I love her.

THERAPIST: But you hate what she is doing. [I was trying to help him see that he could still love Julie even though he hated something she was doing.]

PATIENT: Yes—what she is doing to me. She'll be defensive and smart about it and make me sound silly. Since our last meeting I've been wondering if I'm afraid of asserting myself not because I'll get hurt, but because I'll hurt someone else. If I complain she'll just say, "Let's stop." I have no power over her.

THERAPIST: There must be some way of expressing how you feel without destroying any one.

PATIENT: We went through this at the Reserve meeting. We had a psychodrama and everyone said, "You aren't angry." I said I felt angry. Maybe I have to lose control to let people know how I feel.

THERAPIST: You were making it pretty clear to me.

PATIENT: [*Starts crying*] I've been selfish this past month. Like in New York, when I couldn't work anymore I just stopped. I feel I have to tell her how I feel because I never have been able to tell the person who generated the feelings. Like with my old man. I tried to talk to him but he would never meet me head on about what mattered. With Patricia I threw up all the time but I never even realized I was angry. I never let my parents know how I felt.

THERAPIST: Do you think Julie knows how you do feel now?

PATIENT: I don't think so; I've been too cautious. I told her I felt bad when she first came back and she just said, "I don't know why you want to be around someone who doesn't want to be around you." Maybe I shouldn't get involved with people like her who are too strong. When she gets upset she just wants to go off by herself and work it out. I'm not like that. She used to be able to tell me how she felt. Now she talks about what she calls a "pure love." It's just detachment, really. She's just trying to get in a position where she can't be hurt and can't feel guilty for hurting others. What I want to tell her is guilt producing. After we went to bed she got scared. Like it was too good for her. But she denies there's anything like that there. If I thought she was going to continue like this for a long time I'd have to quit. Maybe she'll let herself start to feel again soon. I don't want to lose her. It wouldn't be so bad to quit if it didn't cause me to be afraid to care for another girl. Julie is going to be twenty in November. Maybe she does feel too young to get involved. I'm starting to feel the opposite. I'm twenty-six now. I'm desperate. If I don't get involved soon I'll be lonely the rest of my life. Maybe that's not completely realistic. Maybe I get attracted to independent women over and over, like Patricia. Maybe they sense needs in me that they aren't willing to satisfy. For a long time I was afraid to be a man. I don't think I'm afraid any more to accept the responsibility. I sometimes wonder if I can carry it off, but I'm willing to try. Julie seems afraid now, but it doesn't help me to know that she may be going through some turmoil.

THERAPIST: If the relationship could go the way you wanted, where would you take it?

PATIENT: I'd like to marry her. If she really wants to wait ten years she can go to hell, though.

THERAPIST: Ten years is a long time to wait for someone.

PATIENT: Yes, it is, and I think she'd be unhappy. I used to think that for me to express my feelings was asking too much from anyone. I'd be real abstract. Now I feel I don't have to keep everything inside. That's what I meant about the job in New York. When I felt crummy I didn't force myself to continue. Will it help me to tell her how I feel? I think it will. Julie says that in her family they let each other know right away when they are angry. It's always been just the opposite with my family. She lets me know. That's one reason I feel good around Julie. I felt that around Julie it was okay to have feelings, but I'm afraid that if I tell her how I feel it will set the policy for all time. If I say I don't want to see you tonight and then want to tomorrow, I'll wonder if I can come back.

THERAPIST: Is there a rule that feelings are for all time?

PATIENT: [Laughs] No, but I have that idea. I feel better now. Six months ago I wouldn't have even realized how I felt. But I just feel shitty.

THERAPIST: Which way do you think is better?

PATIENT: Well I would have just been numb before. I know it's better this way. The price was too high the other way. I want your approval. I want you to tell me to go tell her how I feel.

THERAPIST: I think you're both angry and jealous. If you are ready to tell her you will.

DISCUSSION

In this session, Paul started to sound more like a man and less like an adolescent, even though he vacillated between the two. For the first time, he is prepared to think about becoming involved, getting married, and facing the responsibilities such steps lead to. Six months ago he would have been frightened by thoughts of that much intimacy. Then he wanted a more superficial relationship with a woman.

Paul has also become much more aware of the feelings he is experiencing. During the session he made several contrasts. When he was with Patricia he used to vomit and not even realize that he was angry. Now at least he sees that his vomiting is a substitute expression of his anger. He also contrasts himself with the way he was when he first started therapy. "Six months ago I wouldn't even have realized how I felt." Six months ago he would have just been numb.

Paul not only described more clearly the emotions he experienced away from the sessions, he also expressed his feelings more directly in the session itself. When he talked about his anger at Julie, he actually became agitated and angry. When I said to him, "You are making it clear to me," he started to cry in response to his sense that someone understood him.

The one feeling Paul is experiencing now that he is not aware of is his intense jealousy. I did mention his jealousy at the end of the session to help him start thinking about it. When Julie said, "I don't want to marry for ten years, I want to experience a lot of different things," Paul responded by stating that he doesn't want to wait until he is thirty-six years old to get married. That is probably true, but what he didn't say was that he is very concerned about what Julie will be doing in those ten years and with whom she will be doing those things.

Paul and Julie are starting to have problems because they are at different places developmentally. When they first met, they were both very much adolescents. Paul is starting to come out of his adolescence a little and progress into adulthood. Julie, based on Paul's report, is not ready to make a commitment to real intimacy. Since Paul is just starting to be ready for this kind of commitment, there are going to be many vacillations in the relationship.

In assessing Paul's progress, two main points stand out in this hour: First is the evidence of his movement out of adolescence into adulthood. Second is his new-found ability to understand and, to some extent, to express his feelings.

SESSION 23, OCTOBER 14   **"I CAN'T TOLERATE TOO MUCH
                                            SUCCESS"**

PATIENT: I told Julie my feelings about her after I met with you last Monday. I felt a lot better until I saw her again on Thursday. I was nervous and self-conscious then. I felt rotten on Friday. Saturday night she came over to a friend's house. I left after half an hour. I was shaky. Nothing pisses me off more than a stubborn woman with a phony show of strength. Just like my mother. Maybe I was afraid that I would smack her. I'm going to stay away from her for a while. I'm going to start writing my paper this afternoon.

THERAPIST: You are setting up an either/or situation. Either you can have a relationship with Julie or you can write your paper. Can't you do both?

PATIENT: As you were saying that, I wondered if I just can't tolerate too much success at once. I think I'm doing things to keep Julie from becoming too important to me again. I don't want to be hurt again.

THERAPIST: Yes. And, you are uncomfortable with competing with the man in New York.

PATIENT: Oh, God, yes! Every time I see Julie I think about him. Julie said that she likes me and this other guy because we are both unusual people. The guy in New York is in philosophical analysis. Now she wants to be a philosopher. When she was my student she wanted to be a sociologist. She doesn't want me to have any weaknesses, like seeing you. She likes her father, who is strong, a lot more than she likes her mother.

THERAPIST: What is your reaction to her saying that your seeing me is a weakness?

PATIENT: When I want her to like me I agree with her. I'd like to get it over with. Therapy with you doesn't have bad effects. I've learned a lot and felt some new things. Having a relationship with Julie and seeing you doesn't have to be either/or any more than Julie and work. I saw Thompson out there. [Mr. Thompson is a psychiatric social worker whom the patient had seen briefly at the University Health Service where he and I were now meeting.] I was uncomfortable because I used to see him. I felt I had to explain why I was seeing someone else. I wanted to say to him, ''There's nothing wrong with you.''

THERAPIST: You think that Mr. Thompson won't like your seeing me.

PATIENT: I know. I feel the same with Julie now that I don't want to see her for a long time. It reminds me of a friend of mine who wanted to borrow a hundred dollars. I really felt I had to explain to him why I wouldn't loan him the money. It made me feel very uncomfortable. It's the same old business. I feel if I do something I want to do, I'll hurt someone else. I got so emotional I didn't know what I wanted to do about the money. It was partly Julie's influence that helped me not loan the money to him. It was the night we went to bed together. Back in August I was starting to feel that I was strong. Then, about a week before Julie returned, I started having the bad feelings about women again. I wanted her back immediately. Maybe I sensed something on the phone.

THERAPIST: Your feelings about yourself as a man are partly riding on her response to you.

PATIENT: Yes. A woman has to need me. She can't just like me or appreciate me. I don't like her independent strivings. I always felt guilty about mother's eyes and felt I had to make it up to her. I used to only go with girls who had something wrong with them.

THERAPIST: There's some question about what you deserve.

PATIENT: Yes, but does it mean that I feel not worthy, or is it that I come from a family where love worked that way? I have trouble feeling anything for someone who is independent. Maybe I'll feel differently after I do those papers.

THERAPIST: Maybe.

PATIENT: I'll feel stronger. I cleaned up my desk this morning so that I could get going. I have to assess myself when I'm feeling strong. What kind of woman do I want then? They gave me a year's leave of absence, but I want to finish those papers and get back in next semester.

DISCUSSION

A question the therapist must always keep in mind during a session is, "Why now?" Why is the patient making progress now? Why is the patient sliding back now? Why does the patient have a particular dream now? Why does the patient present a particular dilemma now?

Last session Paul seemed to be making progress. He seemed to be more mature in his attitude about himself and about his relationships with others. He was starting to make plans about how to work effectively toward obtaining his degree. He made use of the last session to be able to share his feelings with Julie about their relationship and about her affair with the other man. In this session, however, he reported that over the course of the week he reverted to his old patterns and his old way of seeing himself. Paul was again putting himself unnecessarily in either/or positions. He was pushing Julie away and was starting to see himself as weak. Why does he undergo this regression now? The patient made two statements during the course of the hour that answer that question: "I just can't tolerate too much success." And, later in the session, "It's the same old business. I feel if I do something I want to do, I'll hurt someone else." The possibility of being successful started to loom ahead and Paul became frightened again. The old issue of competition with other men became very strong.

Once again, Paul is seeing all of his relationships as triangular. The most prominent triangle seems to be Paul, Julie, and the man in New York. When Julie identifies with the man in New York and wants to work in his field, Paul is convinced that he is losing out in the competition. Paul is in conflict. If Julie prefers the other man, Paul sees that as a repeat of Mother preferring Father. But if Paul wins Julie, then he is hurting the man in New York. That possibility resonates with his old fears that if he won Mother either Father would retaliate or he would lose Father. Paul also sets up triangles between himself, Julie, and me, between himself, Mr. Thompson, and me, and even between himself, Julie, and writing papers. Paul and I were continuing to work through his conflicts about love and work.

SESSION 24, OCTOBER 21   "IT'S OKAY TO DISLIKE YOUR RIVAL"

PATIENT: I'm still in conflict about Julie. I spent a lot of time with her yesterday. She's happy around me but doesn't get turned on. I think she is really in love with this other guy. Should I quit seeing her, see her once in awhile or what? I got sick again, had the nausea and vomiting. This morning I decided I should really hustle her without trying the physical thing. She said she was sure she would have married me if she had never gone to New York this summer. I feel the masculine thing would be to really try to get her. But she gets turned off if we try to make out.

THERAPIST: You had the nausea and vomiting again this morning. That seems to happen every time you get angry. Instead of expressing your rage it comes out as vomiting.

PATIENT: Yes. I felt angry, but I like being around her. I did feel better after doing some work on my papers. She's going to New York to see him this week. [Paul listed all the things she said she liked about him vs what she liked about the man in New York.]

THERAPIST: I'm surprised you can calmly make intellectual lists like that.

PATIENT: I don't have the feelings of sexual inadequacies like I used to and I'm feeling pretty good about myself as a person, but I do get hung up in regard to her. I think the sickness is related to rage, because when I get a little angry I can eat.

THERAPIST: Last week you said you were afraid you would hit her.

PATIENT: I think I still have that fear. When I told her that I was ticked off she went home and had a nightmare that I was going to kill her. I guess she must have felt guilty.

THERAPIST: Or frightened.

PATIENT: Yes, she said that I frightened her. Today I worked hard for three hours. That's another way for me to handle my anger. I did hand in a rough draft of one paper last week. For a while I was fooling myself. I thought I was trying to help her understand her relationship with him. But really I was just trying to talk her out of her relationship. I am angry and some of it is directed at myself because I'm afraid to be assertive. To really hustle Julie. I feel somehow it would be wrong. I equate hustling with boorish assertiveness. I get turned off by male assertiveness. For the first time I really feel I can love. I do love Julie but I don't want to push love on her. I feel like a nervous, scared little kid.

THERAPIST: That's one of the two choices you give yourself. The other is being a man who ends up all alone.

PATIENT: That's true. If I could really pull it off as a man, and I just don't feel ready yet, I'm afraid I couldn't find anyone to love. Irrationally, I feel no one else could be as attractive or desirable as Julie. Really she is just a skinny little girl. This is the first time I've ever become so involved with a girl, the first time that the sexual aspect has taken second place to the personal thing. Yesterday Julie said, "I'm just starting to realize how strong a person you are." That made me feel good, but it didn't last because she doesn't love me.

THERAPIST: What does pulling it off as a man mean to you?

PATIENT: I see being a man in this case as either saying to her, "If you are going to be that way it's over," or, the other thing is to say to myself, "I really love her. She's what I want and I should try my damnedest to get her." It's the first alternative that makes me feel alone. The second alternative scares me. I don't feel that business about being a man means being alone as much any more as I used to. In some ways I think it is like a little boy sulking in the corner. It would be taking a chance, but I think I am getting subtle hints from her to try to win her.

THERAPIST: She's really tearing you up.

PATIENT: Oh, yes. She'll say one thing to encourage me, then another that makes it sound hopeless. She said a lot of nice things about me yesterday. Like how patient I was with her when we were first having intercourse. Somehow I'm terrified by this situation, but I don't understand it.

THERAPIST: What's going to happen to the man in New York if you win her back?

PATIENT: [*Laughs*]

THERAPIST: My comment made you laugh.

PATIENT: I guess I laughed because it would make sense that I would be afraid of screwing him up. He may be alone the rest of his life if Julie gives him up. But I think I'm more afraid that he will win. I don't like him and he may really be a nice guy.

THERAPIST: It's okay to dislike your rival.

PATIENT: [*Laughs*] You're right. Why should I like him? You know, I feel a lot better.

DISCUSSION

In spite of Oedipal conflicts that Paul is living through with Julie and the man in New York, there has been some easing up of work inhibition. He handed in a rough draft of one paper last week and reported working hard for three hours on another paper today. For Paul to hand in even a rough draft was significant progress.

The main issue in this session is the two sides of the Oedipal conflict that he is experiencing. He is angry at his mother, as represented by Julie, for not choosing him. He is angry at his father, as represented by the New Yorker, for winning in the competition for Mother. He is experiencing a severe struggle in the triangle now because for him to win in the competition for Julie is like winning his mother and defeating his father. In his mind, if he had really taken mother away from father, his father would not have had a wife. We see this exaggerated kind of thinking when Paul makes the statement about the man in New York: "He may be alone the rest of his life if Julie gives him up." Partly, of course, this is projection of his own fear that he is going to be left alone for the rest of his life if he loses Julie. Although the original Oedipal conflict with his mother and father is under the surface, the derivatives with Julie and the man in New York are clear.

Some of my interventions in this session were aimed at helping Paul become consciously aware of his fantasies about Julie's lover in New York. The first time that Paul laughed in the session was when I said, "What's going to happen to the fellow in New York?" I suspect that a very violent fantasy went through his mind which he then toned down by saying, "I'd be afraid of screwing him up." He next laughed when I said, "It's okay to dislike your rival." That laughter seemed to express the relief that came with my giving him permission to dislike someone and compete with him. To the extent that Paul was in a father transference with me, my comments along these lines were going to have a great deal of impact. In the transference Paul is experiencing a father who is letting him know that it is all right to equal or surpass him, that it is all right to compete for what he wants.

With Paul, as with all neurotics, we observe both the rational adult mode of functioning and the repetitive, childhood, primitive mode of functioning. In Paul's unconscious there is only one woman in the world, his mother. In his current situation that kind of thinking leads to the idea that either he wins Julie or he is left alone with no one. A related problem for Paul is that he not only has very high self-ideals, but he also idealizes his objects. At one point in the session he expressed the feeling that no one else could be as attractive or desirable as Julie. The adult part of him is able to label this as irrational. Julie is a very special person for him, but he also realizes that in reality she is replaceable. For Paul to be able to recognize what is irrational in his thinking is a further sign of progress.

SESSION 25, OCTOBER 28   WORK STARTS TO GO WELL

PATIENT: Saturday night I had a dinner party for several people, including a good girlfriend of Julie's. Julie is in New York seeing the other guy. Funny, I just had the thought: Once I got so mad at my brother that I came after him with a butcher knife. I don't recall how old we were. A couple times when guys pushed me into a fight, I really tried to hurt them physically. Anyway,

Julie's friend had her head in my lap. I felt rotten the next day. Today I've been manic but I feel good. I like to work. I would also like to be psychopathic and just brush things off. I think what bothered me Saturday night was being close to this woman but feeling that I shouldn't take her to bed. I can handle myself much better now with men than with women. By the way, I got my paper back. I got a B on that rough draft. The professor said that if I want to revise it a little he will give me an A. That really made me feel good. But, I still have that problem with intimacy. I can't handle that any better than I did last spring. When Julie loved me, I felt cool toward her. Now I love her obsessively.

THERAPIST: The big change in your feelings toward Julie occurred when the other man came on the scene.

PATIENT: That's right. I never knew whether his involvement made me more depressed or more terrified. There was hate there, too. Twice I've had the fantasy of mashing her up. I don't know what will happen if Julie does come back to me. Maybe I won't want her.

THERAPIST: What are your feelings about the other man?

PATIENT: [Pause] I very seldom think about him. I think I have very strong feelings about him, but they are directed at Julie. He might persuade her to move to New York. Last session I said that I was concerned about him, but dammit, he pressured her when she was involved with me. Why can't I do the same thing?

THERAPIST: At the beginning of this session you talked about Julie visiting him. Then you thought about coming after your brother with a butcher knife and physically hurting other men when they pushed you into a fight.

PATIENT: Yeah. I want to hurt him but I don't like to admit it. You know, my father would never allow any talking back. He just wanted me to confess. I did stand up to him a little this last time I visited. It's confusing. Father is authoritarian, but he also encouraged me to make up my own mind. He did encourage me to go to college.

THERAPIST: Did he encourage you to go to graduate school, too?

PATIENT: No, but it was all right with him. My mother didn't like it because it meant my leaving home. Maybe it was always my mother who made me feel funny about doing things. I don't know whether I was angry at Julie or just hated him so much I took it out on her. I'm avoiding something. I just can't recall my feelings for my mother. I think she was a bitch, but my father and brother say she wasn't. I don't believe them.

THERAPIST: There are several parallels between the relationship with Julie and the man in New York and your relationship with your parents. You are angry with Julie for becoming involved with him and angry at him for taking Julie away from you. I think that you went through a similar process with your mother and father.

PATIENT: That really makes sense to me. Suddenly I'm understanding how I saw my role at home and how I'm repeating that with Julie and him. I am angry at her, but he could be a machine that stole her and I'd still be angry at him. At first I thought that he must be better sexually than I am, more attractive, more masculine, more mature. At first I thought he was a young, radical, dashing person, more like me than I am myself. But, it turns out he is the same age I am. He's the opposite of me. He comes from a poor family. He is very interested in money and other material things. He is studying philosophy but he works as a systems analyst for a company. Once I learned all that about him I started to see him as a cold person, messing around with Julie's feelings. One reason that I felt more calm in August is that I gave up the romantic image of myself as a talented, dilettantish boy. I had this image of myself that I was so cute and witty that just being there was going to be enough. The funny thing is that I acted that way today and I really don't want to any more. I don't want the same values as my father but I don't have to fight because he really doesn't care. Who am I fighting? I think I'm getting away from that. My relationships with adult men are better and I do have more confidence in dealing with women. I think I could go to a seminar and not be so nervous now because I wouldn't have to prove myself. I feel more like I'm in partnership with my instructors and classmates instead of fighting them. Instructors really do want to help. I feel it's my work and whether or not it's good is up to me.

THERAPIST: You are stripping your work of all the extra meanings that you attached to it in the past.

PATIENT: Yes, and it's much nicer. I've made plans for my specialty paper and I've really enjoyed working on my papers. Graduate school just doesn't seem to be a problem now. I'm close to being able to work a full day in a relaxed way. Maybe I shouldn't become involved with a girl until I have work really squared away.

DISCUSSION

Psychotherapy has cleared up many of Paul's problems with competition in the work area. His rough draft was good enough for a B, and he was told that with a little revision that could be an A. More important, he seems to be enjoying his work now. It is a significant advance for Paul to be able to see his instructors and classmates as partners, rather than as people he has to fight. He has eliminated most of the extra meanings which led to his work inhibition in the past.

His difficulty in competing with another man for a woman is a different matter. For Paul, competing for a woman is still a matter of who is going to castrate whom, or who is going to kill whom. Paul's association to Julie going to New York to see the other man made this very clear. His thoughts went to chasing his brother with a butcher knife and to physically hurting other men in a fight. He is afraid both of his own hostile–aggressive impulses and of retaliation from other men. Fortunately, we now have an excellent opportunity for working on the problem. The best time to explore and understand his sexual inhibition is when he is involved in an obvious triangle, as he is now. If Paul decides to give Julie up to the man in New York "like a little boy," we can deal with that. If he decides to compete for Julie, we can explore his anxiety and hostile impulses.

Paul correctly stated that he cannot handle intimacy any better than he did last spring. He has not yet been in love. He still sees women as objects to satisfy him; he does not deeply care about them and their feelings. He has, from time to time, approached real intimacy with Julie, but each time he has backed away from it.

Once again we see Paul's need to remember his mother as a cold, rejecting bitch. We have evidence that his mother had trouble letting him separate from her, but not that she rejected him. When Paul wanted to follow Patricia to Aspen and San Francisco, his mother didn't want him to go. In this session he recalled that Mother's only objection to his going to graduate school was that it meant he would be leaving home. Paul is defending against admitting how much he loved his mother and how much he misses her since her death. I think that the threatened loss of Julie revives the real loss that he experienced when his mother died.

Chapter 5
The Patient Reacts to an Interpretation of His Central Conflict

SESSION 26, NOVEMBER 4   INTERPRETATION OF COMPETITION

PATIENT: I always seem to talk about the thing that most recently bothered me. This week it is the Reserve meeting. A woman captain had a party after the meeting. A black friend in the Reserves, Yale, is a lot like me. We came to the party late. I'm envious of Yale. He's quiet but people are drawn to him. At the party I talked about my political beliefs at length, even though I knew they would antagonize people there. I used to do that a lot. I did the same thing yesterday when I went before a Reserve Promotion Committee. The captain's boyfriend at the party was a colonel. I think I got anxious. I deal with my anxiety by trying to explain myself, but then I talk too much.

THERAPIST: You became anxious with the colonel?

PATIENT: Yes. At least uncomfortable. I really let him know that I didn't like the things that he liked. I should have kept my mouth shut.

THERAPIST: How does Yale fit into this?

PATIENT: I felt he was getting more attention than I was. I feel that other people get sought out and I never do. As a kid I always went up the street to see the other kids; they never came to see me. I think it's another example of feeling inadequate. Then I get anxious and I talk. When I was seeing Dr. Krueger I took out a girl who really attracted me. The next day she was cold to me. Until my next appointment with Krueger I felt terrible. I thought I had pushed myself on her. He assured me that she didn't mind too much or she would have left that night. Whenever I have alcohol I really push hard. Let me tell you about my conscience and hustling girls. I don't think I'd feel guilt if I treated the girl as a person and myself as a person. With Patricia I pretended that all I wanted was sex. After she left I did see her as a person.

THERAPIST: Can you expand on that for me?

PATIENT: Actually I felt more comfortable when I just treated a girl as a sex object, but that's no good. I stopped the relationship because I wanted something more.

THERAPIST: What is the something more that you want?

PATIENT: I don't let personal feelings get involved. It seems safer that way. Maybe I just don't think the girl is good enough, but I stay with her because it's safe. That's more in the past, though. I used to think that if I could get a girl to bed, we would be comfortable, but it never works out that way.

THERAPIST: Let's look at your relationship with Julie in those terms.

PATIENT: Last spring I felt that I'd really like to feel love for Julie. I felt it from her. I liked her and enjoyed being with her but I didn't allow myself to feel much.

THERAPIST: You liked her then because she made you feel good about yourself.

PATIENT: Yes. She made me feel masculine. That's the most important thing to me. The thing that made me feel strong was about a month ago when we had intercourse and it was great. But, we were screwing for a long time and I withdrew and she felt bad. That has really torn me up because I feel that if I had gone longer, I would have won her back. I had already had an orgasm and I felt tired. I think I enjoyed it so much because I was just thinking about my own enjoyment. I felt that if I enjoyed myself she would, too, and she did until I stopped.

Do you think I felt a lot of guilt when Julie told me about the other guy? All that time during August I was telling myself that I don't have to feel any great responsibility to women that I'm involved with. Shortly afterward I got rejected. Somehow I felt my thoughts and my being rejected were related. The more independent I became the more I felt I was doing something wrong. Last week I saw Julie. She came back from New York. She was feeling bad and that upset me. She told me that she really likes this other guy. We went to a movie. Then I told her that I wouldn't be seeing her for a long time, there was just too much crap.

THERAPIST: I'm not sure what you were responding to when she told you she was feeling bad and you got upset.

PATIENT: I think it isn't so much that I'm concerned about her but that I want her to need me. I'm more concerned with her needing my help than with helping her.

THERAPIST: That must interfere with your ability to help her.

PATIENT: Yes. I look for things wrong in her to show her that she needs my help.

THERAPIST: You are in a situation involving Julie and another man. You say that you like Julie but you are dealing with it by telling her, "I won't see you for a long time."

PATIENT: I've been taking out other girls. I might like someone else better.

THERAPIST: Suppose you do find another woman you really like. Inevitably another man will come on the scene, either in reality or in your imagination. Either you will have to give her up or you will have to compete for her.

PATIENT: That really hits home. At a party Friday night there was a girl I wanted to make a play for. She's living with a guy I know but they are not getting along well. I had a lot of conflict about whether or not to let her know how I feel about her. Somehow I have the same feeling with Julie. Like there are too many vines, it's too entangled. I have both feelings—that the other guy will hurt me or that I'll hurt him. He's so unstable that he might try to kill me. But, if I'm successful it means taking something important away from him. You are right. I don't think I'll ever find a relationship where some other guy isn't involved. Even if it's the girl's father. Like with Julie. I met her father a couple of weeks ago. She's very attached to him. He's a very secretive old man.

DISCUSSION

On the surface this appears to be a complicated, fuzzy session. Paul goes through a lot of adolescent carrying on about what is love and whether or not he is exploiting women. I attempt to help him move from a general abstract discussion about these topics to a specific concrete discussion about his relationship with Julie. It does appear that Paul is going through a transition from using women as sex objects to make him feel good to wanting a more mutual relationship with a woman.

Underneath the fuzziness and carrying on, however, is one theme that repeats over and over. The theme is his central conflict with competition with men. During this session he talks about his competition with the colonel, with his friend, Yale, and with Julie's boyfriend in New York. When he suggested that he find a woman that he likes better than Julie, I made the following interpretation, "Suppose you find another woman you really like. Inevitably another man will come on the scene, either in reality or in your imagination. Either you will have to give her up or you will have to compete for her." Paul responded to this intervention by recalling other situations in which he was competitive with a man. First he thought of his acquaintance who is living with a woman Paul finds attractive. Paul not only expressed his competition with this man, but also talked about his fears that either the man will hurt him or he will hurt the man. He actually thought that this man might try to kill him if he developed a relationship with that woman. He ended the session by referring to Julie's father, to whom she is "very attached."

SESSION 27, NOVEMBER 11   A DEFENSIVE DREAM

PATIENT: [*Looks at his watch*] I'm five minutes late. Sorry. I was so engrossed in my work that I forgot about the time.

THERAPIST: Your being that engrossed in your work is a sign of progress, but you have never been late for a session before. You may be resisting something in the therapy, too.

PATIENT: I don't know. I've been thinking about competition since last session. I took your advice, if that's what it was. It's funny. You never gave me advice before. Julie and I went out for dinner. She got upset, so I reacted by getting upset too. Saturday Julie and her girlfriend and I went out to support the carnation strike. We were supposed to go out to dinner that night. I told her that I would call her, but I didn't. About midnight she called me. She said she wasn't angry or hurt but just worried that something had happened to me. I don't believe her. I don't think that it's fear of competing with another guy that bothers me about her. It's her refusal to admit her emotions. I'm still going to see her, though.

THERAPIST: What advice had I given you?

PATIENT: You said, in effect, I was staying away from her because of fear of competing with the other guy. I agreed. I took that to mean I should compete. By the way, I found out his name. It's Larry. But, anyway, I think I react to her closing off rather than to fear of confrontation with another man about her. I had a long dream that Saturday night which I wrote out. I don't know if it was before or after Julie called. A lot of the things I felt in the dream, I really felt.

In the dream my brother and I and Julie and several other people were driving around a lake near Omaha. We came to a familiar cave. I was throwing rocks in a muddy pond. I was looking for a resort. I always get anxious talking to proprietors, you know, lying about being married. We ended up near a bay. This lake was several feet lower than the next lake. Julie jumped into the water with her clothes on. I wanted to jump in, too. She jumped in first because I had to put on a swimming suit. It irritated me that she jumped in before I did. Maybe this means that I was irritated because she had an affair before I did. Julie was wearing a light blue wool sweater. I noticed her breasts and the nipples in particular under the sweater. While she was swimming I saw that my brother had his penis out of his pants. I was going to say "pecker" but talking to you I felt I had to be more correct and say "penis." It was erect and very fleshy. He was masturbating. The whole scene made me very uncomfortable. I told him to cut it out. That's all I can remember of the dream.

Something just came to my mind that I haven't thought about in years. When I was about ten my brother forced me into fellatio. He was about fourteen or fifteen then. What was Bobby doing in my dream anyway? The thing about Julie jumping into the water. She often does things and then I feel compelled to do it, too, even if I have the idea first. For example, I decided to buy a lampshade but then I thought, "that looks just like Julie's shade." I bought it anyway. There were other people in the dream too. They were indistinct. They could have been any group of friends.

THERAPIST: You, Julie, and your brother, Bobby, are in the dream. You don't see how Bobby fits into the dream.

PATIENT: He was back in the distance not doing much while I was there trying to do things. I feel that I wasn't threatened by his masturbating. I just felt it was stupid of him in front of all those people. I'm quite sure this dream occurred after I talked to Julie. I had been reading *Sickness unto Death* by Kierkegaard. I was telling her how great it was, how good he is at talking about the self. She said, "Of course." That really pissed me off. What she meant by that is that philosophers are better than sociologists. I'd like to think they are all thinkers.

THERAPIST: Larry is a philosopher and you are a sociologist.

PATIENT: Yeah. But, it's more that Julie thinks that she's a philosopher and that I'm a sociologist. I'm a much clearer thinker than she is. But, I feel that I'm more in competition with Julie than with Larry or my brother. I get irritated when she talks to someone else. She's purposely trying not to pay too much attention to me.

THERAPIST: During the course of this therapy I've heard very little about your brother.

PATIENT: Bobby works for the same company as my Dad but in a different city. If I were competing with him . . . [*pause*] I've always been taught to feel sorry for Bobby. [*Pause*] He never did anything as well as I did. But, maybe I was competing for attention. I wonder if I fabricate things wrong with me to get attention, like he did. In some ways I was a spoiled brat. I performed and someone applauded. That's part of the problem now. I need someone to applaud, to tell me that I'm cute and talented. Maybe jumping into the water represents growing up. Julie is trying to be independent, trying to get into the swim of things. That irritates me. I'm older and I'm just starting to do that. I am stronger than Julie, more self-aware, but she comes across stronger because she won't admit weaknesses. She is stubborn and defiant.

THERAPIST: In the dream you had her wear a blue sweater.

PATIENT: To me, blue means purity. It makes me think of a little girl, of innocence. I do think of Julie as a little girl.

THERAPIST: And you do wish that she were more innocent, in other words, not having an affair with Larry.

PATIENT: Yes, I do.

THERAPIST: And how did the dream end?

PATIENT: By my saying, "Cut it out" to Bobby. I felt in control. [*Smile*] When I said, "Cut it out" now, the phrase "Cut it off" went through my mind.

THERAPIST: Seeing his penis in the dream reminded you of his forcing you to do fellatio on him when you were ten.

PATIENT: Yeah. I blew him. I remember I cried and felt bad and was really angry at him. It was in a bedroom. I was on the floor and he was sitting on the bed. I even remember the taste I had in my mouth. It's very similar to when I have my mouth on a girl's breast. That night I had intercourse with Julie after she got back from New York, she blew me. I thought she was trying to fall in love with me again. I withdrew because I had had an orgasm. I cleaned myself off and then she blew me. It made me feel good. Then she went home and she's been cold to me ever since. Maybe my brother in the dream is really me. Sometimes I feel guilty about masturbating. Work is going pretty well and in general I'm feeling better.

DISCUSSION

All of this session is an attempt to deny the validity of my interpretation the previous session that he has conflicts about competing with men. Many times during the session I was tempted to make an intervention such as, "My suggestion that you have trouble competing with men seems to have hit a sore spot." Each time I thought of doing so, I realized that his defensiveness was so massive, so acute that it was not time to make that intervention. To have made that intervention in this session would have been wasting a perfectly good interpretation. I decided to save it until a later session when he was still defensive but not to such a great degree.

My first clue that he was going to be defensive this session was his being five minutes late. Paul's being five minutes late may sound trivial, especially since this was the first time he was late in twenty-seven sessions. Lateness in psychotherapy, however, is never an accident. If his lateness had been a pattern I certainly would have pointed that out. Instead I first acknowledged his excuse that he was engrossed in his work. I thought that it was just as important to reinforce his working as it was to deal with the resistance suggested by his lateness. However, I also commented on the resistance aspect because I wanted to help Paul become conscious of his resistance.

During the session he repeatedly denied that his problem was with competition with men. His most frequent way of denying this was to say that he was really competing with women. He not only described ways in which he was competitive with Julie but even reported a dream in which he was competitive with her, rather than with a man. The second way that he denied his competition with men was to dredge up a memory of a homosexual experience with his brother when he was ten years old. In effect, he was saying to me and to himself, "See, I'm not competitive with men; I even had a sexual experience with my brother once." His third way of denying his competition with men in this session was to bring up his competition with his brother, Bobby. This was especially striking, as we had heard almost nothing about Bobby before in the therapy. By bringing Bobby into the picture, Paul was able to compete with his brother instead of with his father. He defensively regressed to pre-Oedipal sibling rivalry to avoid dealing with the Oedipal rivalry and its derivatives.

This session and the week reported since the last session are beautiful examples of the intense struggle a patient will go through to keep from coming to grips with his central conflict. Paul not only spent his waking time during that week looking for arguments against my interpretation about his conflict around competition with men, but from the dream we see that he spent some of his sleeping hours in that same endeavor. Resistance of this type should not be discouraging to the therapist. On the contrary, working through the resistance with the patient is one of the most useful ways of helping him to deal with his problem.

This dream was one of the most detailed that the patient had brought into the therapy. He actually brought a sheet and a half of written notes about the dream with him. He was going to read the dream from his notes but I asked him to tell it to me instead. He told me the dream and handed me the written notes. The reason for handling the written dream in that way is that it is often very significant to see what the patient either adds to or forgets about the dream compared to what he has written down. In this case, except for some very minor changes in wording, Paul reported the dream almost exactly as he had written it. There were many details in the dream which we could have explored, had we more time. For instance, the castration anxiety theme was in this dream. Paul had to put on a bathing suit in the dream to protect him from castration and exposure. There was evidence for this in his associations as well. In the dream he says to his brother, "Cut it out." When he talked about that later he associated to "Cut it off." Toward the end of this session he made the statement, "Maybe my brother in the dream is really me."

SESSION 28, NOVEMBER 19   INTERPRETING THE DEFENSE

PATIENT: For some reason I feel like asking you how you are, but I know that's not part of our job descriptions.

THERAPIST: It sounds like you would prefer to exchange our job descriptions.

PATIENT: I have felt less of a desire the past few days to talk about myself and more desire to act. I don't think it comes from fear of talking about myself.

THERAPIST: No?

PATIENT: No. Somehow it's associated to what I planned to talk about today. I can't recall what it was. Oh, yes. I used to feel impotent. Now I feel I can do things but I don't know the right thing to do. I met a girl Friday. I took Julie out Saturday and she told me that she wrote Larry in New York, saying that it was over with him. I took the other girl out Sunday. When I got home Julie called. It was about eleven p.m. She wanted to come over to spend the night, because she "couldn't study." She came over and slept on the couch. About 3 AM I woke up. I didn't know whether to have intercourse with her or not. Finally I decided to. The next day the test wasn't as bad as she thought it would be. Then I think she regretted sleeping with me because she only did it out of nervousness. Last night I was with two women. We smoked some grass, laughed, and really had a good time. I wondered if that was right or should I appear strong? My conflict used to be: Should I work or enjoy myself? Now I feel I can do both. Both of those women are friends of Julie's. Julie is going to live with them, which bothers me because they like me and I have designs on them. But, I'm afraid because it could get really complicated. I think it would just make me more attractive to Julie, though. Like Saturday. I told her I was going out with other women. That's one reason she went to bed with me Saturday night. A lot of the feelings that I attribute to Julie are really projections of my own feelings. I compete with her.

THERAPIST: How did you feel about her breaking up with Larry?

PATIENT: I don't know. I felt it would happen. I know that the problems we have together are a long way from being resolved.

THERAPIST: What do you see as the problem you have together?

PATIENT: On my part, I fight her. Anything she brings up threatens me. If Julie says she wants to do something I feel it's an attack on what I'm doing.

THERAPIST: Let's look at the hour so far. You began the hour by wanting to reverse our positions. That's a kind of competition with me. Then you denied that you were avoiding looking at your problems. Finally, you started talking about competition with Julie.

PATIENT: Yes. I'm competing with everyone. Where does it come from?

THERAPIST: My mentioning your difficulty competing with men two weeks ago really hit a sore spot. Last week you insisted that you were competing with Julie and other women and not with men. Now you are saying that again.

PATIENT: I know I want to compete with men, but I'm afraid to. If I'm just talking to one other man I don't seem to be competitive, but I am if women are involved. Even if there is no man I will compete with some imaginary man who doesn't exist. But, that's unreal because if a woman is desirable there must be other men who want her. I wouldn't mind competing if it didn't mess me up so much. Even when competing with Julie I compete with her expression of Larry's views. But, then I express views that aren't even mine. I get so defensive. Actually, if I don't give up I do well in competition, but competing makes me nervous. I worry about making mistakes. If I would just relax and be myself, I would do well.

THERAPIST: That's true. We have to find out what keeps you from relaxing and being yourself.

PATIENT: Yes. My whole life is being nervous about competition. When I was in high school I thought I was a rotten athlete. But, I'll bet if I went back and got some honest opinions they'd say I was a good athlete. I talk a lot about being emotionally deprived as a child. What I don't talk about is that I was a spoiled brat. I was special—cute, talented, tall. My brother was always small and did poorly in school. Maybe I still feel I have to be something special.

THERAPIST: Is your appraisal of you and Bobby realistic?

PATIENT: Well, he is older than I am. Even though he was little for his age he was bigger than I was and could beat me up. This inferior guy could do that—make me suck him off. [This is said with great anger.] He always felt inferior. Maybe I identified with him. There is something wrong with my mother and with my brother. If there isn't something wrong with me I'll be left out.

THERAPIST: You had a lot of emotion when you talked about your "inferior" brother making you suck him off.

PATIENT: Once I took his bike. An older guy was driving a car. I was chasing the car. I ran into the car when he turned the corner. I spent the rest of the day trying to fix the bike. I was really afraid, but I can't recall what did happen. The feeling was similar to when my old man would come home and I hadn't finished mowing the lawn. They always said Bobby looked like Dad.

To satisfy me they'd say I looked like Mother. Actually I didn't look like either one of them. Maybe my brother was considered more important than I was. Now I see him as having a lot of problems. He was about five feet two inches when he graduated from college. I was five feet ten inches in the ninth grade. I used to worry about not having hair on my chest. When I saw my brother in Cleveland this summer I told him I was miserable. He said, "Maybe I'm to blame. I picked on you a lot." He was a little sadistic towards me. [*Pauses*] That dream. I still see it as Julie jumping into things and I'm not. That's the only dream I recall that Julie was in. I got angry Sunday when we screwed. I had an orgasm and she had several. I got tired and withdrew and she got angry. That made me angry. She doesn't think of me. It kind of spoils it for me if I have to keep going after I've had an orgasm. Maybe I should let her know how I feel. But, I used to always feel I have to keep going, really perform, then she will want me over someone else.

THERAPIST: That's another example of the competition with men issue.

PATIENT: I have fantasies about her finding someone massively endowed. Whenever I compete I quit enjoying it but I can't stop competing. Maybe part of the competition is with my brother and I don't want to compete any more.

THERAPIST: A lot of the competition is coming from inside you.

PATIENT: Just about all of it is.

THERAPIST: Recognizing that is painful for you.

PATIENT: Admitting that the competition comes from me means that I can't blame the problem on others any more. But, there is a positive side to it, too. If it's coming from me I should be able to change it.

THERAPIST: Today you talked about competing with Bobby, but also associated to your father.

PATIENT: [*Pauses*] I was really upset. I feel sorry for Bobby but really pissed off at him, too. He didn't have to pick on me. I have some feelings when I think about competing with my father. [*Pauses*] I don't want to any more, but unlike my brother, I often think that my father is still competing with me. I feel now that all my competing with them, and with all the other people that I really don't have to compete with, is a waste of time and energy. I have a lot of guilt and fear associated with competition. With Bobby and my dad, rather than get angry I would cry and go along with what they wanted. Oh, I found out today that I have to go on another interviewing trip. I'll be leaving November thirtieth and won't return until December twenty-sixth.

THERAPIST: That means we will have only one more session before a very long break. I'm going to be away the last week in December and the first week in January. We will meet next week and then not again until January thirteenth.

PATIENT: That really is a long time.

DISCUSSION

Paul was able to continue working with his central conflict about competition with men once I interpreted his defenses against it and acknowledged how painful it is for him to talk about that. We cannot expect that a single interpretation of his defense will eliminate it once and forever, but it certainly enabled him to deal with the conflict in the session. At first I pointed out how the defense was manifesting in this session. Then I helped him trace its origin and manifestations over a long period. I helped him see that he started to become defensive two weeks before when I mentioned his difficulty competing with men. I also acknowledged to him that that "hit a sore spot." I wanted him to know that I was aware of the pain involved in his examining and remembering his difficulties around competition with men. I also showed him how he was similarly defensive in the previous session.

Paul was then receptive to my interpretation that a lot of the competition was coming from inside him. It is a critical point in the therapy when the patient realizes that his conflict is intrapsychic rather than caused by the environment. Many patients become temporarily desperate with this realization. For years they have blamed others for their problem. Now they have to face the problem in themselves. Paul recognized this dilemma, but, unlike many patients, was quickly able to take the positive step of recognizing that he can change what's inside him, even though he can't control other people in his environment.

I had planned to tell Paul about my upcoming vacation at the beginning of the next session. I was not aware that he was going to be away for almost four weeks himself until he brought that up at the end of this session. Since he had brought up the issue of a break in therapy, I used that as an opportunity to tell him about my plans. This was a deviation from my usual rule of not bringing up administrative matters at the end of a session, but in this case it did seem timely.

**SESSION 29, NOVEMBER 25   DEFENSE AGAINST COMPETITIVE
                                  FEELINGS TOWARDS THE THERAPIST**

(Pertinent background for this session is that I was twenty minutes late.)

PATIENT: You have never been late before.

THERAPIST: Can you stay twenty minutes beyond our usual time at the end of the session?

PATIENT: Yes, I don't have anything else scheduled.

THERAPIST: What was your reaction when you found out that I would be late?

PATIENT: While I was sitting waiting for you I wondered why you were late. I assumed that you had an emergency with another patient, but I still had feelings toward you like I do toward Julie. I was angry that you were late. The anger isn't justified, but I can't stop feeling it.

THERAPIST: It isn't justified?

PATIENT: When I got here the receptionist told me that you had called to say that you would be late. I know you are not an inconsiderate person. I especially should know Julie isn't inconsiderate. She never has been.

THERAPIST: You tell me that the feelings are not justified instead of expressing the feelings.

PATIENT: I feel that I am not desirable enough for someone to make an effort to be on time for me, or to even see me.

THERAPIST: You had the fantasy that I was late because I was seeing another patient.

PATIENT: I have the same problem with Julie. I can't believe that she prefers me to other guys. Like Tuesday night I stayed at Julie's place. It looks like things are going well between us, but not inside me. We will be making out and she'll say, "Don't, Paul." Saturday she came to my office and wanted to make love right there. I said that we couldn't. Then she wouldn't spend the night with me. This has happened several times. I can't work. I'm upset. I think she is going through the same thing. Last spring she couldn't work, so she's trying not to get so involved. I feel that I'm always begging her. I don't think that she feels that way.

THERAPIST: Your feeling that you are always begging her seems related to your feeling that you are not worthwhile enough for me to make an effort to be on time.

PATIENT: I've always felt that way. I used to have dreams that Patricia was with these wild guys while I'd be an emasculated, studious, hard-working student. Whatever I am I think the opposite is more desirable. Julie will talk about groovy professors and I'll feel really threatened. I try to explain away their qualities.

THERAPIST: That is more of the same thing. You're not feeling sure enough of yourself.

PATIENT: Yeah, and it's the same with work. I shift so often I can't do anything. I can't seem to work and have a girl at the same time. For a while I was feeling that I could have both, but now I'm back to feeling that I have to give all my time to one or the other. If I'm confident that the girl really cares for me, I'm no longer attracted to her because she must not want very much.

THERAPIST: Did this come up today because I was twenty minutes late and we won't be meeting again until January?

PATIENT: I was wondering, "Does he care?" If I really thought you didn't care what happened to me, I would feel worthless. I still get angry with my old man when he says he has no problems, that he can handle everything.

I interpret that as his not caring about me. Once I told my father how beautiful Colorado is and he said, "Omaha is pretty nice, too." Sometimes I feel that what I have to say is completely worthless, unless it's to people below me, like my students. There was a guy in my neighborhood who was good with puns. I felt he was better than me. I've just got to tell myself to quit tearing people down.

THERAPIST: Or recognize your own worth.

PATIENT: That really would help more, wouldn't it? When I get excited I breathe hard. Bobby used to imitate me. When I think about it I want to kill him. He did a lot of things like that. He would say, "If you are going to chew gum, close your mouth." All these things would make me feel worthless, trivial as they are. I can't take ridicule. The one thing that does make me feel worthwhile is that I feel I'm becoming more self-aware. I used to blame others for everything. My work isn't going as well as I would like. I should get in another paper. I can't get over the idea that it has to be perfect. I know they consider me above average.

THERAPIST: But what if you hand in a paper that isn't perfect?

PATIENT: They'll have a lower opinion of me.

THERAPIST: I wonder if that is realistic?

PATIENT: No, they just want me to produce something. The same thing is true in interpersonal relations. Julie made a judgment about me a long time ago and so has my professor. But, I feel like I'm being constantly evaluated. I guess I haven't said anything new today.

THERAPIST: The other side of that is some anger at me for not helping you to say anything new.

PATIENT: That's true. I do that with Julie, too. I say, "You are not important in my life." But both of you are. Why can't I stop that?

THERAPIST: It's protective for you, but it also increases the likelihood of Julie leaving you.

PATIENT: That's right. I put myself in a bind. The way I try to avoid being hurt increases the chance that I will be hurt.

THERAPIST: We didn't talk about the long break we are going to have in therapy.

PATIENT: This is hard for me to say. I'm going to miss you but I also feel good about being on my own for a while.

As the patient left, he said, "Good-bye, I'll see you in January," and I said, "Good-bye" to him.

DISCUSSION

In most relationships outside of psychotherapy, a person would apologize for being late. Apology functions to assuage the feelings of the person who has been wronged. Rather than opening up a topic for conversation, an apology is designed to seal things over. Since the goal in psychotherapy is to help make the patient's thoughts and feelings available for discussion, apologies and reassurances are usually avoided. Paul has a great deal of difficulty discussing the hurt and anger that he experienced when I was late, even with my encouraging him to discuss it. Had I apologized for my lateness the topic would have been completely sealed over, rather than discussed. Paul revealed his discomfort about my lateness and his desire to avoid the topic in his opening statement of the session when he said, "You have never been late before." He was trying to excuse my lateness rather than looking at it.

By asking Paul if he could stay for twenty minutes beyond our usual time at the end of the session, I acknowledged that I was late and that he deserved to have the time made up. I had also asked the receptionist to tell Paul that I would be late so that he would not have the added discomfort of wondering whether or not I had forgotten an appointment. Had either Paul or I been unable to make up the time that day, I would have suggested that we make it up at the next appointment. These are considerations that the patient deserves that do not prevent his expressing his feelings. They are neither excuses, apologies, nor explanations for the lateness.

In addition to my lateness causing Paul to feel angry, it emphasized his being a patient and my being the doctor. That immediately generated feelings of competition with me, which he defended against. One defense that Paul used was to tell me how impotent he is with women and with his work. The other defense was to displace the feelings he was having toward me to Julie. With the first defense he was saying in effect, "Don't worry about my being competitive with you. I'm so impotent that I'm not a threat, anyway." With the second defense he was saying, "I don't even have those feelings about you, I have them about Julie." Those are defenses that Paul has used in countless situations that we have observed before. Several of my interventions were aimed at helping Paul to see that his talking about Julie and about his weaknesses were related to my being late. In retrospect I think it would have been more effective if I had more directly interpreted his defense. The intensity of Paul's need to appear impotent and worthless was highlighted by his comment, "If I'm confident that the girl really cares for me, I'm no longer attracted to her because she must not want very much." That statement was reminiscent of Groucho Marx's famous remark, "I wouldn't join any club that would have me as a member."

An additional issue during this session was the long break in therapy we were about to experience. I made two attempts to bring up the topic of the interruption, but there was little response on Paul's part. Paul's feelings about the break in therapy were somewhat dampened by the fact that he had initiated the interruption. I did not press the issue more because I also wanted to encourage his independence. I wanted to avoid his perceiving me as opposing his separating from me in the way that his mother opposed his leaving home, first to go to Aspen and later to go to graduate school.

When I did bring up the topic of the therapy break near the end of the session, Paul was able to express his ambivalence about the separation from me. As he was leaving he was able to say, "Good-bye," but at the same time was thinking about saying "Hello" in January.

Chapter 6
The Last Struggles with Competition and Success Before Termination

SESSION 30, JANUARY 13   **"I CAN'T LET IT ALL HANG OUT YET"**

PATIENT: I have a lot of things I want to tell you. Let me start with what happened between Julie and me. We went to Omaha even though her parents told her not to. We got along well and she said that she loved me. New Year's Eve she called me and said, "Let's get married." I said, "Let's talk about it when you get here." She got back about ten days ago. At first it was great. Then about five days ago she said she wanted to move out. Now she's pretty cold. I feel we could keep this up over and over with one of us getting turned off and then on again. The romantic thing is for me to save all my feelings for Julie. The practical thing is to go out with other girls. Then I could find out that I'd have the same kinds of feelings for other women, too.

THERAPIST: By practical you mean doing what will keep you from becoming really close to Julie.

PATIENT: I know. I often numb up around her. I don't tell her how I feel. What I'd like to do is live together longer and see how things work out.

THERAPIST: This time when she pulled away you didn't start throwing up.

PATIENT: There's no competition this time. She told me that she likes me better personally and sexually than the guy in New York.

THERAPIST: You won that competition.

PATIENT: It makes me think of the problem more as hers than mine. I used to feel that she had something beautiful with this guy. Now I feel that she would have problems with anyone unless she changes. Usually I'm concerned about making the relationship work. I do feel that I love her, but it's a dangerous feeling. I have to protect myself. Like when she said, "Let's get married," I didn't say yes because I knew a week later she might feel differently. But also, I've always felt that she loved me more than I loved her, and that I used her to make me feel worthy. Yet I'm on guard. I think that if I responded in a more loving way, she would have a lot less upheaval.

THERAPIST: Something keeps you from showing her that you love her.

PATIENT: I'm afraid she will reject me. It's the old masculinity thing. I can't let it all hang out yet. I still feel it may get chopped off. I just remembered the dream I had last night. In the dream I was driving with my father and uncle in my uncle's car. My father asked my uncle if he were still drinking a lot. Probably the reason I had that dream last night is that I just found out that my uncle has been hospitalized for a bleeding esophagus. In the dream, he said that he had a few drinks, so my father said, "Stop the car; we are getting out." I said, "I'm staying." He said, "The hell you are," so I got out. Earlier in the dream there was something about railroad cars. A faster train went by. The two trains almost hit each other. A lot of things come to my mind about that dream. My uncle does work for a railroad. Julie and her father really like trains. I've been in cars with people who've been drinking. I've wanted to tell them to stop, but I never have. My father would, though. I often resist doing things that he would do, practical things. Like I said the practical thing would be for me to go out with other girls. If I'm hanging on to Julie just to rebel against my father I would stop seeing her.

THERAPIST: Do you somehow see having a relationship with Julie as rebelling against your father?

PATIENT: Sometimes I do. But, I don't understand it. We all got along well in Omaha but sometimes I think Julie tries to find things that are right in a situation. She doesn't like a struggle. Like we were having a fight about politics driving to Omaha, but then we stopped in a motel for the night and she started blowing me. I wanted to keep talking about our disagreement and she just short circuited it by making love.

THERAPIST: In the dream you started to struggle with your father but then you went along with his demand.

PATIENT: I tried to be a man with him but I ended up being a little boy again.

THERAPIST: Yes. You thought about the dream today after expressing fear that your penis would be chopped off if you let it all hang out.

PATIENT: Yeah. It's dangerous to stand up to my dad.

THERAPIST: In your dream you and your uncle acted in such a way that your father belittled both of you. It was very much like the story you remembered from your childhood about you and your father and your uncle on a boat.

PATIENT: Oh, yes. When my father said my uncle's penis was so small that he would need a microscope to see it. Those trains in the dream, one faster than the other. That's like who has the bigger penis.

THERAPIST: The dream brings up important issues about competition and about your self-image, but we are out of time for today.

PATIENT: Oh, I may have to go to Montana next week. I'll call you as soon as I know. I hope you had a good vacation.

DISCUSSION

In spite of a seven-week interruption, continuity in the therapy is retained. Both consciously and unconsciously Paul does therapeutic work between sessions. He quite quickly returned to the theme of competition with men. Compared with the previous session he was much less defensive. He talked both about his fear of rejection by a woman and about his fear of castration.

The point in the session at which Paul recalled his dream from the previous night was significant. He had just said, "I can't let it all hang out yet. I still feel it may get chopped off." The dream involved a weak, alcoholic uncle with whom the patient had previously identified in terms of their belittlement by his father. In the dream the patient has a competitive struggle with his father, but backs down. Since there was very little time left in the session, I was quite directive in my interpretation of the dream. When I reminded the patient of when he thought of the dream in the session and of the story he had told me about his father, his uncle, and himself, he was able to recall the story in detail. He was then able to go on to see some of the symbolic meaning of the trains in the dream. At the end of the session I underlined two of the important issues in the dream, competition and self-image, knowing that we would return to them in future sessions.

As the session ended, Paul stated that he might have to be away the following week. With patients who have less capacity for working on their own between sessions, the frequent interruptions of the therapy would be very disruptive. With patients, unlike Paul, who could not maintain continuity with missed sessions, I would have more actively discouraged the interruption. For Paul it seemed more therapeutic to encourage his independence and his functioning in his job.

A few days later Paul did call to say that he would be out of town for two weeks. The next appointment was arranged for February 3.

SESSION 31, FEBRUARY 3   INTERPERSONAL OR INTRAPSYCHIC?

PATIENT: I took some LSD since I last saw you. I didn't think there was anything wrong with it until I started thinking about telling you. I think I want you to admonish me for it, or I want you to say it was a good thing. I want to either fight or align. I mainly just want to make a decision about LSD. I had a good time and no adverse effects. I had been afraid to take it, but I didn't have any paranoid thoughts like I get with grass.

THERAPIST: You said that you didn't think there was anything wrong with LSD until you started thinking about telling me. But, the idea that there is something wrong with it came from you, not from me. I hadn't said anything about LSD.

PATIENT: I guess it has something to do with my father, but I can't put my finger on it.

THERAPIST: First you tried to make it into a battle between you and me, and now between you and your father.

PATIENT: I knew you wouldn't make any evaluation, but I felt I had to justify it. But, I really don't want to justify it. Mainly I just had a good time.

THERAPIST: You knew I wouldn't make an evaluation, yet you felt you wanted me to either admonish you or say that it was a good thing.

PATIENT: Yes. I want you to ask me if I thought it was good.

THERAPIST: All right. Did you think it was good?

PATIENT: I thought it was. Things were funny and pretty for about eight hours. The last four or five hours were quieter. It lasted from about three in the afternoon until seven the next morning, but I didn't sleep until the following night.

THERAPIST: You say that you think taking LSD was good, but there is still a struggle going on inside you about it that you want to attribute to me or your father.

PATIENT: When I was a teenager I missed out on a lot of things because my father was so strict. At least, that's what I always thought. Now you are making me wonder if it was my own strict conscience that was holding me back. Dad once caught me coming home when I was fourteen years old. It was one in the morning. He asked me for the time and I lied to him. I was so scared I couldn't sleep the rest of the night. I just spent fourteen days in Montana. I did a lot of thinking there. The thing I became most aware of was that I always feel I have to justify my opinions. I often feel Julie is in a groovy, beautiful scene, and I am not. Taking LSD made me feel less like that. I feel I've done a way-out thing. Like I've eclipsed some of my teenage friends who used to do things that I was afraid to do. I want you to agree with me.

THERAPIST: There are two things going on this hour, what is happening inside you and what is happening between you and me.

PATIENT: I've been having a lot of feelings about you lately. I really like you and think the way you do, but I get pressure from my friends to be more judgmental, to be against future-oriented things. I think it is important to be somewhat goal-directed, but these friends seem to be the most interesting people around. They read a lot and have a lot of wild ideas.

THERAPIST: Where are your ideas about me coming from?

PATIENT: From watching you.

THERAPIST: But you really don't know that much about me, do you?

PATIENT: You do seem pretty relaxed, and the people I'm talking about aren't. I have the feeling that you accept things. Like you accept the evil in the world as the way people are. Maybe I do project my feelings onto you. I like Julie a lot. She's sensible. We both dislike things about the world but sometimes she gets very negative and rejecting.

THERAPIST: You came in today with the feeling that I would admonish you. That was a projection of your feelings onto me, too.

PATIENT: I know that's important, but it makes me uneasy. I'll come in with an idea about a paper, for example, but then I get frightened. I think the professor won't accept the idea. If he supports it I feel good about it, but even if he resists the idea I sometimes go ahead. Now I'm starting to feel a little more autonomous. Like if you take a neutral stand I can make my own decision. Like I've decided not to take any courses this semester. I'm doing research and have a part-time job. Also, I feel I'll be able to handle courses better by Fall semester. Since I've been seeing you I've been feeling gradually better, more capable of handling a course with tests and papers. In the past I would have gone to my professors with a long prepared explanation for this decision. Now I will discuss it with them if anyone asks, but don't feel that I have to go around justifying my decision.

We have talked a lot here about my problems with competition. I've been afraid to win for a long time, but I never understood that before I got into therapy. I've noticed that I have been feeling less that way since I won against Larry, the fellow in New York. But, there's still some of it. I think of asking girls out and immediately feel I have to prove myself, instead of just seeing if we can have a good time. This is the one subject, competition with men, that really gets me upset. If I can think of just dating a girl to see how we get along I feel okay, but as soon as I feel I have to prove something I get afraid.

DISCUSSION

Paul started out the session with a superego projection. He attributed to me his own feelings that there is something wrong with taking LSD. He was trying to turn the intrapsychic conflict between his id impulses and his superego into a contest between him and me. Paul was right in thinking that I considered LSD a dangerous drug, but he had no way of knowing that. He gradually realized that it was an intrapsychic conflict, but not until he had also tried to turn it into a contest between him and his father. Finally Paul was able to say, "Maybe I project my feelings onto you." He was then able to see how he had also tried to set up contests with his professors, projecting his own concerns onto them about his ideas and his plan to take no courses that semester.

Paul also made what I thought were some accurate assessments of changes that were taking place in him. He is becoming less judgmental. He does seem to have identified to some extent with the psychotherapy model which values understanding, insight, and the reality principle. He correctly identifies the one subject that still upsets him, his competition with men, and he seems to have made significant progress in that area. He has become much more aware of how the problem with competition has inhibited him in the past. This seems to have freed him up somewhat to compete in a constructive way.

SESSION 32, FEBRUARY 10   "SHE HAD A PENIS"

PATIENT: Something happened at Reserves, but something more important happened with Julie. A friend of mine told me that the only change he wanted in the world was to be able to get a good piece of ass easier. I told Julie and she got upset. She told me that she had gone to bed with him about ten days ago. Then she got very cold toward me. The next day I told her I thought we should break off because the relationsip was too one-sided. I listen to her feelings and problems but she can't listen to mine. I told her I get jealous when she talks about other men. She admitted it would bother her if I did that. I haven't seen her since. I think I'll go out with other women, but I know if I get at all rejected I'll return to Julie. I feel frightened of being rejected.

THERAPIST: You feel rejected by Julie.

PATIENT: Yeah. It makes me feel something is wrong with me. Like I have a weakness if I tell her a problem. She admitted that she really liked me last spring when I said I didn't know how I felt about her, but that she quit being excited by me as soon as I liked her. I think she is a little perverted. She gets turned on by our screwing in a car or with clothes on or in the middle of the day. I don't mind that except that it seems contrived. I want her to feel I'm more important than anyone else. Somehow I keep feeling Julie knows what life is all about and that I don't.

THERAPIST: I don't understand that. You are more experienced in life and older than she is.

PATIENT: But I've always felt I'm really not part of the group.

Whenever she suggests something a little different from what I believe, I feel really threatened. I got strength from her loving me and I feel weak when she rejects me. I was jealous when I heard about her going to bed with Dennis. I was jealous but I can't let myself get mad. I tried to solve my feelings by trying to make her but she wouldn't have any part of it. I always do that when I have a problem with a girl. I try to do something sexually.

THERAPIST: What kept you from letting yourself get angry?

PATIENT: I did get angry that night but I didn't want to continue being angry, because then I couldn't get her out of my head.

THERAPIST: Did you throw up this time?

PATIENT: Just the night after when we were going to meet and she didn't show up. Later she told me that she didn't come because she didn't want to face me. By this weekend I felt pretty calm. This Saturday I was being hustled by a thirty-two-year-old woman at Reserves, and Saturday night I planned to hustle a girl who works at the University Grill who I've always wanted to meet. But, during her break she sat with another guy. Actually, I've never let myself go up to a girl I didn't know. Is that all right? Why am I asking you? I think it's all right. I'm anxious about being assertive with women. I feel a little guilty. Mother used to make me feel guilty when I wanted affection from her. When I get rejected I'd like to be able to just forget it, but I dwell on it. That's one reason I'm afraid of being rejected.

THERAPIST: Do you remember an example of your mother making you feel guilty when you wanted affection from her?

PATIENT: There was that time when I left home and wanted to kiss and hold her and she just turned away. I'm sure there are earlier examples but I just can't recall them. I try but I can't. The only early memory I have is the one I told you about the big trees, but I have no early interpersonal memories. I'm hiding something. I want to recall it but I can't. Hey, I just recalled a dream that I had as a kid when I was about eight or ten years old. There is a boy I used to play with. I'd have a dream about his sister and she would have a penis. It was like a boy's penis only it was kind of wound up inside her vagina. That confused me. I wasn't quite sure what girls did have there. She was about three or four years younger than I was. I think we were playing doctor in the neighborhood. There was a different girl who was our favorite subject. I remember the table but I can't recall actually examining her. By the way, she used to beat me up. We were about nine years old then. A little later I heard rumors that some of the older guys were screwing her, but I don't think that was really true. It's funny. I haven't talked much about my childhood. I do when I feel good, like last spring and summer, and now I felt good the last few days. I feel like trying to figure things out again.

THERAPIST: Why do you think you had a dream in which a girl had a penis?

PATIENT: I have some ideas but no real feelings about it. I didn't know whether girls were girls or boys. Being scared by women seems different. They might have something weird and wonderful and terrifying. That's odd. Women usually feel that way about men.

THERAPIST: Maybe there's another explanation.

PATIENT: I wanted her to be like my father because my father was more affectionate than my mother. He thought I was important. [begins to cry] I feel relieved saying that, but not quite as much relief as that time I started laughing when I talked about castration.

THERAPIST: Could that dream have anything to do with castration?

PATIENT: I know it does. At that time I felt I belonged to the little girl group, not the little boy group.

THERAPIST: Why did you have a dream about a little girl having a penis?

PATIENT: So if I turned into a girl I'd have a penis anyway. Of course, that's how I'd first get the idea of losing a penis. It would be to see a girl without one. Somehow that fits in with my feeling that Julie has the real insight into life.

THERAPIST: Girls have something awesome and wonderful and frightening.

PATIENT: Yeah. [laughs] The bitches! You know, I feel a lot better.

The patient then informed me that he would again be out of town for ten days. I told him that I would be away the week of the twenty-fourth. We made an appointment for February 21.

DISCUSSION

Paul continues to work through his central conflict of competition with men. At this point in the therapy I listed in my mind a possible series of steps in interpretation that would be useful to the patient in the course of the next several sessions. I saw as a first step helping Paul to realize that he experiences rejection by a woman as a defeat rather than as an object loss. The reason he experiences rejection as defeat is that whenever he is attracted to a woman he assumes there is a bigger, more powerful man in the background whom she prefers. The next step would be to help him see that he then feels like a little boy. A further step would be to help him see that the bigger, more powerful man represents his father, but now he is a big man himself. His father can no longer hurt him and neither can any of the other "big" men. Eventually we could more directly interpret his castration fear. He touched on his castration fear again this session in the childhood dream he recalled and his associations to it.

To some extent this hour was characterized by the feeling of mastery on Paul's part. But, it was tenuous enough that he wanted some confirmation of his mastery from me. At one point in the session he asked me if it was all right to go up to a girl he didn't know. Interestingly he made his own interpretation about this, pointing out that he knows that it's all right and he doesn't have to ask me, and that the problem is the anxiety he experiences when he tries to be assertive.

SESSION 33, FEBRUARY 21   REJECTION BY A GIRLFRIEND–A LOSS OR A DEFEAT?

PATIENT: I took out a girl for the first time that I know from the lab. I really pressed her for sex. We didn't have intercourse, but I feel bad that I spoiled the chance for a good relationship.

THERAPIST: That conclusion comes from you. You think that because you pressed her for sex you have spoiled the chance for a good relationship.

PATIENT: Maybe I didn't. She was friendly this morning. But, I felt I was pressing too much. About a year and a half ago I met a very attractive woman who drove me home from a party. I was drunk and was really persistent. She got very pissed off. I don't think I have a morality hang-up about sex, but I do feel that a girl who screws on the first date does have some problems. I don't like to be a prude, yet some things both excite me and make me feel they are wrong. I still think that the girl I took out, Mary, might be mad about my wanting sex.

THERAPIST: Anyone else mad about your wanting sex?

PATIENT: That question really jolted me. The thought had just gone through my mind that my father wouldn't do that. The night before he got married we had this party and he was drunk. He said to his future wife, "I just want to get into your pants." So, here he was, about to get married and he still hadn't. I'm just concerned about Mary's feelings. The only way I see another man in the picture is that he may be more of a gentleman and win. I just feel bad that it might end the relationship.

THERAPIST: The other man would win. If a relationship with a woman ends, you feel more defeated than rejected.

PATIENT: I certainly feel that with Julie. There's a dope pusher who lives below her and is interested in her. I really dislike him. She thinks that he is charming and I think that he's a phony. I'd like to really mess his face up. One thing about competing, if I apologize to Mary, that will be a form of competition, too, because I'll be saying, "I'm a sensitive, concerned person, unlike the other guys you know." She actually turns me on more than Julie does. That makes me feel good. Julie really confuses me. When I think about her I get mad, scared, and anxious. Today I thought about Mary and I mostly had good feelings.

THERAPIST: It is near the end of the session for today. I want to remind you that I will be away next week.

PATIENT: It's funny. I feel very differently about our not meeting next week because you are going away than I did about missing last week when I went away.

THERAPIST: You have been talking a lot about rejection this session. I think you feel rejected by me, too, because I'm going away.

PATIENT: Suddenly what you said earlier today about my feeling defeated rather than rejected when it ends with a girl really makes sense to me. If things end with a girl I do feel that some other guy has beaten me out. But with your going away I feel like I'm losing something. I'm going to think more about that while you're away.

DISCUSSION

My first intervention in this session was aimed at helping Paul see that his conclusion that he had spoiled his chances for a good relationship with Mary came from his superego, and did not necessarily have anything to do with reality. He confirmed it was not reality by recalling that Mary had been friendly to him that morning. Nevertheless, Paul persisted in feeling that there is something wrong with being assertive sexually. He again expressed the thought that Mary might be angry at his wanting sex. Since the evidence has been that his problems are with men about women rather than directly with women, I asked him, "Anyone else mad about your wanting sex?" Paul was jolted by that question, because the idea that his father would be angry about it had just made its way into his consciousness.

Paul then tried to deny that another man was involved in the relationship in his mind. But he did so in such a way that it became even more more clear that there was competition with a phantom adversary. At that point I was able to interpret to him that the ending of a relationship with a woman is experienced as a defeat by him. Paul responded with several confirmatory associations. In addition he made clear the amount of hostility involved in his competition with men: "I'd like to really mess his face up." This interpretation had even more meaning for him at the end of the hour, when he realized that he was experiencing my leaving as a loss which was very different from the defeat that he experiences when a girl leaves him.

SESSION 34, MARCH 5   **"NO ONE BUYS *PLAYBOY* FOR THE ARTICLES"**

PATIENT: Your mustache grew fast. I have things to say, but for the first time in a long time, I'm feeling that I talk too much and don't do enough. I am doing more, though. I'm working and I'm going out. The whole thing has to do with sex. I think and worry about it too much. I got here early today so I went to the drugstore and looked at pictures of women in a magazine. I wish I wouldn't think about it until it's appropriate. I know it's okay to think about sex when not screwing, but if I get sexually interested in a woman I get anxious around her. Sometimes I can get rid of the anxiety just by saying I have no reason to be anxious. I want to ask a girl out who works at the Red Coach Grill and I haven't been able to yet.

THERAPIST: You said that you don't do enough. Now we see one area in which you are inhibited, approaching women, and that anxiety inhibits you.

PATIENT: I used to attribute feeling more relaxed after masturbating to being free of all the need to confront women sexually. No sexual desire equals no anxiety.

THERAPIST: You think you will be punished if you express sexual desires.

PATIENT: Yes. Like even looking at those magazines, I felt nervous and anxious, especially if someone was watching. I pretended I was interested in the articles.

THERAPIST: No one buys *Playboy* for the articles.

PATIENT: Yeah. I guess I realize that. I didn't feel guilty when I masturbated, I just felt unmasculine. Like the big tough guys were out screwing. I realize now that they probably weren't either. Somehow it seems secretive and sneaky. Instead of propositioning a girl I'd have to let it happen. I couldn't just say, "Let's go to bed." I still kind of feel that way. But I've noticed that I'm less anxious around people and less confused. I can disagree with people without feeling threatened now. But I'm still afraid of being forceful. I'm afraid people will think I'm pushy. I have more of a desire to be around straight people recently. With dope, people just make exclamations. I'm seeking out more adult people. Somehow this is all related. I feel inadequate. I'm enjoying my research. I'm studying sexual attitudes, but my subculture thinks that's worthless. I want to be groovy but I want to have my personal integrity, too. It's a tough problem. I think I want to be a rational sociologist but I'm afraid that if I am I won't be able to get women. Like as a kid it was the guy who broke windows who got the woman.

THERAPIST: The anxiety you experience with sexuality around women again comes down to competition with men.

PATIENT: But the woman might tell me I'm not groovy enough to be propositioning her.

THERAPIST: That, too, implies that there is a guy groovy enough that you are competing with.

PATIENT: That upsets me. That's related to Dad somehow, but I can't go any further with that. It scares me. Like if a girl is involved with another guy, I think about him and he scares me. Or, it can just be some vague guy in my mind who doesn't even exist.

THERAPIST: It appears that you feel like a little boy in those situations.

PATIENT: Yes. Yes, I do. Like I'm pleading with the girl for something. I want something from them that I'm supposed to ask for but other guys can just demand. That makes it sound like those other guys are my father. It's all right for them to demand it but not for me.

THERAPIST: Yes. Fathers can demand things from mothers but little boys can only ask, and they have to be careful what they ask for.

PATIENT: I feel that way even with younger girls.

THERAPIST: That's the second time this session that you have talked about being older than some of your companions.

PATIENT: I am feeling that way. I feel a strong pull toward growing up. I want to work; I want to get married.

DISCUSSION

Paul's opening comment about my mustache was his only reference to my being away for a week. He was comparing himself to me and was competitive with me in regard to the mustache. That opening comment was a tip-off that this hour would again be about his competition with men. Often a patient is least defensive during his opening or parting comment of the session. Several times during the session Paul went back to his defense that he has a problem with women rather than a problem with men related to women. Each time that I challenged his defense he was able to look more directly at the competition with men. Eventually he was able to see some of the genetic roots of the competition in terms of the original triangle with his father and mother. Throughout the session there was the theme that a strong man was lurking somewhere who would punish him if he had sexual desires toward women, even if they only involved looking at women in magazines.

At the end of the session Paul said, "I feel a strong pull toward growing up. I want to work; I want to get married." This was an explanation of what he meant at the beginning of the session when he said, "I don't do enough." Fear of men and of his superego interferes with his ability to work effectively and to form a sexual, intimate relationship with a woman. He correctly labels those as tasks in the growing-up process. Paul has grown up but his super-ego hasn't. His conscience is still eight years old, still trying to defend against sexuality. The fact that he is experiencing a strong pull toward growing up, however, suggests that some progress is being made along these lines.

SESSION 35, MARCH 12   BEING MORE ASSERTIVE

PATIENT: I came down with Julie today, so I didn't have much time to think about the session in advance. I've been smoking a lot of grass at Julie's. I seem to get insights from grass. I went skiing yesterday. Afterwards I went to Julie's. Julie wasn't there, but a groovy girlfriend of hers was. I always get afraid when I'm taking grass. My defenses are lifted. I feel the fear of my feelings about women, fear of money, fear of cops.

THERAPIST: You and a woman got high last night. What feelings did you have?

PATIENT: This girl has always turned me on sexually and I know that she has admired me for a long time. I had the desire to make out with her. At first I felt that I couldn't do that. I told myself that it would interfere with my relationship with Julie. But then I became aware of some anxiety I was feeling and I realized I was concerned because she is involved with another guy. When I realized it was another guy bothering me again, I said, "The hell with it. If I want to make out and she does, we don't have to worry about her boyfriend or about Julie." We both undressed and danced to loud music. I got an erection and drew an arrow on it with a green Magic Marker. I really strutted my penis around. I looked in a mirror and decided that mine is as big as anyone else's. Telling you about that episode made me a little anxious, but that's part of the same problem. It's competing with you.

THERAPIST: Yes, but you were able to tell me.

PATIENT: [*Laughing.*] And nothing bad happened to me. I must feel the threat of competition all the time. It's just more apparent when I'm high or when I'm talking about it with you. I used to feel that competing was a bad thing. Now I find that I can be more assertive. Feelings of competition used to inhibit me but I've noticed that Julie likes me to be assertive.

THERAPIST: Feelings of competition did inhibit you, but you appear to be overcoming that inhibition.

PATIENT: I used to just sulk when I got into a competitive situation. I'd say, "Let her decide." Now I stay in the game.

THERAPIST: Before you were putting all the burden on the woman. It's like you were saying to yourself, "I'm a good little boy. It's not my fault if she picks me. Daddy can't blame me." Now you are saying, "I'll go after what I want."

PATIENT: I get a good, free feeling, an assertive, even an aggressive, nice feeling when I let myself compete. I notice that I've been smiling and laughing a lot more these days. I was pretty assertive the other day. I saw a reporter interviewing people. I went up to him and said, "I have a few things to say." The next day my picture and comments were in the paper. I used to have anxiety about any kind of assertive activity. Now I can be assertive in a lot of areas. I still get anxious being assertive sexually, though. I had that breakthrough last night but I was high on grass then. The next step will be asserting myself sexually when I'm sober.

It was the end of the session. As the patient was leaving he said, "It's hard to stop at the end of this session. I'd like to talk to you about that sometime."

DISCUSSION

Termination is in sight. Last session Paul complained that he talked too much and doesn't do enough. In the week between that session and this one he turned his words into action. More significant than what he did was the process that enabled him to act. With the woman he was initially as inhibited as ever, but was able to make use of the work he had done in therapy to understand and overcome his inhibition. Initially he justified his inhibition by saying that it would cause problems with Julie. Indeed it might have if Julie found out but it might have just made Paul seem more desirable to her. The real cause of his inhibition came to light when he recognized his anxiety. He realized that the anxiety was caused by his fear of competing with a man and the fantasy that the man would punish him. Having recognized that, he was able to deal with it and overcome the inhibition.

Paul's being able to approach the reporter was equally impressive. That, too, led to a success. His picture and comments were in the paper the next day. Most impressive to me were the processes he went through that allowed him to assertively compete and the "good free feeling" that he experienced when he let himself compete.

When I commented at the beginning of the discussion of this session that termination was in sight, I was not suggesting that these two successes meant that Paul's problems were all worked through. Paul himself recognized that there was more to do. At the end of the session he said, "I still get anxious being assertive sexually. I had that breakthrough last night but I was high on grass then. The next step will be asserting myself sexually when I'm sober." What Paul didn't realize, but which can be predicted with great certainty, is that he will experience some defensive back-sliding. The assertive acts themselves are not of primary importance. Paul could have counter-phobically forced himself to do the same thing early in therapy. The important difference now is that some change has occurred inside him. His superego has been tempered so that it is less harsh; he has come up with new solutions to his conflicts about competition.

For most of Paul's life he had a representation of his penis size that bordered on a delusion. Consciously he knew as an adult that his penis was of normal size and yet part of him was convinced that it was small. In 1791 Boswell wrote in his *Life of Johnson,* "This distinction was made to me by the late Professor Gaubius of Leyden, physician to the Prince of Orange, in a conversation which I had with him several years ago and he explained it thus: 'If (said he) a man tells me that he is grieviously disturbed, for that he *imagines* he sees a ruffian coming against him with a drawn sword, though at the same time he is *conscious* it is a delusion, I pronounce him to have a disordered imagination; but if a man tells me that he *sees* this, and in conster-nation calls to me to look at it, I pronounce him to be *mad.*' " Paul was never mad, but he did have a disordered imagination about the size of his penis. The mating dance that he went through the night before this session helped him correct that disordered imagination.

Just because the therapist thinks that termination is in sight does not mean that the patient shares his view. We saw only a hint that Paul had any awareness that he was approaching the time to start considering termination. At the end of the hour he said, "It's hard to stop at the end of this session." I heard this as his also saying that it was going to be hard to stop at the end of therapy. General aspects of the termination process will be discussed in an essay before the next chapter. I will make specific comments that apply to Paul's termination in the discussion of the particular sessions.

PART III

Termination

A Brief Essay on the Termination Process

INTRODUCTION

Scheherazade told a thousand and one stories to avoid termination. So do many patients. Others are willing to end the therapy, but want to do so precipitously so as to avoid dealing with the termination process. Still others avoid termination by concealing improvement from their therapist. Usually a patient wants to say good-bye to his therapist in the same manner that he has said good-bye to people all his life. Most people build a hello into their good-bye. When I graduated from medical school I recall many of my classmates saying to me, "Good-bye. See you at our fifth reunion if not before." In therapy the patient has the rare opportunity to deal with terminating from an important person in his life over an extended period of time.

Often the termination phase of therapy is analogous to a curtain call at the end of a play where all the characters come out in their costumes. In therapy the patient reruns his old symptoms and defenses. This is sometimes interpreted as the patient's way of telling the therapist that he does not want to terminate. I think the return of old symptoms and defenses has a much more important and dynamic meaning. When the patient becomes aware that he is soon going to be without the help of the therapist, he temporarily regresses. He experiences something akin to what a child in the symbiotic phase experiences when his parent leaves. The rerun also allows for a final burial of the old symptoms and defenses and a consolidation of the gains.

So far I have emphasized the resistance to termination and a temporary regression that occurs. For patients who have undergone successful therapy there is also a feeling of freedom. The patient looks forward to independence from the therapist and to the chance to invest the energy he has been putting into therapy into new endeavors. From a practical standpoint most patients are quite happy to look forward to the time and money they will be saving when therapy ends.

Termination is an integral and important part of psychotherapy. The particular form that termination takes depends on the dynamics of the individual patient, including his previous experience with losses and separations, the intensity of the transference relationship, the therapist's ability to help the patient terminate, and the way the therapy was conducted. If the therapist has acted as an advisor, the therapy can become interminable because the patient will not have learned how to function on his own. There are, of course, psychotic and borderline patients whose egos are so deficient that the therapist does have to provide some of the ego functions. These patients may indeed need therapy at least periodically all of their lives. For the neurotic patient, however, the goal is growth and development, which is achieved by helping the patient learn to do for himself rather than doing for him. The therapist's goal is to make himself unneeded. When that goal is achieved, termination can proceed.

INDICATIONS

The indications for beginning termination, of course, vary with the patient, the type of treatment, and the treatment goals. At one extreme is extremely brief psychotherapy. For four years I was Director of the Student Health Psychiatry Service at the University of Colorado Medical Center. During that time I did the initial evaluation on over 400 medical, nursing, and graduate students who sought psychotherapy. Approximately 15% of those students I saw for only one or two visits without referring them for further therapy. A typical example was a freshman medical student who came to see me after spring break. He complained of being sad, tired, apathetic, unable to sleep, and unable to concentrate. He said that these symptoms had come on very suddenly. He went to an internist at the Student Health Service, who could find nothing physically wrong and suggested that he see a psychiatrist. I commented that those were typical symptoms of depression, just like chills, fever, and a cough are typical symptoms of pneumonia. I then asked him if he had lost someone important in his life. He became teary-eyed and said that his girlfriend had left him over spring vacation. Curiously he had not associated her leaving with his symptoms. We spent the rest of the session talking about what her leaving meant to him. When he returned a few days later for another session he said that he was symptom-free. Once he understood the cause of the symptoms, he was able to use his own resources to deal with the problem. He thanked me for my help and we said good-bye. One could look at that extremely brief psychotherapy encounter as having no termination phase, but actually the only purpose of the second session was to bring our relationship to an end. From that standpoint 50% of the therapy involved termination.

At the other extreme is psychoanalysis, where indications for termination have been quite clearly elucidated. Signs that the patient is ready to terminate in psychoanalysis include his working more independently, having a greater capacity to free-associate without resistance, being able to do much of the work of interpreting his own dreams, and carrying out self-analysis in between and during sessions. Usually the analyst experiences less transference distortion from the patient and is seen as more of a real, contemporary object. The transference neurosis has been experienced and worked through, leading to a re-solution of the infantile conflicts, including the Oedipal conflict as relived in the transference neurosis. Dewald[1] points out that the goal of psychoanalysis is change in both core psychic structures and their derivatives. He describes how to assess structural change. Hurn[2] talks about disposition of the alliance during the terminal phase. By this I understand him to mean disposition of the psychoanalyst, that is, the patient starts being able to do self-analysis and the symbiotic relationship grows less and less necessary. Also, during the termination phase of an analysis the patient becomes better able to visualize a future without the analyst.

In between brief psychotherapy and psychoanalysis is a medium-length psychotherapy on a once- to twice-a-week basis of the type described in this book. Blanck and Blanck[3] list the following criteria for termination of psychotherapy:

1. Attainment of identity: they define identity as "differentiation between self- and object-representations, and the capacity to retain the representation of the object independent of the state of need."
2. Relief from the presenting problem.
3. Acquisition of a more competent defensive capacity.
4. Object relations approach object constancy.
5. Indications that structuralization has proceeded, in that higher levels of internalization have been reached.
6. The ego exercises more and more of its own functions.

These are excellent criteria for termination of the psychotherapy of a psychotic or borderline patient. For the neurotic patient, however, most of these goals have been attained before he ever seeks therapy. He already has a fairly firm sense of identity, as defined by Blanck and Blanck, and has attained object constancy. Before terminating, the neurotic should have obtained relief from his presenting problem or at least gained the tools to solve it on his own. The goal with the neurotic is to free his defenses, rather than to strengthen them. Ideally he would be left with sublimation as his major defense. The growth and structuralization that would be sought for the neurotic would be a mature and reasonable superego and ego ideal, a competent ego, and the capacity to discharge his drives in a socially acceptable manner.

Other indications for initiating the termination phase for a neurotic patient would be signs of freedom from sexual, work, and social inhibitions; in other words, the ability to love, to work, and to play. He would not be expected to be problem-free, but rather to show signs of being capable of mastering problems as they are encountered. Similar to the patient in psychoanalysis, the neurotic in psychotherapy should have developed considerable capacity for self-therapy by taking over the therapist's role in the working alliance. He should have re-solved his infantile conflicts, including the Oedipal one, at least at the level of their derivatives.

FORCED TERMINATIONS AND "NATURAL" TERMINATIONS

In addition to natural terminations which come about as the result of the indications described above, there are also forced terminations due to changes in the external reality of either the patient or the therapist. Forced terminations precipitated by the therapist most commonly occur when a therapist in training completes one phase of his training and moves on. Reider[4] describes patients who deal with being transferred from one therapist to another by becoming primarily involved with the institution rather than the therapist. Dewald[5] describes the forced termination of twelve psychotherapy patients when he made a geographical move. He stated that the anticipation of forced termination served as an impetus to further therapy in some of his patients, led to unanalyzable regression in others, and seemed to have no noticeable effect on a third group. Patients are sometimes "forced" to terminate because of financial reasons or geographic moves. Often what appear to be plausible reasons for a forced termination are really resistances on the part of the patient and, I suspect, sometimes on the part of the therapist.

STAGES OF TERMINATION

The termination of psychotherapy seems to take place in four fairly discernible phases. Usually the therapist becomes aware of the indications for termination before the patient does. The termination process then begins without the conscious awareness of the patient. Next the patient becomes aware that he no longer needs psychotherapy. At that point the therapist and the patient agree to terminate. Usually there is some delay between the agreement to terminate and the setting of a termination date. When a date is agreed upon, I usually add, "Barring unforseen circumstances." I do this so as to not lock us into a very rigid termination date, should something unanticipated occur. A patient in psychoanalysis and I set a termination date for approximately four months after he was to take his State Bar Examination. When I added my clause, he retorted, "Yes, barring not passing the Bar."

The final phase of termination is the actual conscious termination work. Often the setting of a termination date serves as a catalyst for increased therapy work. Before the termination date is set, the patient often has given little thought to what the therapist and the therapy situation mean to him. During this phase he will often work through the meaning of the therapy and the therapist, realize that he no longer needs either, and more actively seek relationships outside of the therapy. Whenever possible the date is set so that it will not coincide with an external event that would have caused a separation between the patient and therapist anyway. If the therapist customarily takes a long summer vacation, it is best not to terminate with patients just before that vacation. Most patients would not fully experience the impact of the termination under those circumstances until the end of the period of the therapist's vacation. By then the patient would no longer be in therapy, where he could deal with that experience with the therapist. The termination is more fully felt if it occurs when the patient knows that the therapist is still at work in his office and has probably replaced him with another patient.

The therapist and the patient together have to determine how much time should be allotted for termination. Often, however, the therapist has to be a fairly firm guide, since many patients would prefer to avoid the pain of termination. Few people relish the work of mourning, whether it be mourning over the loss of the therapist or someone else in their lives. Usually the longer and more intense the therapy, the longer the period that is needed for termination. Especially patients who have had difficulty dealing with separation and losses in the past need a long termination phase.

Some people have advocated decreasing the frequency of sessions during the termination phase, in effect weaning the patient from therapy. In my opinion that serves no function in insight psychotherapy except to dilute the work of termination. I often find it helpful to ask the patient for his fantasies about what his life will be like after therapy is over. This helps him to think about the time when he will no longer have therapy or the therapist. One experienced psychoanalyst frequently asks her patients in analysis what they are going to do with her after the analysis is over. I have found this useful with my therapy patients as well. One particularly insightful patient of mine responded to that question with, "I will no longer have you but I will have what I learned from you. I suspect that for a while after therapy is over I will periodically think about what you would have said in a given situation but after awhile I probably won't need even that. I'll be able to do it all on my own." I think that is an accurate description of what usually does happen in the post-therapy period for a patient who has undergone successful insight psychotherapy.

If the patient raises the possibility of obtaining more therapy in the future, I ask him for his ideas about indications for additional therapy. This usually leads to a discussion of his fears and of what he thinks has been left undone in the therapy. It also helps the patient to think about what the future holds in store for him. In forced terminations, of course, it may very well be that the patient should have more therapy. If the patient is psychotic, or even borderline, and he requests more therapy, the therapist may have to help him transfer to another therapist. With a neurotic patient in insight psychotherapy, however, more can be gained by going through the termination process. If, after the therapy is over, he still thinks that he needs more therapy he is perfectly capable of finding it on his own.

WAYS IN WHICH TERMINATION IS EXPERIENCED BY PATIENTS

Each person experiences termination a little differently, but three aspects of termination seem to be experienced by almost everyone, often simultaneously. Termination is experienced as a death, as a recapitulation of separation–individuation, and as a commencement. It may be seen as the death of the therapist and/or of the patient. This aspect of termination leads to grief and mourning. Death is the end, the ultimate termination.

During termination the infantile prototype of separation–individuation is re-experienced, as well as the important separation–individuation phase of adolescence and of each new life change. There is a wish to leave and be independent coupled with the wish to stay and be taken care of. Increasingly, the patient sees the therapist as an equal rather than as a parent. Finally, the patient is able to give up the therapist to go off on his own.

Termination is also seen as preparation for a new beginning. The therapist's way of working is introjected and the new tools are tried out. The ceremony connected with the conferring of degrees or diplomas is a termination but it is called a commencement, a time of beginning. This is true of therapy termination as well. It is the aspect of therapy termination which leads to the patient's feelings of euphoria and the therapist's feelings of satisfaction. Termination experienced as death leads to sadness and mourning. Termination experienced as separation–individuation leads to ambivalence and separation anxiety. But, termination experienced as commencement leads to the excitement of a new adventure.

Termination As Experienced By The Therapist

So far I have emphasized the effect of termination on the patient. In some ways termination is easier for the therapist than earlier phases. The patient is now capable of doing much of the therapy work on his own. Since the therapist is now experienced more realistically, he need be less concerned about the effects of his interventions on the transference. He also has the satisfaction of observing the growth and development that have taken place in the patient.

Schafer[6] points out some of the difficulties that a therapist can have during the termination phase. "It is during termination that all the unspoken promises, expectations, transferences, and resistances on the part of both persons in the therapy relationship may come to light." Schafer points out that during the termination phase the therapist must face the limitations of both what he and therapy can do. The therapist's own narcissistic investment in the therapeutic results must not go beyond what can reasonably be expected. He continues, "One of the best protections against disruptive counter-transference responses to the terminating patient is a reasonable and stable sense of one's own goodness," and "If the therapist's confidence in himself is lacking or easily undermined, he is likely to intensify rather than turn to advantage the crisis of termination."

The therapist also experiences many of the same emotions that the patient does. The therapist is also ending a relationship into which he has invested a great deal of his energy and skill. A two-way kind of empathy develops between the patient and therapist. The therapist knows a great deal about the patient and knows the patient very well. The patient usually does not know much about the therapist, but through experiencing the therapist's empathy, he does know the therapist very well. In terms of separation-individuation, the therapist is in much the same role as a parent. He must not only be a parent who is able to help the patient grow and develop, but also a parent who can allow the patient to separate and individuate. If the therapist has suffered significant object losses in his own life, no matter how well they were analyzed, he is going to have some re-experiencing of them during the termination phase. When both the patient and the therapist want to avoid the experience of loss, there can be an unspoken, often unconscious collusion to not deal with that aspect of termination.

I cannot emphasize strongly enough the importance of the termination phase. If the patient and therapist have not worked through the termination phase, it really cannot be said that the patient has undergone psychotherapy. In this brief essay I have been able to only touch on the indications for termination, the different types of termination, the stages, the way termination is experienced by the patient, and the effect of termination on the therapist. For further reading on termination I recommend, Glover[7], Fleming and Benedek[8], Weigert[9], and Firestein[10]. Two additional articles specifically on forced termination are by Weiss[11] and Schwarz[12].

REFERENCES

1. Dewald PA: The clinical assessment of structural change. J Am Psychoanal Assoc 20: 302–324, 1972.
2. Hurn HT: Toward a paradigm of the terminal phase: the current status of the terminal phase. J Am Psychoanal Assoc 19:332–348, 1971.
3. Blanck G, Blanck R: Ego Psychology, Theory and Practice. Columbia University Press, New York, 1974, Chap. 17.
4. Reider N: A type of transference to institutions. Bull Menninger Clin 17:58–63, 1953.
5. Dewald PA: Reactions to the forced termination of therapy. Psychiat Q 39:102–126, 1965.
6. Schafer R: The termination of brief psychoanalytic psychotherapy. Int J Psychoanal Psychother 2:135–148, 1973.
7. Glover E: The Technique of Psychoanalysis. International Universities Press, New York, 1955, Chap. 10.
8. Fleming J, Benedek T: Psychoanalytic Supervision. Grune & Stratton, New York, 1966, Chap. 7.
9. Weigert E: Contribution to the problem of terminating psychoanalyses. Psychoanal Q 21:465–480, 1952.
10. Firestein SK: Problems of terminating in the analysis of adults. J Am Psychoanal Assoc 17:222–237, 1969.
11. Weiss S: Some thoughts and clinical vignettes on translocation of an analytic practice. Int J Psychoanal 53(Part 4):505–513, 1972.
12. Schwarz IG: Forced termination of analysis revisited. Int Rev Psychoanal 1:283–290, 1974.

Chapter 7
The Termination Process Begins

PATIENT: There was something we were going to continue with from last session but I can't remember what.

THERAPIST: You were wondering why you didn't want to stop the hour when it ended.

PATIENT: I don't want to talk about that now. I don't compete with Julie as much any more. I want to date other girls, but I still can't just sit down and talk to a girl I don't know. Should I be able to? I feel that I have to.

THERAPIST: What is interfering?

PATIENT: I went to a bar the other night where a girl named Joan works. I had talked to her a couple of times when she served me drinks. She was there with another girl but not working. I walked up to her and she didn't seem to remember me. She just brushed me off. I really felt bad that night. I wondered what was wrong with me. If that happens a couple more times, I'll really be afraid. Part of me says, "What the hell is wrong with her?" I was trying to think about that competition business but it didn't seem relevant here. It is a pretty forward thing to do. It makes me nervous.

THERAPIST: I think you answered your own question about what is wrong with you. Being forward and assertive does make you nervous.

PATIENT: The last few days I had a lot of opportunities to approach a couple of girls. But, I always got scared and would find an excuse for not approaching them. It makes me anxious. I don't know what that's about.

[*With tears*] I felt like telling that girl in the bar, "What kind of shit are you pulling on me?" Instead, I joked about her having a busman's holiday. She didn't get it. I wouldn't be so anxious if I had been introduced to her.

THERAPIST: What is bringing on the tears?

PATIENT: It's the frustration. I shouldn't need an introduction to approach a girl, but I really feel it would help.

THERAPIST: What would an introduction do for you?

PATIENT: Make it easier, somehow. My approaching her would be different then. It wouldn't be so much like I was hustling her. But, I would have trouble approaching an interesting man in a bar who I just wanted to talk with. I'm afraid of talking about this. It seems that I've gone through this crap ever since I've been interested in girls. This fear makes me do stupid things at times. I feel cheated; I feel sorry for myself when it comes to this and I haven't been able to stop it.

THERAPIST: Last week you reported some successes, but now anxiety is interfering again with your ability to assert yourself.

PATIENT: Last week I was able to overcome the anxiety by recognizing the competition element. I don't know if competition played a role with Joan or not.

THERAPIST: What's your idea about the kind of guys that Joan goes out with?

PATIENT: I don't really know, but in my imagination I know she goes out with a big, tough, good-looking guy, about six-foot-four, with broad shoulders.

THERAPIST: What would he do about your trying to hustle Joan?

PATIENT: Maybe I'm resisting, but I think *she* was the problem. She's the one who said no. It makes me think about a dream I had last night. In grade school I was madly in love with Helen. I got in a fight with a guy who was interested in Helen, too. He beat me up. But, in the dream last night I won. In the dream the guy kept coming after me, but with very little effort I chopped him down time after time. I wrote a letter to a friend the night before the dream telling him about my problems with women. But I had the feeling that the problem wasn't going to last long.

THERAPIST: In some ways that was an encouraging dream.

PATIENT: Yeah. I really felt good about that dream. Something is changing.

THERAPIST: What about the experience with Joan?

PATIENT: No, that was different, too. I got over it fast. I told people about it. Before I would have thought it was a shameful thing and I wouldn't have been able to tell anyone. Should I be able to approach a girl if I want to?

THERAPIST: Yes, unless, like in the dream, you think it involves chopping down a man.

PATIENT: I have the feeling that by next week I will have done it three or four times.

DISCUSSION

At the beginning I gave the patient an opportunity to talk about his not wanting to end individual sessions. I thought that would be an opening for the patient to bring up termination if it were on his mind. Paul, however, flatly stated that he did not want to talk about that topic then, reflecting his resistance to looking at termination.

Even though I thought that the termination phase had begun, it did not mean that the working-through process was completed. Working through continues to the end of therapy and beyond. In this session we again reworked his central conflict about competition with men. Paul reported trying to approach a woman, being brushed off, but not reacting with the kind of humiliation he once would have experienced. Again he tried to deny and resist my interpretation about competition with men, but he confirmed the interpretation with his childhood memory and his dream.

In the childhood memory Paul gets in a fight over a girl and is beaten up. In the dream he again does combat with a man, but in the dream he wins. I commented to him that in some ways the dream was encouraging. In the dream the man kept coming after him, indicating that Paul was reluctant to take part in the battle. Nevertheless, he was able to win with ease. The dream also suggests an area where more work has to be done. Paul needs help realizing that competition is not one-tenth as hostile as the dream indicates that he sees it. I approached that problem with my last intervention of the session.

SESSION 37, MARCH 26   **"I THINK I'M USING HER TO WORK OUT
MY NEUROSIS"**

PATIENT: I won't be here next week. It's spring vacation. By the way, I didn't do what I said I would, partly because I had a cold and partly because of what happened between Julie and me. We talked about going to New Mexico over spring break. The next night she brought a guy over. That really made me angry. Then another time we were together and I got numb on grass. I got angry and frightened and started crying. Julie started comforting me and has been very close ever since. It's just that she wants someone to need her. That made me angry because I want her to need me, but it's made both of us closer. It's like we feel we need each other. [Paul continued to try to clarify his own thoughts.] She uses me but doesn't want to feel obligated. I'm confused again but at least I recognize it. I'm having feelings like when I was eleven. It's hard to verbalize. I want Julie to give me some of the things I never got from my mother, but at the same time I want to treat her like my father treated my mother. That night I really let my feelings go. I used to be afraid to do that.

THERAPIST: Can you tell me more about those eleven-year-old feelings?

PATIENT: Saturday I felt sick with the cold and hung over. So, for the first time I skipped Reserves. For years I went to school without missing a day. I felt resentful then because other kids would skip when they didn't feel like going. I had always been afraid to skip because I'm so frightened of authority. At first I felt good about being able to call and say that I wasn't coming. But then I started feeling that I should have gone. I had nothing else to do anyway. Somehow this is all related to sex. Everything that bothers me is related to sex. When I was in junior high school [pause] I walked in the woods next to our house. [Pause] I'm really ashamed of this. [Pause] I'd masturbate. Then I'd feel alone and worthless and dirty. Somehow that is connected with the idea of missing work. As soon as competition comes in I think about sex. God damn, it makes me so mad because I think I'm missing out on a lot of enjoyable things because I'm thinking about sex all the time. I can't just have a good friendship with a woman because I immediately sexualize it, and then I get anxious and I act in such a way to ruin the friendship.

THERAPIST: Are you able to put together the sex, competition, and missing out?

PATIENT: It sounds Oedipal to me. I can't remember a time when it was different.

THERAPIST: Probably it ultimately is Oedipal, but as I listen to you I hear a person who has matured physically and emotionally but is stuck with an eleven-year-old conscience. Today you were ashamed to tell me about masturbating in the woods; a few weeks ago you were very embarrassed telling me about looking at the pictures of women in magazines. You have a conscience that tells you that you shouldn't have sexual drives.

PATIENT: Yes. I can have fantasies, but if I approach a girl and get turned down I feel guilty. It's funny. My conscience doesn't push the thoughts out, though. I do have an overly strong conscience. I can't do what I want to do.

THERAPIST: You did manage to stay home from the Reserves.

PATIENT: Yes, and I feel that something more is going to happen.

THERAPIST: What do you feel is going to happen?

PATIENT: That this is going to cease being a problem soon, that soon I'll be able to handle a lot of different things in my life without getting upset, that soon I'll be able to date when I feel like it. But I can't just say I'll do what I want.

THERAPIST: Defying authority, whether at school or at Reserves or whatever, is still frightening to you.

PATIENT: Oh, yes. I don't want to defy anyone. I just want to be able to forget about authority.

THERAPIST: Yes, whether real or imagined.

PATIENT: You know, I think Julie really cares a lot about me, but I can't stand it when she has other interests.

THERAPIST: Especially other men.

PATIENT: Yeah. She has a parade of guys and it pisses me off. I'm fixated on her. I want to date others but I can't. I don't know what I want out of a relationship with a woman.

THERAPIST: Do you see the connection between your problems with authority and your inability to have the kind of relationship you want with a woman?

PATIENT: In my gut I feel that they are connected, but intellectually I see them as separate problems. Authority involves my old man and women involve my mother. Do you think there's a connection?

THERAPIST: Yes. Your trouble with women is your fear of competing with your old man.

PATIENT: I never fear an individual man. It's just that big unknown man.

THERAPIST: Sure. One is reality. No individual man is that frightening to you now. The fear of the unknown man comes from inside you.

PATIENT: When a guy is actually there I feel some hostility and jealousy, but if I have to just approach a girl just sitting there it's anxiety. The other night I was going to approach a girl at the Student Union. My heart started pounding.

THERAPIST: Symbolically you will have to stick out your penis eventually.

PATIENT: But I don't want it cut off. But I'm never physically impotent, yet I relate the two. Like it's two different manifestations of the same thing.

THERAPIST: We won't meet for two weeks.

PATIENT: I think I will go to New Mexico with Julie. I sometimes think that I'm using her to help work out my neurosis.

DISCUSSION

Paul's missing a Reserve meeting was much more motivated by his desire to defy an authority than it was by the fact that he was suffering from a cold. For Paul to miss that meeting involved a struggle with his superego. He used his cold to justify missing the meeting, but he also used it to avoid competition with men over women. His conscience, which is still that of an eleven-year-old, could allow his defying authority as long as it wasn't directly involving sexual competition. Paul correctly realized, however, that the two issues are related: "Somehow this is all related to sex. Everything that bothers me is related to sex." He then told me with much difficulty his association to masturbating in the woods in junior high school. He went on to point out that whenever competition is involved he thinks it is sexual.

When I asked him how he put all these things together he correctly said that it was Oedipal, but that was too broad a self-interpretation to have any real meaning. I focused on one aspect of the Oedipal problem, his immature, overly punitive, antisexual superego. I referred to it as an eleven-year-old conscience because he had recalled in this session the guilt and shame that he had experienced at age eleven when he masturbated. He not only recalled it, but relived it in the hour as he told me about that experience.

When Paul said, "I do have an overly strong conscience; I don't do what I want to do," I reminded him, "You did manage to stay home from Reserves." My point with that intervention was to help him see that the authority that he had defied was not the United States Air Force, but his own superego. This may sound as though I was encouraging Paul to be irresponsible. Not at all. Paul's problem is just the opposite. His intrapsychic structure prevents him from enjoying himself even in a responsible way.

Again in this session Paul gave some indication that therapy will not be necessary much longer. He stated that he feels that the difficulty with his superego is going to cease being a problem soon. He thinks that he is going to be able to handle "a lot of different things in my life without getting upset."

In this session I also tried to help Paul develop a more realistic adult self-representation. Paul commented, "I never fear an individual man, it's just that big unknown man." I responded, "One is reality. No individual man is that frightening to you now but the other comes from within you." The point was that when Paul was a little boy his father was realistically frightening because of their size and strength difference, but now Paul is an adult and as big as other men.

Paul ended the session by saying, "I sometimes think I'm using Julie to help work out my neurosis." That is a correct statement. At the time Paul was more caught up with defeating all the men that she was parading through the house than he was in having her as a lover.

Chapter 8
The Patient Becomes Consciously Aware of Termination

"HEY, HOW MUCH LONGER ARE YOU
GOING TO BE HERE?"

PATIENT: I can't think of any emotional things to talk about today. I've noticed that when something bothers me, I'm able to sense the real problem much quicker. I got back from New Mexico with Julie last night. I started feeling paranoid around her friends. I realized that I was feeling anxious because I thought I had to be like them. Once I was aware of what was causing me to be anxious, I was able to be the way I wanted and not be bothered by it. Last night I had a short dream where my boss said, "Since you can't handle yourself, we'll have to set up regular hours." Sounds like my old man talking to me when I was a kid.

THERAPIST: And like you talking to yourself now.

PATIENT: [*Laughs*] I had been goofing off for two weeks and was a little worried about returning to work this morning. Sure enough, this morning before work his secretary called and said that he was pissed off but it worked out okay, so there is some reality to my concerns. I'll just have to make sure I don't go overboard with my new-found sense of freedom. I'm feeling less and less that something is wrong with me. Now the only time I feel something is wrong is when I'm smoking grass. Then I get negative feelings. Drugs are just an escape. Now I feel more like facing things.

THERAPIST: I wonder if the dream is related to therapy, too?

PATIENT: You mean the missed session. I never thought much about the sessions that I missed until this time. I told a friend that Julie and I were going to New Mexico. She asked if you allowed me to miss sessions. I told her that I never thought that missing had interfered with therapy and that I was sure you would have said something if you thought it had. I'm glad I'm back. Julie was sad about returning. We got along pretty well, but I was thinking about the other girls I wanted to date and was trying to figure out how to do it. Should I say something to Julie or just do what I want? I'm afraid that if I let her go I'll be very threatened.

THERAPIST: Do you feel threatened when you end a relationship with someone?

PATIENT: I won't have a woman. But I don't think that she and I will ever marry. There are too many things that we don't get along about. She wanted to stay in New Mexico; I wanted to come back and work. I like obstacles to conquer; she likes vacations. I want someone more like me, kind of serious. I get this feeling when I'm pretty well satisfied. What bothers me is that I can't really look at what I want in a girl until I have won her. But that happened with Patricia. Then when she left me, which I at first encouraged, I really wanted her back. Now I feel bad about Julie because I feel I'm using her.

THERAPIST: The last time we met you said that you were using her to work out your neurosis.

PATIENT: I said that? I strain to get her to like me but when she does, I don't like her. Partly it's because she changes when she gets turned on. She starts to act silly. That's neurotic.

THERAPIST: Your train of thought last time was, ''She parades a lot of guys in front of me. I use her to work out my neurotic problems.'' In other words, you are more concerned with defeating the other guys than with winning her.

PATIENT: Yeah. That's what I meant by neurotic. When I do win her it's a hollow victory. I need to keep Julie around to have one person who thinks I'm the greatest guy so I can defeat all those other guys. I don't feel that I want to marry her. I want her there, but I want to date other girls at the same time. That scares me. I don't think I can pull that off. We do get along well sexually and I don't want to give that up. I may have to give that up if I date other women now.

You know, we don't even have it that great sexually. It's just that I'm the first guy she could have sex with. It makes me feel kind of special, but it's kind of sick, too. It's like I'm being the good guy who's helping her.

THERAPIST: You feel that you have some special powers as a man because she couldn't have sex with other men.

PATIENT: Oh, yeah. But, I don't like to be attracted to her for that reason. I think that is the main reason, though. At least, I can't tell how much it's that and how much I like Julie for herself. One reason I want to date other girls is to get some perspective.

THERAPIST: I wonder why there is so much similarity between Patricia and Julie and the kind of relationship you had with both of them.

PATIENT: The similarity is in me. They make me feel they need the special qualities I have. [*Pauses*] I can't give up Julie until I understand what my feelings are about.

THERAPIST: Who said that you have to give up Julie?

PATIENT: I don't have to, but I fear approaching other girls either for mysterious reasons or because I will lose Julie. I have a hard time thinking about this topic. I think I have some kind of misconception about what Julie likes in me. When a girl starts to like me I start showing her a lot of attention and concern. Then I think that's what she likes, but the attention is forced, so it becomes a burden. It drains too much energy. But, I'm afraid I'll be threatened if I get involved with someone who doesn't demand this because then I'd feel she doesn't need me.

THERAPIST: Why is it so important for you to feel that a woman needs you?

PATIENT: Mother needed Dad to take care of her. She had those physical problems. She was delicate. Now I feel he needed her more than she needed him. He tried to make me feel the same way toward her. He would say things like, "Mother doesn't feel well. Treat her gently." It's a combination of feeling castrated and thinking that's how love is.

THERAPIST: Castrated? How's that?

PATIENT: My masculinity is threatened pretty easily. It's like sex wasn't for me, combined with this morbid family I have. Like I have to give up things for sex so by the time I get it I don't like it any more. I really feel bad if I'm just enjoying sex. It's like from a distance I visualize myself enjoying it, but when I really have sex I focus so much attention on the girl's wants and needs that I don't get any enjoyment.

THERAPIST: And you see that as related to the way you were supposed to treat Mother.

PATIENT: Yes. Also I feel in order to keep the girl and my masculinity I have to do it this way but then I don't enjoy it. Julie's feelings about sex are at least as screwed up as mine, so I have to treat her delicately and sacrifice for her.

THERAPIST: No wonder you were so worried about losing Julie. Losing her equals losing your masculinity.

PATIENT: Yeah, but it's not as strong as it used to be because I'm seeing some other girls turned on by me. In fact, Julie says all her friends are.

As the patient was leaving he said, "Hey, how much longer will you be here?" I suggested that he bring that up at our next session when we had time to talk about it. He responded, "Okay. I've been thinking about that for a few weeks."

DISCUSSION

Paul began the session by giving an example of his taking over the therapeutic function. He made use of his observing ego and his identification with the therapy process. In his example he recognized his anxiety, figured out what was causing it, and then dealt with it appropriately. When the patient is able to do the therapeutic work himself, he is ready to terminate.

Frequently dreams presented during termination phase sessions are brief and partially self analyzed, like Paul's in this session. Paul was able to see on his own that his boss in this dream represented his father. He was also able to see the precipitant for the dream in his current work situation. He needed help, however, to understand the intrapsychic aspects and the relationship of the dream to therapy. A direct quotation in a dream almost always represents the superego. My intervention, "And like you talking to yourself now," helped Paul see that he was chastising himself. My later comment, "I wonder if the dream is related to therapy, too?" was all that was needed for Paul to have several associations to missed sessions. Earlier in therapy Paul could not have made that kind of connection without a great deal of help from me.

Paul made several references during this session to leaving or losing Julie. I thought that those were also references to thoughts of ending therapy and losing me. He had still not yet, however, made any direct reference to termination. I gently tried to open up that area by asking him if he was threatened whenever he left someone. It was not until the hour was over, though, that he finally admitted that he had been thinking about our ending for a few weeks.

Awareness of termination usually takes place in four steps. First the therapist realizes that termination is in sight, then the patient mentions termination, a termination date is set, and finally the termination work is consciously undertaken. Paul has reached step two.

SESSION 39, APRIL 16   **"I FEEL STRONG NOW BUT . . ."**

PATIENT: I had lunch with one of your psychology graduate students, Joyce. I was surprised at how comfortably I was able to do that. She is really attractive. In the past I would have been too anxious to have lunch with a woman who has a relationship with you. How much longer will you be here?

THERAPIST: Until the end of June.

PATIENT: I have to do interviewing in Wyoming for the next two weeks, so our time together is shortened even more. I have mixed feelings about missing those next two sessions. I feel pretty good about handling things on my own, but I'm also going to miss therapy. Where are you going when you leave here?

THERAPIST: I will be entering the Air Force.

PATIENT: I wonder how I will feel about your leaving. I don't think it will bother me, but I wonder if I'll want more therapy. I feel good and I don't think so, but maybe the good feelings are false.

THERAPIST: Because of my leaving the clinic at the end of June, we don't have the choice of continuing beyond then. We have approximately two months left. What are your thoughts about the timing of our ending?

PATIENT: I feel pretty good, but I don't think I have solved all of my problems yet.

THERAPIST: I don't think you have either, but treatment can come to an end before everything is worked out. Our work together is ready to end when you have the tools to work on your problems on your own.

PATIENT: That makes sense, but I think I secretly had the hope that I wouldn't have any problems after therapy was over.

THERAPIST: You, like everyone else, will run into problems for the rest of your life. But you can realistically hope to be able to master most of the problems as they occur. I think that the main job that we have left is to say goodbye to each other.

PATIENT: I'm just beginning to realize that saying good-bye might be the hardest part of therapy. I had the fantasy that I was going to work through my problems in the sense of a great catharsis, like in the movies.

THERAPIST: Working through equals what we have been doing for the past several months.

PATIENT: You mean dealing with my problems with competition in several different ways. I guess I'm just a little afraid. I feel strong now, but I may run into some blocks after therapy stops. If things don't work out I can get more therapy later. One problem that I still haven't worked out comes to mind: I feel about Julie the way I did a year ago. I like her, but I want to date other girls, but if I do she will be justified in dating other guys.

THERAPIST: And what's so bad about that?

PATIENT: [Laughing] I don't want to take her for granted, but I don't want to start liking her because she likes someone else. I want to like a girl in isolation. When Julie was in love with someone else, I thought I was madly in love with her.

THERAPIST: Madly in love with her or neurotically in love with her?

PATIENT: Yeah. Madly, neurotically. I picked a good word. I still don't quite know what it would mean to love somebody. I have some ink-lings, though. It would mean to be turned on sexually, to have respect for the other person. But, why am I worrying about it? Sometimes I feel guilty, like I don't have the right kind of feelings. Julie makes me feel that way. Something is missing but maybe I should settle for what I have. It's pretty comfortable. I've been going with her for over a year and it hasn't developed into the full-blown thing, so maybe I should throw it off.

THERAPIST: One thing that seems to be missing from your definition of loving somebody is your caring as much about her feelings as you do for your own.

PATIENT: I do feel some of that, but I fight it. I don't want that responsibility. I started to feel that last summer, and then she slept with Larry. I resent that. It fucked me up for a long time. I wonder if I'm just trying to get back at her. I sometimes wonder if I'm keeping her around to punish her.

THERAPIST: You seem to be questioning whether or not to end the relationship with Julie.

PATIENT: I am. I think I can feel more love than I do but sometimes I say, "This is good enough. I'll get my head straightened out and she'll grow up." One of her friends is pregnant. I wondered what I would feel if she were pregnant. I decided I wouldn't want to marry her. I'd want her to get an abortion. I'd resent having to spend the money and effort and concern.

THERAPIST: Are you using contraceptives?

PATIENT: Not always. We should. I think her pregnancy would put too much strain on the relationship. I already think love with Julie is too much work. About one out of eight times both of us want sex at the same time. Then we really pull it off well. Often she stops before we have intercourse. I'll be all excited and somehow she gets turned off and goes to sleep. Then I get angry. I complained and she said, "What can I do about it?"

THERAPIST: You are talking about possibly ending your relationship with Julie, just as you and I were talking about ending our relationship.

PATIENT: I told her to see a psychiatrist. The night before we went to New Mexico we had trouble with sex. I told her to sleep on the couch. She did, but then I couldn't sleep. Finally I made her talk about it. For about fifteen minutes she said she couldn't tell me. Finally she said the only thing that really turns her on is thinking about a guy eating her out and that she thinks that's wrong. I told her that I have fantasies that most people would think are much worse. She liked that. Sometimes I have to talk to her about her problems for eighteen hours before we finally have intercourse. It's too much work. There was a time when I would have had to work that hard and really take care of her to justify having sex. But now I think I could have a relationship with a woman who didn't make me go through all that.

End of session.

Addendum to session 39: A few hours later the patient telephoned me. The following conversation took place.

PATIENT: I meant to tell you during the session that I have been tired a lot recently. I wonder if it's emotional. Could it be depression or that I'm using up a lot of energy denying something?

THERAPIST: Those are possibilities. Do you think they fit?

PATIENT: No. I think I have mono. I'm going to Student Health tomorrow.

THERAPIST: We are going to miss the next two sessions. If you want an appointment before you leave, I'll be glad to see you.

PATIENT: Thanks. I'll go to Student Health first and see what they have to say. If they don't find anyting physical I'll call you.

THERAPIST: I wonder if your calling now is related to what we did talk about in the session this morning.

PATIENT: As soon as you said that I thought about our missing the next two sessions and our ending in a few months. I guess I did just want to touch base with you before I left town. I'll see you in a few weeks.

End of telephone conversation.

DISCUSSION

Paul was aware that his ability to have lunch comfortably with a woman student of mine was a marked change for him. In the past he would have perceived that as competing with me for a woman which would have caused him a great deal of anxiety.

Paul again asked me how much longer I would be available. He then announced that he would be away for two weeks. This is the first time that he had announced an up-coming absence on his part at the beginning of the session instead of at the end. He was then able to react to our terminating until he side-tracked the issue by talking about problems with Julie. My attempts to relate his thoughts about ending the relationship with Julie to our terminating were not very successful.

Paul shared some of his ambivalent feelings about our ending. He also shared some of his magical fantasies about what therapy would provide for him. I have found that many patients withhold their secret hopes of magical, utopian cures until the termination phase. Many patients wait for that "great catharsis like in the movies," but Paul, like most patients, was also able to see what therapy really had done and was able to do.

I tried to help Paul distinguish between therapy goals and life goals. His life goal may be to solve all of his problems. The therapy goal, however, can only be to provide him with the tools with which to work on those problems on his own.

The telephone call from Paul following the session represented a temporary developmental regression. Paul had attained a higher level of object constancy. However, in the face of a separation from April sixteenth to May seventh, to be followed at the end of June by a permanent separation, Paul regressed. He was starting the process of trying to make me into a memory. Hearing my voice again helped in that process. Probably his asking me where I was going after I left the Clinic was also in the service of starting to make me into a memory.

SESSION 40, MAY 7   **"JULIE IS LEAVING, TOO"**

Paul called me on May 6th to check the time of our appointment for the following day. He came to the May 7 appointment in spite of a spring flood which stopped most of the traffic on the highway which he took into Denver.

PATIENT: I got a little ticked off when I talked to you yesterday on the phone. I felt like being friendly and you seemed overly businesslike. I don't know why I felt you should be friendly [pause]. I was feeling some really warm, positive feelings toward you and I felt that you weren't accepting them. What do you think?

THERAPIST: I'm wondering why those feelings and reactions are coming out now?

PATIENT: I thought that myself. I wondered it it's related to our ending. But I'm starting to get ticked off at everyone who doesn't react to my overtures. I guess I'm still not secure enough. I may feel some anger at you for quitting, but surprisingly I haven't thought that much about our quitting; at least I haven't worried about it much. Julie is leaving this summer, too. She is going to Africa for a year. Maybe I'm terrified at everyone leaving me.

THERAPIST: Maybe?

PATIENT: It does bother me. She's going with the Peace Corps. The fact that she is leaving for a reason makes me feel better about it. I wanted to talk about something else.

Usually I feel a lot better. I don't get depressed any more but occasionally I still get anxious. I feel there is some little thing that I haven't found. I thought to myself, "I'll have Dr. Kapelovitz hypnotize me and find out what it is." At a Reserve meeting a social worker talked about homosexual panic. I thought, "That's it!" But, the last few days I've been working well and I feel okay and things have been fine with Julie. When things aren't going well I feel I have to change something. When things are going well, I feel I'm not quite where I want to be, but I can patiently work things out. But, other times I get that mysterious feeling that there was one little traumatic event which is keeping me from really enjoying things. I'm not depressed and anxious all the time like I was last fall. The one little thing is that I can't always let myself do what I want to do.

THERAPIST: That's not one little thing. That's a big part of your psychic structure.

PATIENT: Yeah. Like it's dangerous to do some things. That makes more sense. That is why I became so attached to Patricia and Julie. They gave me the feeling that it was all right to do what I wanted to with them. They would let me screw them. It scares me, but in some ways I'm a little bit happy that Julie is leaving. The day after Julie told me about the Peace Corps, I got a date with Mary. I told Julie, but I was really nervous telling her. I said, "I still like you but you're leaving." We both got upset, but it's funny—it really turned her on. She says she feels better around me now that she doesn't think she will hurt me. If I have a friend who makes me feel I'll hurt him if I do what I want, I get mad at him.

THERAPIST: Your parents used to make you feel that way, too.

PATIENT: Yeah. I told you about my mother, but Dad does it even more. Like now he surprises me. He really gets excited when I come to see him. Julie and I went to see him recently. Then after two days we went to Puerto Rico. Dad really made me feel I shouldn't leave him. It's funny. When Julie and I are both feeling good I really like her. When she got accepted by the Peace Corps she felt good about herself. She became less inhibited and our sex life really got good. When I'm feeling bad I think she is troubled by some demon, like I feel that I am.

THERAPIST: The only demon that we have found is your problem with competition and the related thing that you mentioned today, feeling that it is dangerous to do things that you will enjoy.

PATIENT: Yeah. My projecting a demon on to her allows me to compete with her demon, who is causing her to do things.

THERAPIST: Are demons men or women?

PATIENT: [*Laughing*] They are always masculine, at least for me. There's a real bitch of a secretary in our office. I was complaining to her that women often get cold. She said that men push women, but since Julie has felt good she's wanted sex so much that I had to quit after three days because I hurt.

THERAPIST: We never resolved what you mentioned at the beginning about my not being friendly on the phone.

PATIENT: I just wanted to tell you how I felt. Tell me again, when are you leaving?

THERAPIST: The end of June.

PATIENT: Are you going to be some place where I could reach you if I ever have to after therapy is over?

THERAPIST: Yes, I will, but your thought about possibly wanting to reach me after therapy is something that we should look at further. I will be stationed in Denver.

PATIENT: You really get some good deals.

DISCUSSION

Paul was talking about termination this session, but for the most part once removed. It was easier for him to talk about Julie leaving than to talk with me about our relationship ending. He stated, "The fact that she is leaving for a reason makes me feel better about it." He had already established that I was leaving the Psychiatry clinic for a reason. He takes some comfort in convincing himself that neither Julie nor I am leaving because of him.

Paul stated that his relationship with Julie is very good right now, but that he was disappointed when I didn't respond as he wanted to his overture of friendship on the phone. The desire to form a friendship with the therapist during the termination phase serves a number of defensive functions for the patient. The hidden wish is, "If Dr. Kapelovitz and I become friends, we won't have to end our relationship." Being friendly also covers up all the negative feelings the patient has for the therapist. Another aspect of the friendliness is that the therapist does become less of a transference object and more of a real object during the termination phase. To some extent I have fostered that change by directly answering many of the questions that he asks about me. In response to his questions I told him that I would be going into the Air Force and that I would be stationed in Denver.

Early in the session Paul talked about the positive feelings he was experiencing toward me. A little later in the session he wondered if his anxiety is "homesexual panic." Loewald[1] has pointed out the emergence in male patients of passive homosexual fantasies in regard to their male analyst during the termination phase. The pending loss of the male therapist resurrects the passive longings that the male patient had as a child for his father. During much of this therapy the patient and I worked on his Oedipal problems and their derivatives. I am now referring to what is known as the negative Oedipus. In the positive Oedipus the little boy wants his mother and wants to be rid of his father. There is also a negative Oedipus, however, in which the little boy wants his father's love. Paul also has some sense of this in his current life situation, as evidenced by his reporting that his father wanted him to continue visiting rather than going off with Julie. Related material in the hour is his wish for me to hypnotize him. Being hypnotized by another person involves a passive relinquishment of control to that other person. I think that the hypnosis wish was also related to the wish for some magic from the therapist that often comes to the foreground during the termination phase.

If this had been psychoanalysis, where we had more time, or even if the negative Oedipal material had appeared earlier in the therapy, I probably would have interpreted it to the patient and tried to work it through with him. With only four sessions left, however, I decided to focus on the areas that are of greater conflict for him and to help him experience termination.

The patient has trouble dealing with termination, not only with me but also with Julie. We had evidence earlier in the therapy of his difficulty dealing with loss in that he never really mourned the death of his mother. Instead of dealing with Julie's leaving, he replaces her with Mary before she even leaves. To some extent he is also denying my leaving by asking if I will be available after the end of therapy. Once again Paul asked me when I was leaving, even though I had told him several times before. He is still avoiding setting a termination date. Since we are rapidly approaching the time when we are going to have to terminate, I will initiate discussion about a termination date next session if Paul does not bring it up himself.

REFERENCE

1. Loewald HW: Comments on some instinctual manifestations of superego formation. Ann Psychoanal 1:104–116, 1973.

Chapter 9
Saying Good-Bye

**A TERMINATION DATE IS SET AND A
SUCCESS IS REPORTED**

A few days after our last session Paul called me but I was out of my office. He left a message with my secretary that he had to be out of town on May 14 and 21 but that he would be in for his appointment on May 28. That meant an even greater condensation of the termination process than I had anticipated.

PATIENT: When are you leaving?

THERAPIST: It is curious that you are having so much trouble remembering that. This is at least the third time you have asked in the last two months. Actually you have known since you asked last summer.

PATIENT: I don't want to remember. It's crazy, but I really don't remember. When is it?

THERAPIST: The end of June.

PATIENT: Will June 30 be our last session?

THERAPIST: That is one possibility. What thoughts do you have about how we should decide when the last session will be?

PATIENT: My first reaction is to make it the latest possible date. My next reaction is to leave a little before that. If we go to the last possible time, it makes it more clear that you are leaving me. If we stop a little before that, it's more of a mutual decision. If we stop a week before we have to, there will still be that week that you will be working in your office. If I have some reaction to our stopping after it's over that I don't realize before it happens, I would still be able to call you.

THERAPIST: The last Monday in June is the twenty-fifth.

PATIENT: Let's agree to June 18 as the last session. Is that all right with you?

THERAPIST: That sounds reasonable to me. Having our last session on the eighteenth means that we will have three more meetings after this one.

PATIENT: Isn't that something! Suddenly I'm just flooded with feelings that seem to contradict each other. I'm grateful for all that you have done for me, but at the same time pissed off at you for forcing us to end. I feel almost euphoric about the idea of being on my own, being a man at last, but at the same time I'm feeling very sad. It's going to be kind of lonely when I don't see you any more, and if I get anxious again I'll have to deal with it myself. I do want to tell you about all that has happened since we last met. Julie and I are getting along really well. My job is going well, too. The man I'm working for wants me to work full-time this summer at six hundred dollars a month. That means that I could have about two thousand dollars in the bank by this fall, so that I could take courses but not have to work unless I really find something I like. I may make a grant proposal myself so that I can do my own research for my specialty paper. Another consideration is to stop with an M.S. degree, but I'm sure I'll go for the Ph.D. I really don't like some aspects of the reading and research. I often feel that what people come up with isn't worth the effort. Like this work that I'm doing now. We really haven't found anything exciting regarding reactions to weather modification. I would junk the whole project but my boss thinks he has to report some results. I feel a lot better because I finished that one paper. Oh, the big news. I didn't tell you why I missed the last two sessions. I presented my paper on sexuality to the Rocky Mountain Sociology Association Meeting in Arizona.

THERAPIST: Congratulations. You hadn't told me that you were planning to present a paper.

PATIENT: I was frightened because I had never presented at a meeting before. I don't think I purposely didn't tell you; well, yes, I did. I was afraid that you would say, "If you are healthy enough to present a paper, you're ready to stop therapy right now." It's funny. I had been denying the importance of our relationship until the time to stop approached. The question and answer period after my paper went very well, too. I think I'll be able to do it much more easily the next time. I told Julie that a lot of my work fears have disappeared. Presenting some work that I had done to a group of professionals is about the most frightening thing that I could do with regard to work. Now I feel I can do the work for a Ph.D. and be successful. But, now I'm not even sure that I want to. The important thing, though, is that at least now it's a free decision. I also feel I want to try LSD for a second time. This is related because I used to not want drugs because I thought they were my attempt at running away. But now in work and sex and drugs I feel like I have the ability to choose. If I want drugs for the experience, that's fine. I just don't have conflicts about those areas any more. Before I would wonder, "What do those people think of me now that I'm high or now that I'm doing this or that?" I couldn't enjoy an experience. I was too concerned about the evaluation from others. That is the one conflictual area still remaining—the fear of a negative evaluation. It's not as strong as it used to be.

THERAPIST: The best evidence that fear has lessened is that you were able to present your paper.

PATIENT: I want acceptance by the Establishment as much as I do by the counterculture group. I used to wonder if I was just rebelling against my father, but as I get to know him better I realize that he has some need not to be seen as pure Establishment, either. I used to think Establishment equals good and that my enjoying myself equals bad. Now I think of them as two reference groups and I want the best from both. That's too abstract. If I go too far in either direction I'll be hurting myself. If I become a radical because I think that's cool, I'll be missing out on accomplishments; if I become a hard-working, straight-line sociologist, I'll be missing out on a lot of fun.

The question is, what am I really like? or, am I really like anything yet? I haven't completely solved that, but I do have a much stronger sense of my identity than I used to have. I got pretty excited when I got that paper done. But then I had to go do interviewing again. Gathering more data wasn't much fun. I think now that my concern comes down to, "Can I be as good a researcher or whatever as I want to be?" Three more sessions. I'll be going to summer camp the end of the month, so I'll be leaving Denver about the same time you leave for the Air Force.

THERAPIST: It sounds like you're still struggling with who is leaving whom.

PATIENT: I'd prefer to leave you; but I think it's a combination of being ready to stop and our having to stop.

THERAPIST: I think that's true. You seem to have solved a lot of your conflicts and to have developed the tools to work on the rest. I'm reminded of two symptoms that you mentioned early in therapy that I never heard about again: You said that you had difficulty urinating in public and that you would compulsively list words in alphabetical order.

PATIENT: Those symptoms dropped out months ago. I think the problem with urinating in public stopped when I understood my problems with competition with men and my fear of castration. Then I could pull my penis out to urinate in public without being afraid it would be smaller than some other guy's or afraid it was going to be chopped off. I don't know about the thing with words. I used to do that a lot when I was anxious. It's probably just that as therapy went on, I grew less and less anxious.

DISCUSSION

Once again Paul was unable to remember the date that I would be leaving. When I pointed out how long he had actually known about the date of my departure and his pattern of forgetting it, he was able to see that he was resisting remembering. Within the limitations available to us, I tried to mutually set a termination date with the patient. Paul was very aware of his desire to keep therapy going as long as possible, but surprisingly he was also aware of the advantages of stopping before external circumstances forced termination upon us.

Once the termination date was set, Paul became aware of his multiple feelings about our ending and expressed them as articulately as any patient that I have ever treated. He expressed his appreciation, but also told me about some of his resentment. He described his good, euphoric feeling of freedom, but also his sadness, anger, anxiety, and fear of loneliness.

Paul spent much of the rest of the hour reporting on his life and activities since our last session. This really amounted to an assessment on his part of what was going well in his life and what still needed work. Paul's supervisor was happy enough with his performance to offer him a full-time summer job. Paul even thought of applying for a grant of his own. He was feeling much more freedom of choice about his actions. The big thing, of course, was his presenting a paper at a professional meeting. Paul recognized that the paper signified his mastery over many of his work fears. It was of interest that he withheld telling me about his plans to present that paper out of fear that I would insist on an immediate termination. I think he was feeling some guilt about the gratification he was experiencing in therapy, while at the same time he was not sure he was sick enough to justify further therapy.

He listed three areas in which he felt that he needed more work: He still was concerned about the opinions of others, indicating that he had some further work to do in terms of developing an inner structure for self-evaluation. He discussed some of his continuing superego problems, but they were much less severe than in the past. He gave evidence of a great deal of moderation in his life and greater ability to do what he wanted. The third area in which he felt he needed more work was in solidifying his identity. He had come a long way in this area, but I agree that in the Eriksonian sense of identity he would probably have to do more after therapy terminated. He was sounding much more like an adult and much less like an adolescent. In presenting his paper at the professional conference, he was a grown man interacting with colleagues rather than a bright little boy presenting to adults.

Paul stated, "It's funny. I had been denying the importance of our relationship until the time to stop approached." This is a common phenomenon. Many patients are not conscious of what the therapy situation and the therapist mean to them until the termination phase. Although most patients have occasionally thought of what it would be like when therapy was over, they frequently first experience the impact of that idea on the day that the termination date is set. As I discussed in the essay on termination, many patients suffer a recurrence of their symptoms in the early phase of termination. So often this is interpreted as the patient saying, "See, I'm still sick. I can't terminate." That may be one part of the meaning, but dynamically I think it involves the patient suddenly feeling that he is once again without the help of the therapist. He then momentarily returns to the state of development prior to his therapy. Paul does experience some anxiety, but does not have a reappearance of his old symptoms. Hopefully he has metabolized and integrated the changes sufficiently so that they are now a firm part of his new self-representation.

Near the end of the session I reminded Paul of two of his early symptoms, difficulty urinating in the presence of other men and listing many forms of the same word in alphabetical order. Each of these symptoms had only been mentioned once by the patient and never brought up again. It turned out that both of these symptoms disappeared in the course of therapy, even though no direct work was done with either one of them. Frequently in psychotherapy symptoms are eliminated by dealing with the underlying causes rather than directly with the symptom.

SESSION 42, JUNE 4   **MOURNING HIS MOTHER'S DEATH**

PATIENT: I took LSD again. Julie and I were in the mountains. I got too anxious to enjoy it. I stay high so damn long and I just wanted to stop. I'd been on it for about sixteen hours before I could fall asleep. I couldn't turn off either the inside stimulation, my thinking, or the outside stimulation. Under LSD everything seemed flat, paper-thin. It made me feel that I lacked a strong self which could shut out the stimulation and allow me to sleep.

THERAPIST: Talking about a self seems related to the reference groups you mentioned last session.

PATIENT: Like they are security.

THERAPIST: Yes. And they help you to define self.

PATIENT: Yes, I see. But I don't want to define myself in terms of other people. But to do it myself I need more security. When I do what I feel I should be doing, I feel secure.

THERAPIST: It is curious that the question of security is coming up today.

PATIENT: I'm not sure why it is. If I ever take LSD again I want someone around who can take care of me.

THERAPIST: Someone?

PATIENT: Yes—you. You won't be around much longer. LSD screws up a person's ego. To carry out the simplest plan I had to really work. I could drive but my visual acuity was poor. I had a helpless feeling. I felt very much under the control of the environment. That was upsetting. Some people like that but I like to be more in control myself. Somehow it's related to enjoyment. Others who lose control enjoy it; I don't. I want to be active. I don't want to be a passive-type person any more.

THERAPIST: Does something interfere with your being as active as you want to be?

PATIENT: Yes, but not as much as it used to. I am able to do almost as much work as I want to do now. This summer I'll earn and save some money. I'd like to finish my Ph.D. soon so I can get out and start a job; but when I start asserting myself, I still experience some anxiety.

THERAPIST: How does the success at being active, like presenting that paper, fit into all this?

PATIENT: A success at being active like that makes me feel more like working and less like being passive. I can go to work and have much less anxiety. I feel like I'm in a pretty good place in life because I see a lot of possibilities of being active. Next fall I'll do my specialty paper on the sex stuff. I got some requests for my paper yesterday. One problem with being active is that to do my work I have to be a little callous. I haven't been giving Julie as much attention as she would like. I feel a bit selfish about that. My friend, Jack, said yesterday that one way to look at personal problems is to see what part of you you are rejecting. For him it's sex. He thought I didn't accept that I'm competent, intelligent, and worthwhile. That was certainly true of me in sex and work and everything. It made a lot of sense to me.

THERAPIST: What service does not accepting your competence perform for you?

PATIENT: I think that people will like me better if I'm not too competent. My parents and brother reinforce that.

THERAPIST: How so?

PATIENT: Your asking irritates me. My father needed me to be a kind of fuck-up.

THERAPIST: You have rarely expressed your irritation with me. I wonder why it comes up now?

PATIENT: I hadn't realized it until you asked the question. But I think

I'm really irritated with you because we are stopping soon. I thought I was angry because I thought you already knew the answer to your question.

THERAPIST: I think both reasons are true. You did get angry when I interfered with your trying to blame your parents and brother for the internal problems that prevent you from being as competent as you could be. You are also having a lot of feelings about our ending. I think that the real issue at hand now is our ending.

PATIENT: I agree, but I don't want to talk about that now. I want to talk about why I think people will like me better if I'm imcompetent. I've always felt comfortable as a clown. I'm still not comfortable with the idea of myself having substance as a well-adjusted, competent person. Like at the office. I often act that "don't care screw-off" but lately while working with the sociologist it's been different because I've really been producing. But even then I sometimes play the little kid, the clown.

THERAPIST: You think that pretending that you are still little is safer.

PATIENT: I feel that it is. That way I can argue with someone and pretend I'm not really concerned, or if I screw up I haven't really lost anything because I pretended it didn't mean anything to me.

THERAPIST: We have two more sessions after this one.

PATIENT: Yeah. I've been complaining some today but I've really been feeling pretty good. I don't think I'll take LSD any more. It doesn't hurt me, but it doesn't provide anything new either. It just precipitates things that are already there.

THERAPIST: You are finding it so hard to talk about our ending. I wonder if it reminds you of other relationships that have ended?

PATIENT: [Starting to sob] My mother [long pause while he continues crying] I've never really dealt with my mother's death. I went to her funeral, but I didn't really grieve. I'm bawling like a little kid now. I've been telling you all through therapy how she was cold and selfish and didn't understand me, but really she loved me and was proud of me.

THERAPIST: Yes, if anything she loved you too well. She had a conflict about letting go of you so that you could go on your own and become independent.

PATIENT: That's true, like when I wanted to go to Aspen and when I decided to go to graduate school. A lot of times I feel that Dad is in between me and Mom.

THERAPIST: I think that one of the reasons that you had to see your mother as cold and not caring about you was to avoid competing with your father.

PATIENT: Yeah. If you had told me that at the beginning of therapy I wouldn't have known what you were talking about, but now it's perfectly clear.

THERAPIST: The other reason, since you've been in therapy, that you've wanted to see her as cold and not caring is to avoid admitting to yourself how much you miss her.

PATIENT: [*Crying again*] Mom had her faults and I was never as close to her as I wish I had been, but I did love her a lot and I miss her now.

THERAPIST: We do have to stop now.

PATIENT: Okay. I'll see you next week.

I continued this session ten minutes beyond the normal stopping time. I probably would have continued it even longer if I had not had another patient scheduled.

DISCUSSION

There was marked resistance throughout most of this session. I think that even Paul's taking of LSD was in the service of having something to talk about besides the feeling of loss that he was experiencing. He described trying out some of his new-found strengths and bemoaned some of his lingering problems. Certainly that is part of the termination process. He also made a number of comments which I was able to relate to our ending. Each time, however, he would deal with them briefly, only to become defensive once again.

It finally occurred to me that an extremely important relationship of his had ended before therapy started. He had never dealt with that loss, either. We had talked about his mother's death early in the therapy, but only superficially. There had been almost a complete absence of mourning his mother's death. When I said, "You are finding it so hard to talk about our ending. I wonder if it reminds you of other relationships that have ended?" the floodgates opened. In a very short time Paul did a great deal of work. Not only was the mourning process initiated, but Paul was able to see how he had defensively avoided feelings of warmth and closeness for his mother to avoid competition with his father.

For the most part, sessions should begin and end at the scheduled time. There are times, however, when material demands flexibility. As I was making the intervention about the ending of other relationships, I made the decision to extend the session if the intervention had the effect that I expected.

SESSION 43, JUNE 11   ONE MORE WEEK

PATIENT: Julie left since I last saw you. She and I didn't get along well the last two days. I was irritable about her leaving. As soon as she left I felt calm, but then I missed her. I called her the next day. I have been a little sad but it hasn't been too bad. I can take a loss if it isn't a rejection.

THERAPIST: Your relationship with Julie is the longest you have ever had with a girl.

PATIENT: Yeah, the best, anyway, [*laughing*] believe it or not. I actually knew Patricia longer but I felt better with Julie, closer to her. Anyway, I didn't plan to talk about that today. One funny thing, though: I didn't want sex with her the last few days and she wanted it. I had started looking at other girls already. I wanted to start dealing with her being away for a year.

THERAPIST: Do you usually get irritated with a person when the relationship is ending?

PATIENT: Usually I'm afraid to show the irritation. But I felt safe with Julie. Besides, she's coming back in a year.

THERAPIST: The reason I ask is that you also became irritated with me last week when I questioned one of your defenses.

PATIENT: Yes, I remember that. I was trying to blame my parents for all my problems, but you made me see that I had a lot of control over what happened to me. If I don't get the irritable feeling I get kind of a numb feeling. I think it's healthier to feel the irritation, but I wanted to talk to you about guilt today. I don't know if it's really guilt or just a concern about what other people think. I don't want to completely do away with guilt—that's not me. If I don't pay my bills I feel guilty and then I pay them. But, I'm attracted to a girlfriend of Julie's. I feel something like guilty about making sexual advances toward her. I'm afraid she will reject me, that Julie will find out. Oh, hell, I think it's just the old guilt I feel when I start to make sexual advances. During much of the therapy I felt freed from that, but since we decided to end it has come back a little. I think I'm only going to solve this by doing what I want to do in spite of the anxiety. I really don't want to get too involved with this girl so I feel it's wrong for me to have sex with her. This really bothers me. It's an adult part of me that I don't like.

THERAPIST: It sounds like a parent part of you.

PATIENT: Yeah, I guess it is. Realistically I know it's all right if both of us want sex and if I don't get her pregnant. But if I go too far the other way I'm afraid I'll become a psychopath.

THERAPIST: I don't think you could become a psychopath if you wanted to.

PATIENT: [*Smiling*] Right, but I tell my friend, Jack, who is very inhibited, that it's all right to have sex with anyone as long as you don't rape them.

THERAPIST: I think you were telling yourself, too.

PATIENT: [*Laughing*] I guess I couldn't be a psychopath. I have too strong a conscience in that area.

THERAPIST: What is your idea about how you got a conscience?

PATIENT: I'm afraid someone will leave me if I do wrong. Someone like my parents. Is that your idea of it?

THERAPIST: A conscience is a child's incorporation of what he thinks are his parents' moral standards. But as a child you saw your parents as much stricter, much more moralistic than they really were.

PATIENT: [*Eyes wet*] That really makes me feel grateful. You are saying it's all right for me to enjoy myself. My father never said anything like that to me. [The patient then began a theoretical comparison of Freud's theories and Taoism.]

THERAPIST: Why did you suddenly become so theoretical?

PATIENT: I'm not sure [Short pause].

THERAPIST: I thought you were becoming emotional and wanted to stop it.

PATIENT: Oh! That is it. I didn't want to cry. But it was a good feeling, too. [Once again there was a pause during which the patient seemed to be deep in thought. Normally I would have waited for him to speak. This time, however, because it was near the end of the hour and I wanted to directly focus on termination, I broke in.]

THERAPIST: After a little over a year we are ending next week.

PATIENT: I was thinking about that just now. I don't want to end, but I don't want to be dependent on you, either. I don't think I am too dependent on you. I feel much freer to leave now than I would have six or eight months ago. That reminds me–as painful as it was, our talk about my mother last time really helped, too. I thought about her several times during the week. I was able to love her more, but I also finally started to say good-bye to her. She meant a lot more to me than I had ever admitted.

DISCUSSION

The patient continued to deal with termination, but only indirectly. He began the hour saying that Julie had left, then went on to describe their last two days together. That was interesting, since he had only two more times, including this session, in which to see me. He also talked about being able to take a loss as long as it was not a rejection. I think this, too, referred to both his relationship with Julie and his relationship with me. At that point I thought of confronting him with his indirect way of dealing with our termination, but chose to go along with it instead. In retrospect, I think this was the correct decision. It allowed him to say things about our relationship that he could not have said directly.

Another point in the session at which I was tempted to intervene was when he mentioned that his feeling guilt about making sexual advances had returned. I would have said something such as, "A patient often has a return of symptoms as therapy is about to end. It may represent his unconscious way of telling the therapist that he does not want to terminate." Instead, I made an effort to consolidate the work we had done in previous sessions on his overly strict superego.

That led to the high point of the session, which was the interpretation about the etiology and development of his superego. An interpretation of this depth could be made in psychotherapy only because the ground work had been laid. Not only was it gradually built up to by a series of other interventions in the hour, but also, his superego problems had been dealt with at other levels during many of the previous 42 hours. He reacted to the interpretation with great emotion. I think that the crying reflected a combination of his gaining some freedom from his superego plus the loss of part of his childhood. There was both gratitude and sadness.

The goal with Paul was to transform his harsh, inhibiting childhood superego into an adult, reasonable guide to action. Had Paul indeed been a "psychopath" the goal throughout therapy would have been to build superego where none existed.

I ended the session with reminding him that we had only one more meeting. Paul responded by expressing his ambivalence about our ending. He also confirmed that the last session had initiated the previously defended-against mourning of his mother's death.

SESSION 44, JUNE 18   THE LAST HOUR

PATIENT: I don't know what to say. [*His eyes grow damp*] When I saw you I started thinking. [*Silence.*] I felt something personal rather than my feelings about ending therapy. I had forgotten about our relationship–that part of ending–until I saw you. The personal thing is bothering me. That surprises me. I started crying last night when I talked to Julie, too. I don't know what to do in situations like this.

THERAPIST: Maybe you won't miss *therapy*.

PATIENT: I think that's true. I feel I can do it on my own now. But I've never faced my feelings about leaving someone before. I feel good that I can, but I'm also embarrassed about my feeling of affection for you. I talked to a psychiatric nurse at a party last week. I told her that I didn't have trouble crying, that sometimes I cry when I'm happy. Maybe crying symbolically represents being pissed off. I really don't believe that, but I've heard that theory. The nurse was convinced of it. I think for me it just means that I let down enough barriers to feel something.

THERAPIST: At our very first meeting we talked about your trouble expressing feelings.

PATIENT: Yes, maybe I'm trying to push back to then. But I don't think so. I feel I can go it alone now but also know that I can see someone else if I have to.

THERAPIST: How would you make that decision?

PATIENT: I guess mostly by feeling it, or if I went into the old patterns of being unable to approach people or if I became unproductive in work again or if some crisis came up with Julie. Recently I thought Julie was pregnant. A rubber broke. I don't think it would have bothered me too much. I would not have let her get an abortion. I would have married her. In the past when I thought about that it really made me nervous. But I really felt I could handle it. I don't think I'll run into any problems getting my Ph.D., either. I feel pretty confident. But I did have that dip with that business last fall with Julie. Even with my doubts I think I will turn out pretty well.

THERAPIST: You have some doubts, but for the most part you seem quite confident about love and work.

PATIENT: Yes. There is something, though, that I'm going to talk about even though I have already decided to do it. I'm going to force myself into being more relaxed. I'm in a position now where everything is pretty good, but I'm still kind of jumpy. I have been doing some yoga and it really relaxes me. I'm drinking and smoking much less than I used to. You know, at one time I had some fears of being or becoming crazy. Like I had an empty feeling like Laing says that schizophrenics have.

THERAPIST: A schizophrenic could not have expressed the feeling you did at the beginning of this hour about our relationship.

PATIENT: [starts crying again] Yeah, I really don't have that kind of emptiness. But I often did shut off feelings. [There was a pause. The patient started sobbing and shaking.] I feel reluctant to talk. [There was another pause.] I've been zipping around avoiding talking about our ending and yet really don't know what to say.

THERAPIST: Who's leaving whom?

PATIENT: I don't know. If it were up to me I wouldn't quit for a while.

THERAPIST: What would you want to do with that time?

PATIENT: Just have it. I think the work thing I can easily handle now. There are still a few things with women I'd like to work out. Women seem less predictable than work. [There was another pause as the patient became so overwhelmed by his emotions that he was unable to talk.] Are you feeling at all emotional now?

THERAPIST: Sure.

PATIENT: It makes me feel good that you are, but I feel you aren't supposed to.

THERAPIST: I'm not supposed to? I wonder if that's some of your old strict conscience coming through.

PATIENT: That's funny because what I thought was, "My father isn't supposed to get emotional." You know, psychiatrists aren't supposed to have feelings.

THERAPIST: The truth is I thoroughly enjoyed knowing you, working with you, trying to understand you, and helping you to understand yourself.

PATIENT: Thank you. I think I knew that all along but I'm glad to hear you say it. It's like I told Julie. [Again there was a pause as the patient was overcome by his emotions.] I'm sorry I have to be so indirect about this but I have to now. [Short pause] She was jealous about my seeing you. She said, "Why can't you just talk to me?" I told her that there is no reason to be jealous, because my seeing you really leads to my having a closer relationship with her. I told her I like you because you never tell me what to do but you are not afraid, either, to tell me what you feel. What I'm really trying to say is I like you, you did a good job. You helped me a lot. I know there are a few minutes left but I'd like to leave now.

THERAPIST: All right. I think I understand.

We both stood up and shook hands. Paul touched my arm, said, "Thank you," and left.

DISCUSSION

This was an emotion-filled hour for both the patient and the therapist. Paul started the session by expressing his feelings about the ending of our personal relationship as opposed to just ending therapy. I tried to help him further express these feelings by saying, "You may not miss *therapy*." He correctly understood that statement to mean that the major work of therapy had been completed but that he would still miss our relationship.

The patient encouraged me to express my feelings by directly asking if I had any. Whenever I have presented this session in a psychotherapy conference for psychiatry residents they have expressed surprise that I immediately answered his question. Remaining silent or asking him to think about why he asked that question would have been counter-productive at this point in the last session. The goal here was to facilitate his becoming consciously aware of his feelings about our relationship ending. Letting him know that I had feelings about it, too, helped him to accept his own feelings.

One of the residents, in a psychotherapy conference in which this material was presented, asked me, "What would you have done if, nine sessions ago, when termination first came up, the patient had expressed the intention of stopping without dealing with termination?" It is highly unlikely that this patient would have done that because of the strength of our alliance at that point. If he had, however, I would have dealt with that just as I tried to deal with everything else during therapy. That is, I would have tried to understand it in terms of his psychodynamics. I would have confronted him with the fact that he had never, as he put it, "faced my feelings about leaving someone before." I would also have pointed out that it was a return to the pattern for which he had originally sought therapy, namely, his inability to bring his actions to successful completion. I am certain that this patient would have understood and decided to go through the terminal phase of therapy.

I think that he accurately assessed his growth during therapy when he said that he thought he could handle work easily now, but that there were still a few things that he would have to work out in terms of developing intimate relationships with women. I felt confident that during therapy he had developed the tools with which to do this on his own. The time to terminate therapy is not when the patient has solved all of his problems, but rather when he becomes capable of going on to solve them without more help.

Recalling that Paul and I had only 44 hours together underscores the intensity of the psychotherapy relationship. At the beginning of therapy nothing new could happen in the patient's life. Every person he met, including me, immediately became a transference object, a character playing a distorted role in a rerun of his childhood drama. Although Paul was 25 and a graduate student then, his self-image was still that of an inadequate, poorly equipped little boy. He had few choices and experienced sexual, social, and work inhibition. Every action was determined by his fear of competition, castration, belittlement, and rejection.

Gradually Paul was able to differentiate me from his childhood image of his father as a frightening giant who would hurt him if he asserted himself. Then he was able to differentiate other men, including his father, from that childhood image. As he worked through his problems with competition, including his competition with me, he became more productive in his work and more successful socially and sexually.

In short, Paul experienced changes in his id, ego, and superego and in their relationship to each other, as well as growth and development of his whole personality, his self-image, and his level of functioning. He became consciously aware of many of his drives, acting on some of them within the limits of his reality needs and sublimating others. Paul experienced less shame as his ego ideal became more realistic and less guilt as his superego grew less punitive. His ego seemed to be functioning more effectively as a mediator between the other structures and with external reality.

During the last session I had a very vivid recollection of the patient as he appeared during our first interview. I felt that he had grown during those 44 sessions from a stammering, inhibited little boy into a strong, productive young man closely in touch with his own feelings.

Glossary

Italicized words are defined elsewhere in this glossary.

Abreaction An emotional discharge related to the recall of a repressed experience (see *repression* under *Defense Mechanisms*). Abreaction is therapeutically useful both directly and by adding conviction to one's *insights*.

Acting-Out The *unconscious* expression of conflicts, attitudes, and feelings by actions instead of words. For example, in the course of psychotherapy, if a patient has a sexual affair, he may be acting out both his erotic *transference* feelings for the therapist as well as repressed *Oedipal* desires.

Adaptation Dealing with one's external environment by changing one's self and/or changing the environment and/or leaving the environment.

Affect The subjective feeling-tone associated with drives and their discharge or frustration. Sometimes used interchangeably with emotion or feeling.

Alliance That part of the relationship between patient and therapist which allows them to work together and allows therapy to take place in spite of frustration, pain, and disappointment. The patient's tasks in forming the alliance involve developing a trust in the therapist, investing emotional energy in the relationship with the therapist, and identifying with the therapist's way of doing therapy.

Ambivalence   The simultaneous existence of two opposing *affects*, drives, or ideas, e.g., experiencing love and hate toward the same person. Part of the ambivalence may be *unconscious*, e.g., one may be aware of love while repressing hate.

Anal Phase   See *Psychosexual Development*.

Analysand   A patient in *psychoanalysis*.

Analysis   A synonym for *psychoanalysis*.

Anamnesis   The developmental history of a patient and his illness.

Anxiety   A distressing *affect*, similar to fear, which is experienced both as apprehension and as physical manifestations such as sweating, rapid heart rate, rapid breathing, and diarrhea. Fear is an appropriate response to real external dangers. In contrast, anxiety is a response to an internal impulse or thought which is frightening because of the real or imagined consequences that would follow if the impulse or thought were acted upon. Signal anxiety is a small amount of anxiety which alerts an individual to initiate *unconscious defense mechanisms* to keep the unacceptable impulse or thought from becoming conscious.

Body Image   The conscious and *unconscious mental representation of one*'s body.

Borderline State   An unofficial diagnostic term for patients whose *ego* functioning is better than that of a *psychotic* person, but not so good as that of a *neurotic* person. A borderline individual is more likely to decompensate into a psychotic state under stress than would a neurotic or healthy individual. (See page 51 for a discussion of the four major diagnostic categories: psychoneurosis, character disorder, borderline, and psychosis.)

Castration   In psychiatry, castration refers to the fantasized loss or mutilation of the genitals. Castration anxiety may be precipitated by aggressive impulses toward a real or imagined competitor or by symbolic castrations such as the loss of a tooth or a humiliation.

Cathexis   The investment of emotional energy in an object or idea. For example, one could cathect or decathect another person by investing emotional energy in, or withdrawing it from, that person.

Character   The totality of the relatively stable personality traits and the usual mode of response of an individual.

Conflict   Intrapsychic conflict is the struggle between internal forces, e.g., between *id* impulses and *superego* prohibitions. Extrapsychic conflict is the struggle between the individual and the external world.

Constitution   A person's intrinsic psychological and physical endowment.

Counterphobia   The active seeking out of the feared experience in an attempt to master the anxiety associated with it.

Countertransference   The therapist's inappropriate conscious or *unconscious* repetition in the therapy situation of a relationship which was important in his childhood.

Contraindication   An indication, side-effect, or symptom which opposes a method of treatment otherwise advisable.

Cunnilingus   Oral sexual stimulation of the female genitals.

Defense Mechanisms   *Unconscious* intrapsychic processes carried out by the *ego* to prevent wishes and impulses from reaching conscious awareness or from being acted upon in order to avoid *anxiety* or guilt. Nine important defense mechanisms are defined below.
1. Denial: The *ego* avoids awareness of a painful aspect of external reality by replacing it with wish-fulfilling fantasies.
2. Displacement: An emotion or fantasy is transferred from its original object to a more acceptable substitute. For example, unconscious hatred of a parent may manifest as conscious hatred of a political system.
3. Identification: The patterning of an individual after the personality characteristics of another person. Imitation is a conscious form of identification.
4. Isolation: The repression of the *affect* associated with an impulse or idea.
5. Projection: Emotionally unacceptable wishes, ideas, and impulses in the individual are attributed to others.
6. Reaction formation: A painful idea, impulse, or feeling is replaced by its

opposite, leading to attitudes and behavior that may become a stable part of an individual's *character*.

7. Regression: The return to a behavior and mentation pattern derived from an earlier phase of development. Regression takes place in normal situations, such as sleep and play, as well as in severe physical illness and some psychological disorders.

8. Repression: The mechanism by which impulses, feelings, and ideas are either kept from ever becoming conscious or which, although once conscious, are made *unconscious*. Repression is not to be confused with suppression which is a voluntary withholding from communication of conscious impulses, feelings and ideas. Repression is the basic defense which is supported by all other defenses.

9. Sublimation: Instinctual drives which are not acceptable to the individual or society are converted into acceptable ideas and behavior, e.g., oral sadistic drives may be turned into humor and wit.

Delusion A false belief, not shared by an individual's subculture, which is maintained in spite of logic or evidence presented to the contrary

Denial See *Defense Mechanisms*.

Displacement See *Defense Mechanisms*.

Dreams (see pages 15–20) A normal regressive phenomenon occurring during sleep in which thought processes and *affects* are represented in predominantly visual form. Modern dream research has shown that everyone dreams several times during the course of a normal night's sleep but any or all of the dreams may be repressed. Freud introduced several terms to explain dreams:

1. Dream work: The process by which the *latent* dream is transformed into the *manifest* dream. (See pages 19–20.)
2. Latent content: The underlying wish-fulfilling meaning of the dream.
3. Manifest content: The dream as recalled by the dreamer.

Dream Work See *Dreams*.

Dyspareunia Pelvic area pain experienced by the female during sexual intercourse, usually emotional in origin.

Ego A theoretical construct describing a group of functions. The ego, along with the *id* and the *superego*, constitute the three major divisions of Freud's structural model of the psychic apparatus. The ego mediates between the demands of the id, the superego, and external reality. Successful compromises between these forces mediated by the ego lead to a reduction in intrapsychic conflict and to *adaptation*. Unsuccessful compromises lead to the formation of symptoms. Some of the ego functions which are needed for successful mediation are (1) defensive (see *Defense Mechanisms*), (2) adaptive, including the ability to reality test, that is, to correctly appraise external reality, (3) perceptual, (4) intellectual, (5) executive, and (6) organizing. In common usage, ego is synonymous with self-esteem.

Ego-Dystonic   Aspects of the individual which he considers undesirable, unacceptable, or inconsistent with his total personality.

Ego, Experiencing   See *Splitting of the Ego*.

Ego Ideal   That part of the *superego* which provides a model of what a person should aspire to be and do rather than what one should not be and do. A person usually experiences shame and a loss of self-esteem when he does not live up to his ego ideal, while he experiences guilt when he is or does something which is prohibited by the rest of the superego.

Ego, Observing   See *Splitting of the Ego*.

Ego-Syntonic   Aspects of the individual which he considers desirable, acceptable, and consistent with his total personality.

Empathy   A method of experiencing and understanding another person's *affect*, behavior, or experiences by temporarily identifying with him.

Etiology   In medicine, the cause of a disease or symptom.

Fantasy   Often referred to as daydreams, fantasies differ from other thought sequences by having a wish-fulfilling quality similar to dreams. In addition to gratifying wishes, fantasies may attempt to express and work out solutions to conflicts and help a person prepare for possible future actions or events.

Fellatio   Oral sexual stimulation of the penis.

Free Association   The spontaneous, uncensored flow of ideas which the patient in psychoanalysis is asked to verbalize no matter now illogical or embarrassing.

Genetic (See page 60.) In psychiatry, the infantile and childhood developmental experiences from which adult behavior, personality, and psychic structure are derived.

Genital Phase See *Psychosexual Development*.

Id A theoretical construct comprising that part of the psychic apparatus which contains the unconscious instinctual drives and wishes.

Identification See *Defense Mechanisms*.

Inhibition An unconscious defense against unacceptable drives or wishes which may restrict behavior, e.g., sexual or aggressive inhibition.

Insight Conscious understanding of what was previously *unconscious* or *preconscious*. Insight is more likely to bring about change if it is accompanied by emotional conviction in addition to intellectual understanding. See *Intellectualization*.

Intellectualization A *defense mechanism* which uses reasoning to psychologically bind instinctual drives and to resist achieving emotional *insight*.

Isolation See *Defense Mechanisms*.

Interpretation (See page 60.) An intervention by the therapist which leads to *insight*.

Intrapsychic That which takes place within the mind, e.g., a conflict between *id* impulses and *superego* prohibitions.

Latent Content See *Dreams*.

Latency Phase See *Psychosexual Development*.

Libido Sexual drive energy.

Manifest Content See *Dreams*.

Narcissism Self love; the investment of psychological energy in the *self*. A person with healthy narcissism has the ability within himself to recognize a "good job, well done" and to see himself as a lovable person. But he is also capable of being concerned about and loving other people. For a person with a narcissistic character disorder, a form of pathological narcissism, other people are important only in terms of how they make him feel about himself. Since this type of person has only limited ability within himself to judge performance and lovableness, he is very vulnerable to injury to his self-esteem. Thus he often experiences humiliation and rage. Depending on the response of others, this type of person vacillates between feeling great and feeling worthless. A more severe form of pathological narcissism is seen in those schizophrenics whose self-preoccupation is so intense that they are unable to distinguish self from non-self.

Negative Oedipus Complex See *Oedipus Complex*.

Neurosis Synonymous with psychoneurosis. An emotional maladaptation characterized by disturbances in thought, feelings, and behavior. Neuroses arise primarily within the mind rather than from the events of the external world, but reality may trigger a neurosis if it corresponds to an earlier traumatic experience. In contrast to character disorders and *psychoses*, neuroses are perceived by the patient as *ego-dystonic*. (See page 51 for a discussion of the four major diagnostic categories: psychoneurosis, character disorder, borderline, and psychosis.)

Object Relations The emotional ties which exist between an individual and another person. *Borderline* and *psychotic* individuals exhibit an immature capacity for object relations.

Observing Ego See *Splitting of the Ego*.

Oedipus Complex A complex is a group of associated ideas, drives, *object relations*, and fears. The Oedipus complex occurs normally and universally from approximately age three to six years. The child competes with the parent of the same sex for the love and possession of the parent of the opposite sex and wishes the death or, at least, the disappearance of the parent of the same sex. The child fears retaliation for these incestuous and hostile wishes. The characteristic retaliation feared by the little boy is *castration*, while that feared by the little girl is injury to the genitals.
A healthy resolution of the Oedipus complex is identification with the parent of the same sex. This involves incorporating the child's perception of that parent's moral values thus leading to further development of the *superego*. There is also the expectation that the child will one day have a love object of his own, similar to, but not, the parent of the opposite sex. Althought much of the Oedipus complex is conscious during childhood it is largely repressed

later. But, if inadequately resolved, it may manifest in derivatives such as castration anxiety, fear of competition, work and sex inhibitions, and inappropriate object choice.

Coexisting with the Oedipus complex is its opposite, the negative Oedipus complex, in which the child wishes for the love and possession of the parent of the same sex and the death or disappearance of the parent of the opposite sex. The negative Oedipus is usually less prominant but intermittantly comes to the fore.

Operant A form of learning or conditioning in which a behavior is increased by reward (positive reinforcement) or by avoidance of punishment (negative reinforcement).

Phallic Phase See *Psychosexual Development*.

Pleasure Principle The concept that assumes that the individual instinctively seeks pleasure and wishes to avoid pain. Infants and small children are governed primarily by the pleasure principle but with maturation the individual learns the importance of the *reality principle*.

Preconscious Refers to those thoughts which are not conscious but can be made so by focusing one's attention. See *Unconscious*.

Primary Gain The relief from unpleasant *affects* such as *anxiety* and depression and from psychological conflict attained by the operation of a *defense mechanism* or the formation of a symptom.

Projection See *Defense Mechanisms*.

Psychiatrist A doctor of medicine who specializes in the diagnosis, prevention, and treatment of mental disorders. See *Psychoanalyst* and *Psychologist*.

Psychoanalysis (1) A method for investigating both *unconscious* and conscious aspects of the mind, which makes use of *free association, dream* analysis, and analysis of *transference*. (2) A body of knowledge and a theory concerning human development and behavior. (3) A specialized, intensive, extensive form of *insight* psychotherapy. (See pages 42–46 for a detailed description and comparison of insight psychotherapy and psychoanalysis.)

Psychoanalyst Usually a *psychiatrist* who has had additional training in the theory and technique of *psychoanalysis*. The required additional training includes a personal psychoanalysis, the supervised analyses of several patients, and four or more years of seminars. Non-psychiatrists who have taken psychoanalytic training are called lay analysts. See *Psychiatrist* and *Psychologist*.

Psychologist A specialist in psychology who usually has a M.A., M.S., or Ph.D. degree. Clinical psychologists have additional training and experience in a clinical setting; they specialize in the evaluation and treatment of people with mental disorders. See *Psychiatrist* and *Psychoanalyst*.

Psychoneurosis See *Neurosis*.

Psychopathology (1) The manifestations of mental disorders. (2) The study of the development of mental disorders.

Psychosexual Development The regular developmental sequence of *libidinal* stages from infancy to adulthood. The way in which the major tasks and conflicts of each stage are mastered affect subsequent stages and contribute to the person's eventual personality characteristics.
1. Oral phase: The earliest stage lasting from birth to about age one year. The mouth is the major focus of physical sensation. This phase is subdivided into oral erotic, which relates to pleasurable sucking, and oral sadistic, which relates to aggressive biting. Examples of oral eroticism and sadism are eating and sarcasm, respectively.
2. Anal phase: The second stage, which predominates from about age one to two and a half or three years. The child's interest and concern focuses on the retention and expulsion of feces and on anal sensations. Examples of disguised adult derivatives of the anal phase are orderliness, stubbornness, and miserliness.
3. Phallic phase: The stage which predominates from about two and a half or three to six years. The phallus (penis or clitoris) is the organ of major interest. The tasks include sexual differentiation and establishment of sexual identity. The voyeuristic and exhibitionistic tendencies of this period are seen in disguised adult forms such as gossiping and "showing off." See also *Oedipus Complex*.
4. Latency phase: From about age six until the onset of puberty, there is a period of relative slowing down of psychosexual development.
5. Genital phase: The final stage of psychosexual development, in which genital sexuality predominates except in foreplay. A mature relationship is formed with the sexual partner.

Psychosis A severe mental disorder of organic or functional origin. The organic psychoses are secondary to observable physical diseases such as a brain tumor. The functional psychoses are secondary to psychological, hereditary, and neurochemical factors; they may be either *affective* disorders, such as a manic-depressive disease, or thought disorders, such as schizophrenia. Psychotic manifestations are inappropriate, extreme, or labile affect and disturbances in thought processes such as loss of reality testing, loose associations, delusions, and hallucinations. Also characteristic are an inability to cope with the ordinary demands of life and poor ability to relate to other people. (See page 51 for a discussion of the four major diagnostic categories: psychoneurosis, character disorder, borderline, and psychosis.)

Reaction Formation   See *Defense Mechanisms*.

Reality Principle   With development, the normal individual modifies the *pleasure principle* by taking into account the demands of the external world. Operating by the reality principle often leads to greater total pleasure than operating by the pleasure principle, but may involve postponement of immediate gratification in order to obtain a greater gratification later or to avoid punishment.

Regression   See *Defense Mechanisms*.

Repetition Compulsion   The impulse to repeat earlier, often painful experiences without regard to the *pleasure principle* or the *reality principle*.

Repression   See *Defense Mechanisms*.

Resistance   The manifestation, in the course of psychotherapy or analysis, of a *defense mechanism*. Resistance most commonly occurs when the therapy is making conscious an impulse, idea or *affect* which the defense mechanism was keeping *unconscious*. In the most general terms, a resistance is anything which the patient does that interferes with therapeutic progress.

Screen Memory   A tolerable conscious memory that covers one or more repressed associated experiences which, if made conscious, would be painful.

Second Gain   Unlike *primary gain,* which is the reduction of internal conflicts or painful *affects* by the operation of a *defense mechanism* or the formation of a symptom, secondary gain is the advantage (e.g., increased personal attention) gained from the external world by the same processes.

Self An individual's total person, including his body, psyche, and personal attributes such as attitudes and *affects*. For any given person, everything can be divided into self and non-self.

Separation Anxiety A normal reaction of fear and apprehension in an infant, beginning at age six to eight months, when separated from his mother or other important parenting figure. Separation anxiety cannot occur until the infant is capable of distinguishing between *self* and non-self. Separation anxiety normally decreases in intensity as the child develops the ability to form and maintain a memory of the loved person in the person's absence.

Signal Anxiety See *Anxiety*.

Splitting of the Ego In psychotherapy and psychoanalysis, the patient benefits from the ability to split his ego-functioning into observing and experiencing aspects. This allows him to observe and thus to deal with the thoughts, impulses, *affects*, and behavior he is experiencing.

Structural Theory The psychoanalytic theory of mental functioning which divides the mind into three functional groups; the *ego*, the *id*, and the *superego*.

Sublimation See *Defense Mechanisms*.

Superego A theoretical construct comprising that part of the psychic apparatus which contains the individual's *ego ideals*, as well as the critical and punishing functions commonly referred to as the conscience. The superego is formed by identification with and internalization of real or imagined parental and societal attitudes.

Suppression See under *Repression*.

Therapeutic Alliance See *Alliance*.

Transference The inappropriate repetition in the present of a relationship that was important in a person's childhood. (For a more detailed definition and discussion, see pages 66–69.)

Unconscious Mental content of which the individual is unaware. Unlike mental content, which is *preconscious*, unconscious material cannot easily be brought into conscious awareness. The unconscious drives, *affects*, and ideals are dynamically kept from conscious awareness by *defense mechanisms*.

Working Alliance   See *Alliance*.

Working Through   The psychological work which enables insight to effect significant and stable changes in a person's attitudes, behavior, and psychic structure. (See pages 79–83.)

Index